THE ENCOUNTER

THE ENCOUNTER

A HANDBOOK OF POETIC PRACTICE

Edited by Jon Thompson

Parlor Press
Anderson, South Carolina
www.parlorpress.com

Parlor Press LLC, Anderson, South Carolina, USA

Printed in the United States of America on acid-free paper.
SAN: 254-8879

Library of Congress Cataloging-in-Publication Data on File

1 2 3 4 5

978-1-64317-298-9 (paperback)
978-1-64317-299-6 (pdf)
978-1-64317-300-9 (epub)

Cover image: "Lozenge Composition with Yellow, Black, Blue, Red, and Gray" by Piet Mondrian. 1921. The Art Institute of Chicago. Use by permission.
Interior and cover design: David Blakesley

Parlor Press, LLC is an independent publisher of scholarly and trade titles in print and multimedia formats. This book is available in paper and ebook formats from Parlor Press on the World Wide Web at https://parlorpress.com or through online and brick-and-mortar bookstores. For submission information or to find out about Parlor Press publications, write to Parlor Press, 3015 Brackenberry Drive, Anderson, South Carolina, 29621, or email editor@parlorpress.com.

Contents

Preface

This book collects essays by a wide range of contemporary poets who reflect upon an encounter, or set of encounters, that has opened up poetry's possibilities in some telling, enduring way. The remit I offered to poets was to reflect upon *any* poem, book, individual, art object, moment, condition, event or happening of any kind that shaped their thinking about poetry. What came back, as you will see, is a startling, rich, diverse set of personal essays that illuminate the ways in which contemporary poets think about poetry, and the ways in which they write poetry—and an equally rich and diverse set of insights about how poetry might be written.

Many poetry handbooks are guides to form, or the formal dimensions of writing poetry. These matters are crucial to understand, and, if one is a poet, to master. *The Encounter* is not that kind of book. While the essays in this book turn out to have a great deal to say about the formal elements of poetry, they don't set about doing so abstractly or schematically. Rather, what distinguishes *The Encounter* from many others is that all of the essays in it are rooted in the lived experience of these writers. They underscore just how much of the writing life depends upon various kinds of unexpected encounters—unexpected relationships—that come to shape what gets written. Collectively, the essays here testify to moments that flash into new kinds of awareness of what poetry might be. And then is.

A note on the text: These are personal, rather than academic essays. When quoting other texts, citations are provided in footnotes. To make them as unobtrusive as possible, we did not ask poets to provide citations to their own poetry; for similar reasons, we did not ask for citations for epigraphs to the essays.

—Jon Thompson

Meetings

Rae Armantrout

My mother read poetry to me when I was small. In a way, my life story begins with that. Poetry was a lilting rhythm, a familiar voice. It came with magical illustrations. Poetry was old. The owl and the pussycat went to sea/in a beautiful pea-green boat." Poetry was a way of singing to yourself, even if you couldn't sing. It had rules. Little children like rules. Teenagers like them less. When I was twelve or thirteen I was already trying to write poetry, but I had traditional meters stuck in my head. I think I composed a book report in the meter of Hiawatha. I could be wrong. I was ready for something else.

I wish I could point to one encounter that changed or even formed my idea of what poetry could do. In my experience things rarely happen that way. Instead there are a number of what people now call "inflection points." Because I liked poetry, my seventh grade English teacher at Lewis Jr. High in San Diego, Mrs. Hancock, gave me an amazing gift—a poetry anthology called *Modern American Poetry* edited by Louis Untermeyer. My whole life I have believed (and often said) that I discovered William Carlos Williams in that book along with what they used to call "free verse." I just looked up the anthology on Amazon, using the "Look inside" function to see which WCW poems Untermeyer had included. To my amazement, I found plenty of free verse there (much of it by people I had never heard of), but nothing by Williams! Still, somehow, I remember reading "Metric Figure" in that book and discovering how good poetry could sound without formal devices, how immediate it could seem. How could such an anthology omit Williams? Did a later edition of the same anthology include that poem? Was I dreaming? I also remember encountering Dickinson and Pound in that book and they *are th*ere. The Dickinson poems, of course, are reproduced with made up titles and no dashes. They look strange. There I first read #585 (Fr) which begins, "I love to see it lap the miles—/And lick the valleys up—." What interesting verbs those are! Here a train is consuming space like a rapacious kitten—menacing and cute. Did my (nearly) lifelong fascination with Dickinson start when I read this? Maybe. I don't mean to imply I had flawless taste at such a tender age. I was also taken with Stephen

Crane and Sara Teasdale. I'm pretty sure that if my teacher hadn't given me an anthology of modern poetry, I would have lost interest in writing– though there is no way to be certain.

When I was a senior in high school my English teacher, I can't remember his name, told me "Women can't write poetry." Nevertheless, I persisted.

When I was a sophomore at San Diego State College, a daring young professor, probably adjunct faculty, assigned Ginsberg's" Howl." In 1967, as you might expect, that poem could still provoke outrage. I found it exciting. I loved the propulsive syncopated rhythm of phrases like, "teahead/joyride neon blinking traffic light." Ginsberg and other poets (and singers) were pointing the way out. I didn't worry much about the fact that the poem begins with the "best minds" of a generation being "destroyed by madness." I started looking at poetry anthologies. Eventually, like many people then, I came across Donald Allen's *New American Poetry*. That is where I first read Denise Levertov. I particularly recall "Overland to the Island" in which a dog's gleaming fur is "a radiance/consorting with the dance."[1] The words consorted with one another. Soon I would apply to UC Berkeley where Levertov was teaching. If I hadn't moved to the Bay Area, I doubt I would be a poet.

When I arrived on campus, she had one space in her class, and she was conducting interviews to fill it. I got there so early that I was first in line. When she called me in, I told her I had come to Berkeley specifically to study with her. I didn't actually know she was teaching there until I arrived. I wasn't in the habit of lying, but the words just popped out of my mouth. She looked at a couple of the not-so-great poems I had written and announced to the (by then) long line of waiting students that the place had been filled. It was the year of the invasion of Cambodia, the campus strike, and the People's Park demonstrations. Most of what she taught us wasn't formal. But she did advise me to think harder about line breaks. Like many beginners, I hadn't given this much thought. The most important thing I got from Levertov's class though, honestly, was something quite different. The path takes a detour at this point. I met Rochelle Nam-

1. *The New American Poetry 1945-1960*, edited by Donald Allen, Grove Press, 1960.

eroff in Levertov's class and, when I went to visit Shelley at home, I met her then husband Ron Silliman. I learned and have continued to learn a lot from Ron. He seemed to *get* my poems in a way no one else had. For instance, when Shelley asked why a poem called "Re-lease" (which was later published in my first book) ends with "re-call," Ron pointed out that several other words in the short poem also begin with the prefix "re." (In retrospect, I can see that Shelley might have been questioning the value of the hyphen which *is* a bit heavy-handed –but I got the feeling then that Ron was interested in words down to the level of the syllable, as I was.)

Ron was only one year older than me, but he was a lot more sophisticated about poetry and the "poetry world." He had probably read everything Williams ever wrote—or so I imagined. He was well versed the New American Poets: Black Mountain, the SF Renaissance, the New York School, the Beats. I knew a smattering and thought that was enough. I remember he was shocked that I hadn't read Olson's essay "Projective Verse," so, of course, I did. I'm not going to look it up now. What I remember is the oddly phrased maxim that "one perception must move instanter on another."[2] I liked the kinetics but disliked the authoritative tone. (Still do.)

I should have been thinking about what I would do after college. The word "career" wasn't part of my working vocabulary then. I should have been applying to grad schools or law schools, something.

When I graduated, I moved back to San Diego and married my long-time boyfriend, Chuck. He was finishing college there. I got a job as a teacher's aide at a high school. Ron moved to Buffalo with Shelley—and then back. They soon divorced. I didn't know any poets in San Diego, but I kept writing. I stayed in touch with Ron to some extent. I only know this because it was Ron who suggested I send work to Bob Grenier for his new magazine *This* and to Clayton Eshleman for his journal *Sulfur*. I'm sure I wouldn't have known of these publications if it weren't for him. As it happened, I was published in both and thus had some reason, for the first time, to think of myself as a poet. In 1972 I applied to grad school at San Francisco State and was

2. Charles Olson, "Projective Verse." Dana Gioia et al., editors. *Twentieth-Century American Poetics: Poets on the Art of Poetry*. McGraw-Hill, 2004. p.175.

accepted. When Chuck and I arrived in SF, I got in touch with Ron, who had moved to the Haight Ashbury, and showed him the poems I'd been writing. I can't recall now what they were. He had published a book called *Crow*. It may be surprising to those who haven't followed his career, but, back then, Ron was a minimalist. I enjoyed the way his early writing broke "ordinary" language apart to examine it more closely. I *liked* it, but I admit I wasn't blown away by it. That would come later.

In 1974 (?) I gave my first public reading at a bar in Oakland called The White Horse. Ron read too. David Melnick (who had also taken Levertov's class) was the MC, I think. There were probably other readers but I don't remember them. Ron read from the manuscript of *Ketjak*. That book-length prose poem was structured in a way that was immediately audible and completely new. The first paragraph was two sentences, the second was four, the third was eight. Each paragraph after the first repeated the sentences in the previous one, often in an extended form, while interspersing an equal number of new sentences. It was like watching (well, hearing) the growth of some new life form. Each sentence in itself was a small act of attention to the recognizable world around us, but none related directly to the one before or after. He hadn't shown me any of this work in advance. I was amazed. I knew I had heard something that was going to make a difference in how poetry was read and written. (Ron, by the way, says he has no memory of this event. The past is a fragile thing.) I was very pleased that he dedicated the poem to me. Soon Ron would dub this kind of writing "the new sentence" and other Bay Area poets, such as Lyn Hejinian, would be working in a somewhat similar way. I tried the style myself briefly, first in a collaboration with Ron called "Engines," but after a few attempts decided it wasn't for me. That doesn't mean, however, that I wasn't at all influenced by this form, which became, arguably the dominant style of the west coast Language Poets. I began to divide my poems into sections which I saw as modular, separate from one another while part of a larger whole. Even within sections, the movement between stanzas became looser and less predictable. Here are a few stanzas from the third section of my poem "Sense" in *Necromance*:

First the (non)sense

of direction.

"Stones to frogs,
then to princes
who do a circle dance
and turn to stone."

Good-night!

Meaning extends
her arm backwards
ballerina-like:

Do those stanzas look like anything Ron would write? No. But his influence and that of other poets I met through him is there nonetheless. In the 70s and 80s we became a more or less cohesive group consisting of Ron, Lyn. Barret Watten, Bob Perelman, Carla Harryman, Steve Benson, Kit Robinson, Alan Bernheimer, and me. Whether I actually belonged with this group was at times an open question. It was my friendship with Ron that really sealed it. As a group, we were in close contact with other outlier poets like Leslie Scalapino, David Bromige, David Melnick, Erica Hunt, etc.

All such gatherings eventually come apart. I was the first to leave. In 1978 I got pregnant. Chuck and I were financially marginal in a San Francisco that was becoming more expensive by the month. We wanted to stay, but decided we couldn't or didn't want to raise a child in the state of precarity we had accepted for ourselves. Chuck, who had been managing a Dalton's bookstore in San Bruno (where he had employed Carla, Steve, and Alan's wife Melissa Riley) applied for and got a better job as the "general book buyer" of the college bookstore at San Diego State. It offered a better salary and health insurance so we moved back to San Diego. For me, this felt like falling off a cliff. Remember this was well before the internet. Carla warned me that, if I moved to San Diego to raise a child, I would stop writing. That could have happened; it wasn't unreasonable. One thing that kept me going, at first, was correspondence with old friends, including Ron, Lyn, and Steve Benson. Ron invited me to collaborate with him on a new sentence type work called "Engines" which appears in his book *The Alphabet* and in my book *Veil.*

The quietness of my life in San Diego was almost eerie after the excitement of San Francisco. For at least a year I stayed home with our son, Aaron, while Chuck worked. After so many years away, my old hometown seemed strange as well as familiar. There was something about this that was actually stimulating to my writing. My pace of production, which had been quite slow, started to pick up. I needed contact with other people, yes, but I also needed time on my own.

I am still in more or less regular communication with Ron, Lyn, and Bob. I still show Ron every poem I write. If he really dislikes something, I tend to keep working on it. Sometimes his responses are cryptic. He rarely makes specific suggestions. Often, though, after I sit with them awhile, his comments seem spot on. (Of course, there are also times when we don't agree. For instance, not long ago he disliked a poem of mine which I not only kept but published in a recent issue of *Conjunctions.)* To generalize, he prefers me to explain as little as possible and to choose the wilder option where alternatives are given. He also (and this may surprise some people who make assumptions about "language poets") tends to tell me when he thinks no one will get a reference or when he feels some part of a poem has the wrong—or perhaps no—emotional resonance. I sometimes ask Lyn and Bob to read a new poem as well. These three disagree with one another surprisingly often. And I sometimes disagree with any or all of them and quietly ignore suggestions. That's how it is in old friendships. This give and take, which began long ago, is generative. It keeps me from being too easily satisfied and also keeps me from being frozen with doubt. The most important thing for me, though, may not be any particular advice but the fact that our conversation is ongoing.

I didn't exactly choose to be a poet. I just kept answering what spoke to me and this is where it ended up. Many would think it's a pretty strange place, the "poetry world." It can be as cut throat as life in any small pond. But this is also where I have found the closest thing to real communication and community.

All Things Counter, All Things Consonant

Jennifer Atkinson

In 1968, my family lived at the top of a mostly wooded hill in Connecticut. Some eighty acres of woods stretched behind us and lots more forest surrounded us. That conservation land stretched beyond our biggest spruce and down a steepish hill to the reservoir, a wide lake whose water was meant for Bridgeport. (Ours came from a well.) A strange moony sort of girl, when not in school or riding the bus to and from, I mostly read novels or tramped around in those woods. I especially loved the hemlocks. In summer I'd sometimes find crushed grass underneath them, nests where the deer lay down to sleep. In winter the hemlocks' blackish downswept branches would sometimes get so heavily shagged with ice that their tips froze to the snowy ground. An icy crust would form over all the conifers, around the trunks of the deciduous trees, across the leaf litter and moss, the flitches of Christmas fern and whorled ground pine. Dry leaves skittered and scratched in the wind. In the field my father mowed twice a year, snow-crust smoothed the rough ground where blueberry bushes and three dunce-cap-shaped junipers grew. On late winter afternoons, their shadows cast a purplish sheen, and where the sun hit, their branches glittered, not too distantly at all.

In school I was as silent and self-contained as a student could manage. I opened my locker and shut my locker, walked from Algebra to Social Studies to English, Latin, Spanish, French, Biology—as many classes as I was allowed. I kept my head down mostly, and listened or read under my desk when I thought I wouldn't get caught.

The poems I'd been given in school up until ninth grade were rarely mysterious, or if they were, we were encouraged to see their mysteries as problems to solve. Poetry was explained as a pleasant, functionless sort of algebra in which this road means one thing and that road another. Or else poetry was pretty words to decorate otherwise dull things—the fog as cat-footed or the dawn as rosy-fingered. Reading poems, my teachers implied, was more or less like translating Latin—pleasant if irrelevant outside of school and a little fusty.

Latin was for broadening our vocabularies and bettering our SAT scores. Poetry was for making us "well-rounded."

Year in, year out, we read poems and solved for X, and our well-meaning teachers encouraged us to write little ditties, usually of the pretty words for dull things sort. We wrote haikus and end-rhymed quatrains and—don't get me wrong—I enjoyed the task and could usually rack up a + or an A for my efforts. But then one day in ninth grade Mr. Concilio, mild-mannered English teacher (and, it turned out, something of a poetry Superman) changed for me what "poem" meant. He handed out a mimeograph sheet, still damp and smelling deliciously of probably toxic blue ink. He'd managed to fit both Wallace Stevens's "The Snow Man" and Gerard Manley Hopkins's "Pied Beauty" on one page.

"The Snow Man" by Wallace Stevens

One must have a mind of winter
To regard the frost and the boughs
Of the pine-trees crusted with snow;

And have been cold a long time
To behold the junipers shagged with ice,
The spruces rough in the distant glitter

Of the January sun; and not to think
Of any misery in the sound of the wind,
In the sound of a few leaves,

Which is the sound of the land
Full of the same wind
That is blowing in the same bare place

For the listener, who listens in the snow,
And, nothing himself, beholds
Nothing that is not there and the nothing that is.[3]

---

3. "The Snow Man" was published in *Poetry Magazine* originally in 1921.

"Pied Beauty" by Gerard Manley Hopkins

Glory be to God for dappled things –
 For skies of couple-colour as a brinded cow;
  For rose-moles all in stipple upon trout that swim;
Fresh-firecoal chestnut-falls; finches' wings;
 Landscape plotted and pieced—fold, fallow, and plough;
 And áll trádes, their gear and tackle and trim.

All things counter, original, spare, strange;
 Whatever is fickle, freckled (who knows how?)
  With swift, slow; sweet, sour; adazzle, dim;
He fathers-forth whose beauty is past change:
    Praise him.[4]

My teacher must have typed the poems out by hand from his own Stevens collection (*The Collected Poems of Wallace Stevens*, maybe even Knopf's first edition in 1954) and his copy of Hopkins poems, most likely an early edition of the Penguin paperback *Gerard Manley Hopkins: Poems and Prose*, selected by W.H. Gardner.

Mr. Concilio probably introduced them with something about unusual words and whether we knew what *juniper* and *pied* meant. I wasn't listening. I was reading: "One must have a mind of winter . . . junipers shagged with ice . . . rough in the distant glitter," and wondering what it felt like to be cold so long that your mind turned wintery and you felt like a snowman. I was lingering over and over that mysterious, solemn, slow last line, "The nothing that is not there and the nothing that is." *Nothing* and *nothing* at the far-end of a long sentence and an un-foot-printed walk through the snow.

That day when I first read "The Snowman," the landscape of the poem was *my* landscape. I knew it. The scratchy sound of dry oak leaves blowing across the bare snow crust was more familiar to me than the pep rally cheers I was supposed to love to shout. I wasn't a shouter and I hated those school cheers. For me, there was definitely misery in the sound of those avid shouts but none at all in the wind. The poem's spruce and juniper landscape wasn't foreign, as I'm sure

4. The source for "Pied Beauty" is *Gerard Manley Hopkins: Poems and Prose* (Penguin Classics, 1985).

it is for many readers. It's Connecticut. I was at home in the place and the words—what could be more real?—and so when the last line hit, its mysterious *nothing* and *nothing* entranced me.

And then (it was there on the page so how could I stop?) I was on to the next poem, a tiny one. It started out so familiarly, rather like the many "What I Love About ___" poems I'd been asked to hear and write since first grade, except that it leapt quick into music I'd never heard anywhere before: "Fresh-firecoal chestnut-falls; finches' wings . . . swift, slow; sweet, sour; adazzle, dim . . . "

Intoxicated by the blurry blue words on the page, I lost track of everything else for a while, even my adolescent self-loathing. I was head over heels in love. As soon as I got done reading the Hopkins, I circled back to the Stevens, read on down through the *nothings* and onward through *dim*. Back and back. Again and again. The combination of Stevens's stately rhythms and mysterious distant glitter with Hopkins's word-crazed, jerky, dazzling music stunned me. *This*, I hardly thought to think, *this* is interesting.

Returning to those poems now, fifty years later, I remember my keen delight and the almost equally sharp sense that the other students felt nothing. I knew they would deride any outward signs of enjoyment. I kept my happiness to myself, folded it up with the handout and put it away for later. Later that day and again and again ever since I've turned to those poems and poets, amazed.

Now I wonder if anyone else did the same. I've shared "The Snow Man" with countless classes and have seen dozens of students bewildered by it—in a good way. Why? What is it that still draws us? Why is the day I first read them—and together like that—such a red-letter memorable day? It's not like I swore that day at my ninth grade desk that I would grow up to be a poet. In fact, I didn't think you could *be* a poet anymore. Poet, I assumed, was a vanished career, like tinker or wet nurse or monk. But I did realize that afternoon that I wasn't the only one who loved the sounds of words and the ways their sounds and meanings change when they're put next to each other. This Wallace Stevens and Gerard Hopkins did too. Their blank snow and skies and cows and rose-moled trout literally rang true. I saw because I heard or heard because I saw.

The way an image like "fresh firecoal" appears in your mind. When you read those words, your memory is transformed, made new as in a dream, and singular—separate from the remembered experience of a fire burning in a grate. An image, I'd call it now, that ashy coal broken open to pure fire.

And the poem doesn't stop there: it rhymes that firecoal to "chest-nut-fall." Like the dunce-cap junipers and ice-shagged hemlocks in "The Snow Man," I knew chestnuts from experience. I knew how once ripe, they fell from the trees near our house, their spiny husks split wide to reveal the burnished glint of the nut. I think I saw even then how unlike things—a coal broken from its ashen husk and a chestnut ripe in its spiny cover *rhymed*, rhymed as images and as words. The dense alliterative f's and l's, the cross-consonances and assonances among the words enact the image-rhyming of things that are, at the same time, alike and wholly unlike. Through the burred sounds of the rhymes the images stick in the grow, gathering resonances. You find yourself smelling the sweet charry smoke of roast chestnuts.

The poem continues like that, adding finches' wings to the list of rhyming pied things—wings that in my Connecticut-bred mind opened goldfinch-yellow and black—couple-colored, alive with bothness. And not just little things in the poem rhyme. Whole landscapes in their order and disorder, human jobs and the tools that go with them, each designed for its right function, reveal in their forms how they rhyme too, right along with skies, cloudy and clear, animals, scaled and stippled, air and water and fire and field.

"All things counter, original, spare, strange" is not meant I think (now, if not then) to sum up the sestet but to further disrupt a simple reading of the bothness the poem celebrates. Together those four adjectives are more inclusive than a full rhyme would imply; they include what does not rhyme fully or fit snugly in place. The oddness of those not-quite synonyms, not-quite rhymes in their dissimilarities include what is extra, unnecessary, redundant. That "spare" might also suggest leanness in so extravagant (if curtailed) a sonnet makes me laugh now, when I think of it.

The following lines, if I may tire you further with a poem we all know so well, rev up still further. (Those who think theologically will want to add something about the nature of God here, and rightly so, but I'll leave that to them. Surely it had no part in my astonishment at thirteen.) I loved that "fickle" and "freckled" rhymed in every way, the language corroborating the image and vice versa—this at the same time that each of the words was about *un*likeness! I also love (and must have loved then too, even if I couldn't have said so) the rhythm of the opposites line: "With swift, slow; sweet, sour; adazzle, dim" as it prepares for the final notes: "He fathers forth whose beauty is past change:/Praise him." I will leave to theologians the question of "past change" and whether that implies greater piedity or less, and leap to that final resounding full rhyme of "dim" and "him." God and dark are opposites in most Christian poems and hymns, but here they are made consonant, alike and not in equal measure. I mean, if their initial sounds did not differ, we would hear no rhyme. That stuns me still.

Reading and rereading once again I turn back to Stevens's poem and our shared Connecticut landscape, where the same dry leaves blow each winter. There's no god here, nor fire, just snow and wind and dead leaves skittering across a field with hemlocks and pines and junipers beyond it.

One must have a mind of winter to see (or rather to "regard" or "behold") this place as it is, and why would anyone want to? And yet I did. I wanted to get that cold, that un-human. I might have been drawn into the poem's landscape because I recognized it the way in her poem, "Poem," Elizabeth Bishop recognizes the farm in her great-uncle's painting, but I stayed there in the poem-scape because it was *not* the landscape I knew, it was that landscape transformed into language.

Unlike Hopkins's close-ups and sudden long views, Stevens keeps a constant distance, remote in the snow. Unlike "Pied Beauty's" singing rhymes, full and slant, head and tail, rhymes that enact a vision of wide consonance and extreme peculiarity, we hear in "The Snow Man" the level roll of the sentence and its repeating words: "sound" and "sound" and "sound," identical rhymes, plain rhymes whose *lack* of unlikeness means we don't hear them as rhyming at all. The effect is sublime, I might say now. Then it must have felt eerie in its unornamented abstractness. Like a mirror reflecting a mirror, emptiness but vaster.

I fear I've taught these two opposite poems too many times to still feel the rush and surprise of those nothings, both there and not there, or the fiery coal broken open. Sometimes, though, as we read together, I'll see a glint in a student's eye, a moment of sudden apprehension as the words reflect themselves, each other, and the world beyond, as the mysteries refuse solutions. Perhaps they feel as once I felt—caught, like an image between mirrors; caught, like a moth in the sounds—"swift, slow; sweet, sour; adazzle, dim."

On the Threshold-Condition

Dan Beachy-Quick

I want there to be an image that helps me encounter *encounter*. The infant's eyes for the first time ever-opening within ourselves even now, the light-flood in the brain. Open hands. The ears that cannot close even at night, even in sleep: dream that listens. Mouth that opens to eat; mouth that opens to speak; mouth that closes and hides the tongue and teeth. Our senses are the space of the world's encounter. Wound of the body. But the images don't hold, don't rise out of the depth of their phenomenal claim, don't open up into the complex intimacies *encounter* also entails—the personal, the political, the historical; the whole inter-woven, inter-ruptured, penetralium of the human among every sort of other, that links day to day so that the days add quietly up to a life, a life capable of encounter, ongoing forms of encounter, built on the bedrock foundation of being wildly, radically, open to the world, our ongoing, life-long, infancy of the senses.

I want a passage to help me encounter *encounter*. I mean a text; I mean a path, a tunnel, a hall. John Keats does not clarify what I'm seeking, but guides me into the mist. On 3 May 1818 he writes a letter to John Reynolds:

> I compare human life to a large Mansion of Many Apartments, two of which I can only describe, the doors of the rest being as yet shut upon me—The first we step into we call the infant or thoughtless Chamber, in which we remain as long as we do not think—We remain there a long while, and notwithstanding the doors of the second Chamber remain wide open, showing a bright appearance, we care not to hasten to it; but are at length imperceptibly impelled by awakening of the thinking principle—within us—we no sooner get into the second Chamber, which I shall call the Chamber of Maiden-Thought, than we become intoxicated with the light and the atmosphere, we see nothing but pleasant wonders, and think of delaying there forever in delight: However among the effects this breathing is father

> of is that tremendous one of sharpening one's vision into the nature and heart of Man—of convincing one's nerves that the World is full of misery and Heartbreak, Pain, sickness and oppression—whereby This Chamber of Maiden Thought becomes gradually darken'd and at the same time on all sides of it many doors are set open—but all dark—all leading to dark passages—[1]

Learning to think darkens the mind. The out-shining nature of every given thing opens inwardly into its own mystery, a door ajar in the darkness. Keats gives us the counterpoint image to the infant eye open to the sudden light: the eye adjusting to the darkness of the world, and finding in that darkness opportunity. I have thought the first line of every poem is door set open in darkness, and the poem itself is the passage into and through that darkness. I'm not sure the last line of the poem returns us to the thoughtless chamber of our bright origins. The last line may be but another door leading to another dark passage. An infinite series of doors opening onto opening doors. But what Keats does offer is a way of thinking of poetry's relation to encounter. It's different than one might expect. Epistemological and architectural both. So different than the grassy bowers of his poems. Not a bower at all. Not a trellis vined with flowers. Just a door on its hinges open slightly so that one can see the jambs, lintel, and sill. A place that is not a place. A way in that is a way through. An arrival that departs. A departure that arrives. A threshold-condition.

* * *

But what I need is a memory that encounters *encounter*.

I knocked on the office door of the visiting poet who led my workshop my third semester of graduate school. I should admit to a growing wariness in relation to all things workshop related then—a distrust of the pedagogy, of the way community was built and behaved, of the actual poetic possibilities inherent within the space. Poetry felt to me to be elsewhere than where I'd come to find it, and I didn't know what to do with the bewilderment I felt growing inside

1. In *Selected Letters of John Keats*, edited by Grant F. Scott. Harvard University Press, 2002. p. 124.

me, didn't know how to put my confusion to any other use than being confused. I needed a teacher. I needed a guide. I didn't wholly trust I knew how to find a teacher or a guide. I just had this vague, dim-lit, numb, half-mute awareness that I needed some other than what I had given myself and what had been given me. But I knocked on Heather McHugh's door and she opened it and let me in.

I remember her office was in an attic space at the top of the house where workshop was held. That I'd climbed stairs. (Hindsight reminds: "Where do we find ourselves? In a series of which we do not know the extremes, and believe that it has none. We wake and find ourselves on a stair; there are stairs below us, which we seem to have ascended; there are stairs above us, many a one, which go upward and out of sight."[2] But I hadn't yet woken to those stairs; I hadn't yet fallen asleep deeply enough to need to wake up.) What she said to me I'll never forget. She stood in front of me, holding the pages I'd given her. I lingered on the threshold. She bent her head toward me so that her eyes peered over the rims of her glasses. She said one thing: "All *you* need to do is make friends with the dead."

I can't imagine it can be true that I didn't sit down and talk with her for the hour we'd set aside, but the memory lives on in me in this way: I turned around; walked out; the door closed itself behind me; I woke to find myself on a stair. (Hindsight says: "The road up and the road down are one road.")[3] I walked out the door of that house with new eyes opening in my eyes. All pupil, scant iris, sun in full eclipse. (Hindsight recites):

> We grow accustomed to the Dark —
> When Light is put away —
> As when the Neighbor holds the Lamp
> To witness her Good bye —
>
> A Moment—We Uncertain step
> For newness of the night —

2. Ralph Waldo Emerson, "Experience" in *Emerson's Essays*. Harper & Row, 1981. p. 292.

3. In Hippocrates, *Heraclitus, On the Universe*, edited by W. H. S. Jones, Loeb Classical Library vol. 150. Translation mine.

Then—fit our Vision to the Dark —
And meet the Road—erect—

And so of larger—Darknesses —
Those Evenings of the Brain —
When not a Moon disclose a sign —
Or Star—come out—within—

The Bravest—grope a little —
And sometimes hit a Tree
Directly in the Forehead—
But as they learn to see —

Either the Darkness alters—
Or something in the sight
Adjusts itself to Midnight—
And Life steps almost straight.[4]

No dark woods; all dark woulds. No golden bough. No Circe. No bag of blood. No beeswax in ears. No sirens. No Tiresias. No Orpheus. No cave with filled with shadows. No region untrammeled by thought. Just the eyes adjusting to the dark. Just the learning to seek and see the sparrow-fluttering-through-starlight presence of the shades.

* * *

John Keats writes on 19 February 1819: "A Man's life of any worth is a continual allegory— and very few eyes can see the Mystery of his life—a life like the scriptures, figurative—which such people can no more make out than they can see the Hebrew Bible."[5] It's been two decades since that door closed behind me in my actual life; it's been twenty years, and a portion of eternity, that it has stayed open in my allegorical one. The Poet lives in strange proximity to the person who lives their life so as to write a poem, or so I've come to suspect. There is some intimate interstice between the reality of day to day life and this other reality our allegorical life opens—that reality of the

4. Emily Dickinson, *The Complete Poems of Emily Dickinson*, edited by Thomas H. Johnson. Little Brown & Company. 1960. p. 200.

5. *Selected Letters of John Keats*, edited by Grant F. Scott. Harvard UP, 2002. p. 261.

symbol, in which each given thing (the young rabbit just ran under the blue spruce outside me window where I write, the spruce so large it reaches past sight, the rabbit so small it lives in a world of pine) means more than it is precisely because each thing is exactly what it is. The education that Heather McHugh told me to seek, this primary school that is a conversation with the dead, brings me again and again to the fragile boundary between life and death, day and symbol, pulse and shadow, and the ever-more-humbling realization that the poem is the door that keeps open a threshold on that very line.

In *The Dominion of the Dead*, Robert Pogue Harrison offers a brief history of human dwelling. He reminds us that the very word *human* is etymologically tied to *humus*, and that our being is of the earth from which we emerge and into which we return. He points to the archaeological fact that the earliest human habitations were built directly over the graves of ancestors. Fathers, foundation; mothers, bedrock. Life builds itself on top of death, not as denial of it, but connection to it.[6] Words bear their curious allegorical parallel. Each a brick or each a plank. Each holds a breath other lives before our own once breathed. Each made of the timeless mud of others' thoughts we come to know as our own. A mob lives inside a syllable. And as of the ancient "sacrifice of aversion" in which blood was poured into a pit so that the dead could for a short while be appeased of their want to continue living, saying a word as it most is meant to be said, gives back to the dead that eternal *now* of actual attention embedded inside the consciousness a word embodies. (Hindsight in a small voice):

> Perhaps we are *here* in order to say: house,
> bridge, fountain, gate, pitcher, fruit-tree, window—
> at most: column, tower . . . .But to *say them*, you must understand,
> oh to say them *more* intensely than the Things themselves
> ever dreamed of existing[7]

The dead told me a poem is a hut in which they arrive and speak again, and we build it to hear their voices.

---

6. Robert Pogue Harrison, *The Dominion of the Dead*. Chicago UP, 2003. pp. 33–34.

7. Ranier Marie Rilke, *The Duino Elegies*. Translated by Edward Snow. North Point Press, 2000. p. 55.

That thought has guided my poems these many years—the thought that every poem is a form of offering, of form of opening, a space of indwelling and initiation, of refuge and recovery. Not my refuge but another's. (Hindsight points out: "Nature is a haunted house—but Art—a house that tries to be haunted—.)[8] How long invocation echoes through the shady realms of the undergrove. I know I've written a poem when I can taste earth in my mouth. The word for *word* in ancient Greek, *mnema*, also means memorial, burial mound. The word for *word* in ancient Greek, *sema*, also means a grave, the marker of a grave. I turned to ancient Greek in the last decade to be closer to what words say when I say them. I turned to translating so that my mouth can be another's mouth. This morning's work with Sappho feels like a small revelation:

the bedrock

whispers[9]

Yes, I think that's true. The way I've learned to encounter poetry says that it is true. The bedrock whispers. The poem echoes and amplifies that small voice. (Hindsight repeats: "I have a mouth so I can sing another's song.")

8. *Emily Dickinson: Selected Letters*, edited by Thomas H. Johnson. Harvard UP, 1986. p. 225.

9. *Greek Lyric: Sappho and Alcaeus*, Loeb Classical Library vol. 142. Harvard UP, 1982. Translation mine.

Not Even a Name in Prose

Kelvin Corcoran

19 March 2020

Dear Jon

It has taken the almost complete lock-down of Europe because of the COVID-19 virus to make me sit down and write this piece. I'm left with no options, no distractions, and no excuses.

It might be that in trying to write these anecdotes from the past, in order to explain how poetry arrived, half of what I say is made up now having ascribed present meaning to those events from then. Recollection is layered over, piled up, and then partly forgotten—but I would like to sprinkle some facts about. Poetry can arrive it seems in prosaic, unexpected ways from the commonplace and flip the moment into and out of the previously unknown. I think it can also arise exactly as anticipated, but making the predictable unpredictable at the same time. I'm not setting out to suggest a simple line of progression. It's not the story of X happened which prompted Y and here's Z. It's not that these events, years apart, delineate a sort of liaison with the muse.

I savor the smell of early Cape Golliard books, when you stick your nose right in them. Fortunately, they also contained some of the most exciting poetry of the time. I also recall exactly a first sight of the collection of kouroi, the young marble giants, in the National Archaeological Museum Athens. I turned the corner, stopped dead in my tracks—and a while later began breathing again. A few weeks back I heard the classical Iranian singer Hamayun Shajarian in concert. His rendition of Avaz sent us all out of our seats up into the sky. There's poetry already in all of these things. So, simply, at the beginning.

I remember one lesson from school, on Keats's ode "To Autumn." The teacher, Leonard Saffron, was an austere, difficult man, thoughtful, occasionally bad tempered, always formal in his manners. He was also striking in his appearance; he sported three-piece tweed suits, a tidy goatee and spats. Spats! He arrived at school in a classic Citroen car and walked through the place in a detached manner—in spats. None of this was at all typical for teachers in a provincial secondary school in a small market town in the English midlands in the late sixties early seventies. I don't think it was duplicated anywhere in the county let alone in the school.

Mr Saffron took an interest in me. He frequently told me I was bright but lazy and he may have known about my difficult family background. He would have known I'd been suspended from school now and then. In the right mood he would threaten me—*I'll throw you out of the bloody window Corcoran.* Unlike for some of my friends, his bad temper didn't bother me much and I wonder if that was because compared to my alcoholic father's rages, and his entirely destructive behavior, Mr Saffron didn't scare me. I liked him, he was unusual. We all knew he was Canadian and later I found out he'd been a Spitfire pilot in the Second World War. I think I may have sensed he knew something, that he carried with him something from a different world. This aside he claimed to have no imagination and wrote textbooks on grammar, which also had to be survived. Some of this perhaps makes it even more surprising that the lesson on Keats was the first thing that found its way into my usually distracted, stupid adolescent head—but I think he was the first teacher I actually listened to.

So, Keats entered. It was an early summer's afternoon; the classroom windows were open and the smell of the grass from the school fields drifted in. The classroom was always quiet, you did not talk out of turn. What I remember is that Mr Saffron presented the poem under a sort of obligation, some sort of sufferance, teeth not quite gritted. He drew a diagram on the board which illustrated the shape of the poem's argument, the rise and fall of emotional tone, and he read it to us. His rather grand voice delivered the lines with an easy clarity. We read it to ourselves and he talked about it. And I swear this was the first thing that ever lodged itself in my brain. Something happened. This is fifty years ago—and the light was a certain way, reflected off the tops of the desks in a certain way, and we were all quiet with just Keats's words in front of us and in our ears. This experience of really seeing something, of really understanding something, this artifice, this made-up thing, stayed with me and was perhaps the beginning of a hopeless and unavoidable engagement with poetry. I also think, looking back, part of what caught me, why I was so enraptured by the poem out of the blue, was the personification of Autumn as a young woman, " . . . sitting careless on a granary floor,/ Thy hair soft-lifted by the winnowing wind;"[1] I knew that, I saw it straight-away, mistakenly or not, comically or not, that was me all of fourteen years old, knowing I was absolutely in love with the girl I was "going out with." A common and splendid intoxication.

I wonder now, again looking back, whether poetry became such a definite thing for me, because it seemed certain. Whereas what all children want to be certain, what should have been solid ground, family and home, was not certain, it was completely unpredictable. My mother did everything she could for my four sisters and me in the face of my father's alcoholism. She held the family together no matter what he did, threatened or destroyed. And it wore her out and she died in her fifties. I think she was worn out by it. So, the ground that should have been certain and reliable was not—but poetry was. This experience of Keats's poem, courtesy of Leonard Saffron, sewed the seed even in that thin soil and further astonishment followed.

As Ian Davidson says, "Poetry was big at Essex University when I was there."[2] It really was and it was brilliant. This page could be filled with the names of poets, editors, publishers and other writers who were associated with the university during and around my undergraduate time. The ethos in which I studied literature was confident, expansive and driven by generous teachers who were themselves combatants and poets. Boundaries were pushed against and there was perhaps still something in the air of the radicalism of the university's founding in the previous decade. It was also the case then, the mid 1970s, as Ian points out, when creative writing had not yet

---

1. John Keats, "To Autumn" in *The Poems*, edited by David Bromwich, Nicholas Roe and Graham Handley. Everyman's Library, 1999. pp. 233–34.

2. Geraldine Monk, editor. *Cusp: Recollections of Poetry in Transition*. Shearsman Books, 2012. p. 215.

whispered its promises to budget holders in universities as part of the stampede to monetize higher education.

Poets Ed Dorn, Ted Berrigan, Alice Notley, Tom Raworth, Andrew Crozier and Robert Lowell had been in the university. The evident gender profile in this list was also part of that time. I was taught how to read poetry by poets, Ralph Hawkins and Doug Oliver. Ralph set out before us without preconception, Prynne, Olson, Zukofsky, O'Hara, Ashbery, Oppen, Crozier, Niedecker and others. This was far from typical of the poetry on offer in British universities at the time. Ralph did what good teachers do. He set the best work before us and then stood aside almost, so we could think and talk. I was inside the goldmine. Before I even knew they existed the shackles of the narrow, provincial English poetry canon had been slipped off. It was in this atmosphere I went to my first poetry reading. And this qualifies as poetry arriving as anticipated—in a poetry reading after all. However, the experience as it unfolded was previously unknown to me and I knew nothing about the name Basil Bunting either.

> It is time to consider how Domenico Scarlatti
> condensed so much music into so few bars
> with never a crabbed turn or congested cadence,
> never a boast or a see-here;[3]

Bunting introduced himself as old as the century, *and so you'll excuse me if I sit down*. There were about twenty of us in a seminar room. It was early Spring and a blackbird sang outside the open window, it carried on offering counterpoint to *Briggflatts* throughout the reading. I still find it difficult to describe what the reading did to me. It was one of the most beautiful things and it was overwhelming. I was inside an architectonic experience and sensing its point of origin. The reading as with the poem itself exemplified what Bunting found to praise in Scarlatti, the exact placing of each element and the intricacy of the whole work without resort to false claims, a poetry condensed.

---

3. Basil Bunting, *Briggflatts* in *The Poems of Basil Bunting*. Edited by Don Share, Faber and Faber, 2016. p. 56.

Hearing *Briggflatts* opened the door to much else. Initially it led me to study and write at length about the first stanza of the poem. Encouraged by Doug Oliver, I used a recording of the reading to produce a visual trace of the words of the poem as spoken by Bunting. A printed tracing of the sounds, their pitch, duration and volume was produced by an oscilloscope-like machine in the linguistics department. This meant I could look very closely at the length or duration of vowels and consonants, the stress and patterns of sound in the reading of the lines, and in some ways see the pattern of sound and perhaps its relationship to the generation of meaning in the poetry. This was an attempt to look closely, to test, Bunting's own claims for the relationship between sound and meaning in poetry, though he of course would not accept the separation of those terms.

> Poetry is seeking to make not meaning but beauty; or if you insist on misusing words, its "meaning" is of another kind, and lies in the relation to one another of lines and patterns of sound . . . which the hearer feels rather than understands, lines of sound drawn in the air which stir deep emotions which have not even a name in prose.[4]

I think these ideas, adapted, not entirely accepted, perhaps sometimes mangled and only half grasped, are still important when I set out to write a poem. Beyond this immediate curiosity, hearing Bunting read, as with the poets supplied by Ralph Hawkins, opened up further discoveries of different kinds of poetry, and even led me to think I could write poetry. Toward the end of the *Briggflatts* Bunting writes, "Fifty years a letter unanswered;/A visit postponed for fifty years."[5] So, Jon, this essay can be read as a letter answered after fifty years—to Leonard Saffron, and a little less than fifty years, as a note of thanks to Basil Bunting.

4. Basil Bunting, "The Poet's Point of View," *Briggflatts*. Bloodaxe Books, 2009, pp. 42–43.

5. Basil Bunting, *Briggflatts* in *The Poems of Basil Bunting*. Edited by Don Share, Faber and Faber, 2016, p. 60.

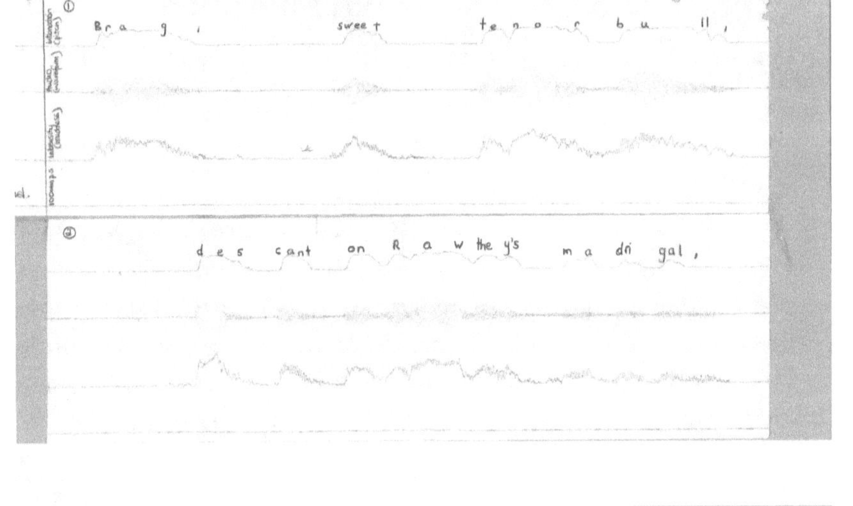

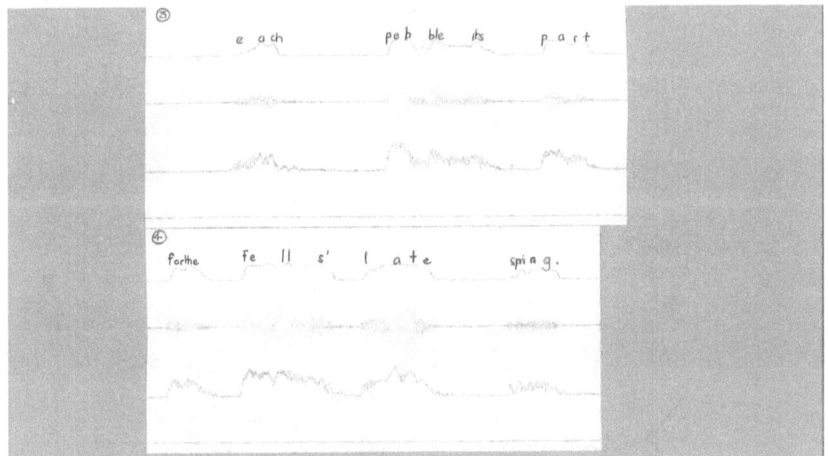

Figure 1. An oscilloscope tracing of a recording of Bunting reading the opening lines of *Briggflatts* at Essex University in 1976.

Encountering a Copy of Edvard Munch's Lithograph *Geschrei* (Berlin 1895) in London, 2019

Martin Corless-Smith

The term *encounter* has an adversarial air. It used to suggests conflict but has weakened now to suggest an accidental meeting, where the greatest danger is surprise or uncertainty. But this uncertainty is still a matter of life and death, like in a gothic tale where specific facts are recounted that still leave us questioning the nature of what is real and what is imagined, and what of the everyday remains inexplicable. The ghosts we encounter in such a tale are both the self and the other. The encounter is an event of knowledge and knowledge's failure.

It is something like the difficulty of comprehending being, together with and against the obvious and simple fact of our apparent existence.

* * *

Munch produced thirty copies of the print *Geschrei*. Or forty-five. Some accounts say four dozen. It was a copy of the painting (which was probably the copy of a pastel) he made earlier in 1893 based upon an event that took place while out walking with two companions above the town of Kristiania (now Oslo).

The print on show comes from the British Museum's own extensive print collection. It was made during a trip to Berlin. The printmaker ground the image off the stone's surface soon after Munch left, without his permission (the preferred limestone is hard to come by and is nearly always ground for reuse. Only images by established, well-selling artists would be preserved).

Munch entitled the painting *Der Schrei der Natur* (the scream of nature) in German and *Skrik* (shriek) in Norwegian. One title suggests the scream is an external force invading from the nonhuman realm; the other that it is a response to those forces emanating from the central figure itself. But actually the image implies that these are identical. And that is terrifying.

The lithographic process requires the artist to draw/paint directly onto a prepared stone that absorbs the greasy crayon or paint. In Munch's print the strokes are evidently both brush and crayon. The medium is unforgiving (even grease from fingertips can leave an impression).

The result gives the impression of a brisk sketch. In *Geschrei* there is a tentative border drawn an inch above the bottom edge of the print that suggests he has adjusted the length mid-sketch. The "error" adds to the sense this is a preliminary sketch rather than a copy and a print.

The grease marks attract an oil-based ink from a roller. Those areas left unmarked are kept wet to stop the ink from sticking. The stone is re-wetted and re-inked and prints are pulled one at a time.

In order to produce a lithograph that copies the original painting's (paintings') composition, Munch would have had to produce a reverse sketch on the stone, which might be done by making a cartoon on a non-absorbent sheet that is then pressed upon the stone to transfer the reverse image and act as a guide. The effort required suggests he saw printing as another necessary version of the image. Most artist prints tend to be reverse-imaged. Some of his were.

The lithographic image we see is one print of a copy of a copy. With that said it is still a thing in the world to be encountered. It is a copy and it is unique. It is not the same as seeing a reproduction. I don't allow it to be the same. I feel more. I engage more.

With an image like *The Scream* it is hard to know what original means, not just in terms of the physical object before us, but because the image is before us a thousand times before we are brought before it.

I went to the show twice. But even if I had been only once it would be hard to say I saw the piece, encountered the piece, for the first time where I stood. The image is as familiar to me as my own reflection.

Perhaps more so as it does not change the way one's own reflection must change, unless of course one accepts that everything changes for us as we change.

On the way up the stairs to the show one encounters a strip of the print on a poster the size of a house. It's ubiquitous. Is it too commonplace to be seen properly, to be effected by, to be encountered?

According to his various written accounts, (one is even partially rerecorded in pencil on a proof of the lithograph owned by the Metropolitan Museum of Art) the composition is a depiction of a particular historical/personal event. But it's hardly a self-portrait.

Munch was very committed to the self-portrait, producing them throughout his life. His tall lanky frame, slightly sunken eyes (with the right eye lid ever so slightly lower than his left) and his handsome, austere, perhaps even stoical square jaw are all very recognizable. Even the many representations of his hands remain utterly consistent from early academic renderings to later brash expressionistic slashes (not withstanding the loss of half a finger).

A genderless ageless face passes out of form, merging into nature. Or, nature floods the self-conscious creature with its vast energy that *he, she, it* is just a small instance of. The separation between self and world is breaking down.

Was it ever there?

Munch is taking his experience and distilling it into a universal experience, because his experience is the experience of becoming universal. Or realizing that he always was.

He is so present to the phenomena of the experience that he is becoming it, and becoming absent. There is something of the Hegelian dialectic, the structure of *Aufhebung* about this image that has transcended the event while harboring specific aspects of the experiential cause. The ghost is Munch because Munch has become a ghost.

The figure hovers over a railed embankment that looks like a jetty or a bridge. It is a bridge between sky and earth and land and water. Munch relied on this diagonal compositional device throughout his work, finding it first in his attempts at impressionist streets scenes seen from a balcony vantage point in Paris. The effect is precipitous.

The two background figures are passive, are not experiencing this ecstatic union. They are still disguised as gentlemen in their top hats. Top hats are an affect of society, which can only function if we ignore, for the most part, our contiguity with death. But we cannot always do this. Nietzsche's Zarathustra has run into the marketplace, and Freud and Jung are about to tell us that our neuroses are really disguising. The men occupy a small wedge, backed into a corner, that suggests their complacency is possible only by ignoring the whole of the scene of nature.

The Scream is at once the reception of the sounds and sights of nature, and the responsive realization that this power is dissolving us. In this it is his encounter with the death of the self in life.

Munch is made and broken by the experience. Munch becomes a figure as it dissolves out of being. The terror is that there is no escaping our mortality in this moment. If we are to live we are to die.

I say Munch becomes the figure, because Munch drew the figure, and in doing so he leaves it behind as his ghost. It is the ghost that both makes him and dissolves him. The scream is the self-consciousness of the death of the painter heralding in the painting. The painting survives us.

So the figure and nature share the contours of the light and sound waves. The sky is blood red: interior and exterior are in exchange. For Munch the pedestrian this is a nearly unbearable synesthetic event. For Munch the painter and for all those that see the paintings (or the black and white lithograph), it is still almost unbearable.

What we do in seeing this iconic image in its basic vocabulary of color and line, is experience something tantamount to Munch's own trauma. In this partial transmigration, in viewing his art, we also experience the dissolution of ourselves.

I don't mean to suggest that Munch's trauma becomes our own, that we suffer a similar transferred anxiety. The transference is nothing like an identity. It's more that the veracity of the work is so affecting it compels us to engage with it. The work's conviction is palpable which allows us to give ourselves over to it. We recognize the truth of it. It is undeniable.

It is something like Levinas's speculation on the face of another. It is the awareness of living otherness *there* that allows us to understand what it is to be human.

The presence of an essential human element in art allows us to notice our own humanity.

It's difficult to know what ingredients a work of art or literature needs in order for us to lose ourselves in it, but we are surely all familiar with the experience, and we can also detect a degree of necessary commitment on our part, a commitment that is not always available; this, along with a necessary set of circumstances. We don't always know why one piece touches us whilst another cannot. It is the same with meeting people.

It's rare that a serious and even difficult artist gains widespread appeal. Sometimes it takes a few generations. And some that were considered important disappear without a trace. Munch's lasting appeal and relevance might suggest that his ability to turn his real suffering into art has managed to hold onto a visceral human experience that we recognize as true.

One should not underestimate mere fame.

Munch is a lyric painter: he uses the personal the same way a lyric poet uses the I. The specific is a key to the universal.

The act of painting is simultaneously an instantiation of experience and a reification of its transformation into a universal statement. It produces and presents evidence of deliberation that focuses on the sensational aspect of being. Painting is an exemplary interaction between material and immaterial being. It delineates the processes that are the *sine qua non* of human consciousness as it interrogates its own coming into being.

The strange familiarity of Munch's scream does nothing to lessen its virtue as a model image for everyone's own crisis of being.

The canvas and the lithographic stone, like the page or the stage, are all an idealized ground. And upon this ground are the specifics that articulate its universality. The marks are of an instant and move beyond that instant, real and idealized simultaneously, necessarily.

The body is also a real and idealized ground. We are self and humanity both.

This ground is the *toward and from* of experience. Without the body we do not sense, without the universal of the symbolic order we do not know. Upon the specifics of experience we encounter the universal. The universal opens the door for the senses to know experience.

The figure is nobody. She is a ghost.

The lithograph *Geschrei* is concurrently the event of seeing it, the memory of having seen it before—a ghost and a ghost—the proof of its making, the history of the world, the paradigm of the human, our own death acknowledged.

Living and dying are identical.

This is what art says. This is the point of lyric poetry. The deixis.

I am specific. I am universal.

Living and dying are identical.

Art is the mirror where the ape sees its human face.

* * *

Walking to the British Museum one is buffeted by tourists, of which one is loathed to count oneself, and despite having been born in England, that is surely what I am now, as I do not live here permanently, do not pay taxes, and I do not work at the British Museum (though I do give a hurried lecture under the portico as an overdue rainstorm empties onto the sizzling piazza off Great Russell Street). I am one of a crowd, without identity.

For all these qualifications of certainty in thinking about the status of his print as original, I am certainly stood before his lithograph. I mean I was. I don't have much time as the show is packed. I have loved Munch for as long as I can remember. He is personal to me. He is personal to everyone else in the room too.

The show is so full I have to back away from the art I want to see because the crowd makes me feel like screaming. I look at the people instead. And I wander, the biggest person in the room, in the middle of the scrum, watching the people watch the art. I don't want to get in the way.

On the way there is the accompanying hover of a police traffic helicopter which lifts one into imagining London from the air, and into remembering the possibility of social discord, of acts of violence, terrorism, accidents and the tentative status of peace in such an oversubscribed conurbation. There is a sense of suspended anxiety. A city functions by staving off myriad calamities.

Protection and suppression in one sound.

I see a lot of living people, but people are dying all over London. I mean some will die today, because all these people are busy dying.

The great pleasure of visiting a museum is to see outstanding works of human craft and ingenuity, and much of it anonymous. The vast majority of them are dead.

* * *

Outside the main show, but before one officially leaves the exhibition, is the shop. I see a small reserved man, English, laughing with unstifled glee at what is on offer. And there is certainly something hilarious about it. I assume the British Museum is in on the joke. The Scream tea towels (I got one), The Scream post-it notes (I got some) . . . a spatula(!), cuff links, silk scarves, kitsch, boutique, tat, artisan . . .

It's kind of a portal back into the world of commerce. But I don't see it as a challenge mounted in favor of capitalism. Munch's work seems impervious to the degradation.

And capitalism is inside the show anyway.

Of Munch's four painted versions of the scream, two have been stolen. One recovered. One sold for what was at the time a world record price. Capitalists, and capitalism are interested perhaps in owning Munch's original(s), and at the same time in benefiting from their reproduction. You can't own the scream. It's already out of the bag.

Munch seemed ambivalent about selling his own paintings, often calling them his children. He often repainted sold pictures as if to reclaim them and returned continually to specific images throughout his career, painting them numerous times, as if each motif had become part of his personal language that allowed him to construct a sense of personal history, to which each new picture might add.

He was perhaps the first great painter/printmaker of his era, in that his graphic works were no less a vehicle for transcendence than his canvasses. It would be a mistake to think of the wide dissemination of his images as a dilution of their appeal. Or value. The value he worried about was not monetary. Nor in a making a single finished masterpiece.

He's not a Warhol or a Koons, joking about the aura of the piece and playing with idea of individual works and mechanical re-production. He's a serialist, and a ritualist. His images emerge from the trauma of being, and offer little consolation even as their presence offers proof of his animal survival and his momentary spiritual transcendence. They are wounds he carries with him. After artistic success comes the hangover. The next day he needs the same fix. It doesn't matter if it is a similar image: he is after all, the same creature that lived into dying the day before. No one blames a dancer for perfecting the same steps. Once Munch finds a motif he holds onto it.

He would have preferred to live surrounded by all his paintings, a perfect record of living, a frieze of life.

* * *

I have a facsimile of two Munch prints. I bought the first at the end of a trip around European art galleries in my early twenties, and I had the perhaps typical twentieth-century student dilemma of having to decide whether to buy something I wanted to keep, or buy food for the next two days. I chose death over life. And of course I survived.

It's a woodcut version of *The Voice*, and is as close to the original as technology and skilled printmakers can manage. It is not worth a fortune, but its effect upon me is still striking after many years of ownership. I didn't buy it as an investment, nor as a decoration, nor as a status symbol. I bought it as a young artist to remind myself of what art can achieve. Perhaps it was a fetish, or a shrine. I suppose Art, like us, is caught between religion and the marketplace. It's surely not unique, but I've never seen another, or even the original it was a reproduction of.

The unique events of a specific life are the only way that humanity happens. The universal requires the specific.

The other facsimile is *Geschrei*.

But often the human, that living/dying phenomenon, can only really see its meager happenstance as universal when it sees and experiences art. Only then does the human encounter its own humanity. You can't own events, even if they are your own. And you can't really own art, because it isn't a thing. It's a ghost. Or a ghost of a ghost. An encounter.

The artist is addicted to dying into the piece of art. When I paint I'm really reaching at something that I feel is true beyond the banal intrusions of my personality. I want to step aside and let the making of it be about the world rather than me. As a writer we write something into being, but really it writes us. Being happens simultaneously to our remarking upon it. Painting is life happening, and it happens to leave behind a vivid trace.

* * *

One evening I was walking
Out on a hilly path
near Kristiania—
with two
comrades. It
was a time when life
had ripped my
soul open.
The sun was going down—had
dipped in flames
below the horizon
It was like
a flaming sword
of blood slicing through
the concave of heaven
The sky was like
blood—sliced with
strips of fire
—the hills turned
deep blue
the fjord—cut in
cold blue, yellow, and
red colors—
the exploding
bloody red—on
the path and hand railing
—my friends turned

glaring yellow white—
—I felt
a great scream
—and I heard,
yes, a great
scream—
the colors in
nature—broke
the lines of nature
vibrated with motion
—these oscillations,
it brought also my
ears into oscillations—
so I actually heard
a scream—
I painted
the picture Scream then.[1]

—*From* the Private Journals of Edvard Munch.

* * *

The Scream is a symbol. *Symbolon* is from the Greek for *syn*, together and *bole*, a throwing or casting, (compare to bolt), so meaning "thrown together." The term was originally used to describe a token which matched another held as proof, and allowed the bearer entry into a secret creed. A symbol is half of a metaphor.

With the scream we feel we know exactly what the figure is experiencing, what the painting means and yet we also know that we cannot know for certain. The figure is our avatar, our doppelganger, staring out at us as if out of a mirror. We know the figure and we cannot.

A glimpse of the other reveals the true terror of existence. We see that all we know of being is this glimpse of otherness. We shockingly see that the self is just such a stranger, albeit one we have lived alongside for a while.

1. J. Gill Holland, editor and translator, *The Private Journals of Edvard Munch*. niversity of Wisconsin Press, 2005, pp. 64–65.

This is the encounter art offers. A full embrace would annihilate us, just as with Rilke's angel.

This is true for the artist and the viewer.

Keats had to return from the easeful death of his *Nightingale* (the day before I had given a talk at Keats's house in Hampstead).

In the painting Munch has cast aside the skill of draftsmanship and naturalistic color to allow a raw scar to emerge in its place. He has given away himself—sacrificed his status and training. He has become as fundamental as a scream.

A scream is not articulate. It is a pre-linguistic alert.

In order for the painting to work we must abandon ourselves to the viewing. We might do this in delight or in terror.

If we don't see the work this way, if we don't encounter it, it doesn't matter. It is nothing. We are not there.

Bataille considers the drama of the assailed self in his masterpiece *Erotism*. The "discontinuous" being is threatened by their awareness of the vast continuity that they must eventually return to. The border between self and otherness is the boundary where all human drama is played out. Two things threaten the self's integrity: Love and Death.

Munch's scream was to be a part of his lifelong project, The Frieze of Life, which accordingly was to be about, Life, Love and Death.

We might consider the threat to the self offered by Love as Beauty, the threat to the self offered by Death as the Sublime.

The Scream is not a symbol made from idealizing existence. It is not a platonic ideal. It is a reduction to the core self at the instant it is assailed by overwhelming nature. It is the sublime of death.

In the background two passive figures look over the harbor. Two passive ships are anchored in the fjord, part of an unresolved trinity.

Even the town is reduced to waves of catastrophic energy. There is nowhere else but this event, no place to retreat. The steeples push upwards as if to escape, but they only distort the forming power of nature.

* * *

Anxiety is the emotional state of our current zeitgeist. It might not have been our only overwhelming reality (see how Nietzsche describes the Greeks, bearing in mind that the "happy" Alexandrians had slaves, every era did, we still do), but it is apparently now the most prevalent.

Greed, anxiety and guilt overwhelm pity, joy and love. We all wish it were not so.

One could structure a defense of anxiety as the natural state of the paranoid animal, other than it not being apparently the case for animals at all. Dogs have their battles and settle back to lick their wounds.

Anxiety is peculiarly human.

Anxiety seems to be the dominant energy surrounding the embattled connection between the symbolic self (soul, self-consciousness) and the animal. How do we settle this conundrum? It is the state of the exhausted, world-choking faithless self: guilt, anxiety, greed; a shuffle that never quite alleviates any one of those states.

The major source (or at least an acceptable theory) for anxiety today might not be the fear of nature overwhelming us, it might be that we have overwhelmed nature. But it still spells out our death. Capitalism breeds anxiety with its necessary inequalities, manufactured conflicts and its aimless amoral fluctuations. Different sources, same anxiety.

* * *

Really it's too late to worry about the human dilemma. It always has been.

I don't mean we shouldn't try to be good, or better, save the planet, feed the poor, it's just that we are always swirling in an eddy down the sinkhole. History finished the morning it began, and culture danced out its dithyrambic death the moment a self reflected.

All we can do is worry, a choking acknowledgment of our catastrophic fate.

Munch's figures know this. Beckett's too, only his don't scream, they straight-face our hilarious degradation.

Eliot's intellectualize in a frozen impotency, Pound's indulge in a delusion of history and economics. . . . Bacon's wrestle in the blood and shit of erotic desire, Rothko's suicide, Berryman's drink, Hemingway's kill, Betjeman's giggle, Auden's simper, Larkin's snicker, Proust's reflect . . . Joyce's carouse.

* * *

But it is not a sensation of anxiety that grips me now, as perhaps it once was. I seem to recall my first impressions of the image being one of shock and near panic. I was young, and had perhaps not seen, or been allowed to see adults (even "tortured artists") acknowledging their true despair. The anxiety I felt was both personal and cultural. It was something like seeing the burgeoning punk movement, which was coincidental for me.

Now I feel pity: pity for Munch, and pity for any human who has ever felt fear and loneliness. Everybody.

And gratitude.

When we leave the gallery we are not changed and we are. Post-trauma. We have been electrified by the clear vision of one who dwelt in anxiety. We cannot live there to the same degree that he did. Only rare artists and saints (or the mentally ill) maintain that proximity to death. And we can be grateful for his gift as we are charged and exhausted by our new knowledge. Even old knowledge can be new.

The proliferation of the image of *the Scream* could be seen as an attempt to co-opt and dominate the figure into a neutralized cartoon. That seems to suggest a purposeful agenda for what must surely be a thoughtless surge in mindless productivity. Capitalism has no plan, like a virus has no plan.

Capitalism does want to end the anxiety of death and replace it with material accumulation. But it always fails to alleviate anxiety.

Munch's *Scream* tears through the tea towels and the post-it notes. That's the great joke of the exit shop. We can't help but be implicated by the image. And its trivialization. We know both tendencies. To feel and to ignore.

And the truth is the scream can be viewed as hilarious. And it can be seen as a cartoon. And it is still capable of being engaged with as an artistic achievement and a cultural phenomenon of great power.

Like the image of the cross, its proliferation is not the diminution of its power, but an aspect of its success. At any moment we can choose to look or not to. Either way we disappear.

Is this image the modern crucifixion, with the self as the new Christ?

* * *

Some of Munch's pictures are not "good." He got tired of being good. He wants to paint his own death and his own jealous love as banal set pieces from a drama he has not written.

Very soon one understands that mastery is really only useful so that the self can get out of the way. A brush can be trusted to do what is required. If art is self-expression, great art is expression that is no longer hampered by banal vanity, or mere technique.

In *Creation and Anarchy*, Giorgio Agamben expands on an idea of Deleuze's to point to a description of "mastery" in art. All artists are artists in potential, which simply means they are capable of making art. In balance with this potential is their potential-not-to. Masters understand (consciously or not) that in order to not merely obey their technical ability to make they must also resist, otherwise art is mere "execution," proceeding with false confidence towards a completed form. According to Agamben "mastery is not formal perfection, but quite the opposite, it is the preservation of potential in the act."[2]

Without the will to resist, art would be mechanical entailment.

Consciousness acts as a resistor (Lyotard).

Great art accepts resistance to eloquence as a necessary trait.

The "scream" is not and should not be eloquent. It must accept its trembling nature.

Eventually Munch seemed to dash off paintings, unconcerned with closure as such. Instead he was indicating the briefest glimpse of being. Art was not asked to reformulate these glimpses as fully realized. All life was passing into painting, all painting into life.

The best piece at the show is his first masterpiece, *The Sick Child* (1885) painted when he was twenty-two. It depicts his favorite sister's death. He never recovered.

It's replayed in a later academic success *Spring* (1889), similar composition, window to the right with light and air entering the deathbed scene (not at this show). Only in *Spring* there is a hint of the rejuvenation of the seasons. The curtains billow with actual air. If anything it is a step backwards, a loss of faith. With *the Sick Child* the colors are a vibrating green and red, but the green is drab and bilious. The window offers no fresh air. It is a stab of cold ice in the ferment of the battling colors. The painting never settles.

2. Giorgio Agamben, *Creation and Anarchy*. Stanford University Press, 2019, p. 19.

There is no consolation for dying but forgetting, living. Which is dying.

* * *

Sitting passively afterwards, on a sweltering tube ride west, I am slumped in my animal. My flame has dwindled to a flicker. If the tube crashed into a tunnel wall I would slip out of consciousness as easily as a sigh.

Addendum

As the next summer of my life approaches, I review this essay written at the end of the last one. It is nearly ready. But since it was written the world has accelerated towards demise or an overwhelming acknowledgment of it, with a febrile intensity not known for decades. We have been sitting like exhausted children after the party, docile in the back seat in a post-euphoric coma. And now we see no one has been steering.

I think that poems and paintings have punctuated my life with moments of sublimity and beauty. Even now the temporal pressure of another approaching summer is lifted by the floating truth of Munch or Keats or even by lesser known, less universal artists and writers. Even in isolation I populate my emptying society with blessed company that is ageless. I find myself alive as a self in the company of the dead and see that this has often been the case. The encounter of the poem and the encounter of the painting is the self hovering above the body, seeing it's self in passing.

When we sit on the underground train we look over and see the self reflected back at us, anonymous and passive. The face is distorted and colorless, like Munch's famous mask. The drama of life is suspended, the trials of sustenance float away. The underground carriage is empty, and the monadic eye has at last accepted that life has been nothing but a passing encounter, even with the phenomenon called self.

Cotton

Eduardo Corral

I move through life undiagnosed. Each time I read a book, letters leap out of some words, fracturing sense and music. I have to blink a few times to make the words legible again. Some letters—especially vowels— disappear right before my eyes. I constantly misspell words and I find it impossible to scan a line of verse—my ears cannot distinguish between stressed or unstressed syllables. I misremember proverbs. My tongue refuses to properly pronounce words: I mumble, I stutter. Sometimes I have to reread a word a few times to unlock it. I call people by the wrong name. Even family members.

* * *

In fourth grade, I was taught the three "Cs" of the Arizona economy: citrus, copper, cotton. (Those industries are long gone). When I read the word *cotton* in my state history textbook, my eyes often didn't register the two vowels. I'd see an incomplete word: "c tt n." My inability to read like my classmates made me fearful of class presentations, books. I became a very quiet student. Inside me, though, bewilderment spiraled like a dust devil. Then I learned I could suppress my anxiety if I willed myself to stop thinking about my learning disability. (When Bill Clinton revealed he compartmentalized his feelings, I realized this wasn't a healthy coping strategy. Thanks, Bill.) The fear of being labeled a student with a learning disability also fueled my emotional suppression. If I dwelled on my difference, I might tip off my teachers. I didn't want that. What if they blamed my parents? What if they dragged me to a doctor?

* * *

The list of words I can spell correctly on the first try is not extensive: mestizo, pulmonary, Barcelona, avalanche, Duchamp, cigarillo, mesquite, Paraguay, nodule, villanelle, taxidermist, tableau, hemisphere, Mireya, mercado, haboob.

* * *

Southern Arizona has two seasons: summer and not summer. In July, at the height of the monsoon season, the temperature often rises to over one hundred degrees. As a child, I explored the neighborhood with my siblings in the morning and at dusk. If we felt reckless, we played under the scorching sun. The coal-hot sidewalks burned the soles of our feet and the lack of shade drove us into the cotton fields behind our house. Curled in the shadow of still-green cotton plants, we cooled our bodies, pretended the distant roar of cars was the sound of an approaching dust cropper.

* * *

In a poem whose title I don't remember, Robert Vasquez calls the mouth, eyes, and ears "organs of intake." In eighth grade, I changed the way I took in language. I flipped a bookmark length-wise, placed it underneath a line of language, which isolated it from the rest of the text. I deciphered—word by word—the line. Then lowered the bookmark. This method allowed me to sense, for the first time, the propulsive force of sentences. Words clicked forward. A phrase branched into a complete utterance. Reading had been, until that moment, a series of pauses, hesitations. This method also instilled a tactile-rich relationship with language—to understand a word, I sometimes have to touch it.

During lectures, I looked away from the face of the person speaking. I learned not to jot down everything—too much language overwhelmed me. I wrote down key phrases. By directing my gaze to the page, I was able to watch my right hand write out what my ear took in. I processed language twice, which hardwired my mind to transform key language into a kind of hyperlink. When I poured through my notes, I recalled most of the unwritten information by "clicking" on the language: by putting pressure on key phrases, my mind retrieved other language, more information.

* * *

Ampersand, infrared, gossamer, pharmacy, Maradona, peninsula, hoarfrost, clementine, dyslexia, parachute, avocado, ocotillo.

* * *

In 1997, at Arizona State University, I signed up for a Mexican American Literature course. On the first day, the professor announced we'd be writing poems mid-semester. This didn't appeal to me. So after class, I hurried to the registrar's office to drop the course, but I decided against it because the class met twice a week at 1:00 p.m. "I could do that," I told myself. (Full disclosure: I'm not a morning person.)

The poem I wrote was horrible. But that doesn't matter. What has stayed with me is this: the shock of recognition as I struggled with language, not to glean meaning, but to create meaning. My learning disability, up to that moment, was a disadvantage, a secret I never shared with anyone. But as I worked on my first poem, I began to relish the way my mind scrambled syllables, slowed down sentences. Language, under my pen, felt different: malleable and exciting. I realized my learning disability had been teaching me—from elementary school to college—to scrutinize syntax, to dwell with bewilderment, to seek different angles of approach.

Most importantly, though, that first poem compelled me to rethink my disability. It was an asset—a life-changing asset. Yes, it often halts my reading, which never fails to annoy me. But it instilled an attentiveness to language which made possible a life as a poet.

* * *

Last summer, while reading a novel by a Mexican author, I encountered the word "cotton." Once again, my mind deleted the vowels. Then it transformed the gaps in the word into tiny heaps of snow. I touched the word. It was cold.

Wind Rose

Laura Da'

Over an opened road atlas, my dad gently traces my child's finger along highway routes and tells him stories of all the bluebirds in Bickleton and the size of the sturgeons in the Columbia River. Watching them brings the feel of the paper under my own skin. These tender memory palaces offer directives that compel and confound me. Opening a book to an intricately inked world of the imagination seduces me into dizzy infatuation; gazing at an allotment map with my grandfather's name crossed out in pale violet stills me with grief. Considering poetic encounters bends my mind into a wind rose curving to the cardinal directions of my steering influences.

North

I grew up on the north side of a mountain. No city, no ambient light, no noise of traffic. In one ear, I could hear the humming cascade of burntboot creek scuttling off the side of a rock face, and in the other, the Snoqualmie River's branching.

My affinities for poetic structure split into recognizable directions. My dominant hand sends each poem to navigate rolling meanders. I have a tendency to branch, and long, segmented poems are a predilection I'm always dipping my toes into. My desire for symmetry rounds the edges, so each stanza holds a taste of my childhood home: concrete foundations laid in the moist green grass of the Cascade foothills and the frank sound of a hammer.

I slept on bare mattresses laid down on subfloor for years. The back of the house where my bedroom was squared out gaped unfinished against the backdrop of the mountainside. Playing hide and seek with my neighbors, I once crouched into the folds of a tarp that had been stapled across the boards. When I fell out along the bottom seam of the blue vinyl, I landed with a thump and was quickly found.

Long two by fours of downy skinned cedar siding were always propped on sawhorses. I remember working constantly, wearing a white shirt over my clothes that had been laundered so many times that the elastic of the neckband tore apart from the shirt itself like a grimy necklace.

When I looked out of any window, my sight was hemmed by the dark blue of the mountainside, the spikey green of the cedars, the marbled, velvety down of ubiquitous rain.

That early eye-scape makes its damp way into my poems with their boxy stanzas and flooded obsessions. The poetic structures I am drawn to were probably set within the confines of my northern childhood where my nostalgic affinities perch precariously on a damp green mountainside.

East

Western maps are oriented to the east; the function and binary is embedded in the word itself. I turn my head to the east to consider the roots of my poetic traditions and to bow to its inevitable comfort of community and weight of grief.

For many generations, my family conceptualized Shawnee Territory inside the tender paper prison of maps. A return to home cost a long drive plotted through the coffee wringed pages of a road atlas. When I think of my tribe, I can feel it first in my body—there is the blazing heat of vinyl seats under my thighs, the waxy smell of my hands sweating over the steering wheel. I would tumble out of the car onto the dusky green of Northeastern Oklahoma and breathe its funky air, whining for a cherry limeade from Sonic.

Writing and being Shawnee are twined in my memory. Listen, when I say all my Shawnee relatives are poets I'm not speaking metaphorically. My uncles read poems to their beloveds at every funeral and the parlors murmur with sighs; my aunt writes letters that make me laugh unto the point of pain; I have an ancestor who wrote letters to congress each Friday for most of his adulthood.

About a decade ago, I was drifting away from poetry, and it seemed like my lost words were erasing me from being Shawnee. During this time, my tribe started a community initiative to send tribal members to visit our traditional homelands. It was summer and my best friend was going, so I signed up. There were about one hundred of us and we stayed in Chillicothe, Ohio. The subtext of this point on the map is that Chillicothe is the principal city of the traditional territory of the Shawnee Nation.

We rode together in chartered buses. At one point, the driver refused to go on until he was provided a slice of pie and a cup of black coffee. On the eighth hour of the drive from Seneca, Missouri to Chillicothe, Ohio the chief finally let the head-piece from the sound system drop to the velour seat at the front of the bus, and instead of quizzing the crowded Pullman on lineage and Shawnee history she began murmuring quietly with a friend about the best foods to eat during chemo therapy.

Disorienting cities are a function of colonial violence and erasure. There is a dominant narrative of indigenous people as unsettled and un-gathered. In Shawnee, there are many words for city. Shawnee cities are balanced by their own measures. There is a Shawnee word for city—Chillicothe. If you trace your finger along state atlases throughout the middle of America, you may find Chillicothes. There is one in Ohio; there are Chillicothes in Kansas, in Missouri, in Texas. The names of our villages live far from us now; the Shawnee of Chillicothe are only passing through.

The grief of returning to a stolen homeland ripped the capacity of narrative from my mouth. On that trip, I did not sleep for days. I picked fights with my best friend in the musty Midwestern motels as we moved from one historical site to another.

On the third night, I started writing the fractured images of the day on the rough drag of the Quality Inn and Suites stationary. Shawnees at Prophet's Town burnt signal fires to protest the signing of the Treaty of Greenville. Clustered cabins buffered by listing expanses of corn for five miles along the Mad River channeled messages up and down from village to village. Soldiers marched in through smoke and left in smoke, torching the cornfields. That village sits underground at the Shawnee Prairie Preserve. The re-created prairie is reseeded with over 100 grasses and plants native to Darke County.

Prophet's Town: two rivers flowing into a confluence and gravel mounds cropped within the prairie openings fringed with trees. I woke up at the desk the next morning, having slept contorted in a dark and dreamless void, a history of words inked all around my head.

South

When I am writing poems in the hazy stew of deep, deep infatuation, a trill begins with the plotted dot of the pencil hitting paper, that dot goes on a quest, and the poem quickens around an image as a gesture of honoring potential.

There is an expanse to the skyscape of Northern New Mexico that woos me. It is impossibly vast. South from around Pojoaque into the approach to Santa Fe talks to me about the margins that I had always imagined hemming the fabric of reading and writing and living and speaking; it makes a proposal that those limits are negotiable. I have never fallen for anything quite so hard as that narrative of open sky and red rock. Each blank page gives me a sliver of that light, and a whisper of that potential for freedom.

Images are the poetic territory of joy. There is a southern vision that I'm always writing my way back to: my child was almost two when he was given a name that had been held for him for three generations. At a museum opening to honor his ancestors, there was a picture of his grandfather as a small child in the arms of a woman. I was carrying my son like that and everyone stopped and laughed. My son looked so much like his grandfather in the photograph that we became ourselves the dynamic image. Inside the exhibit, we became the exhibit.

The next day, we sat with relatives on the rim of a plaza's dusty parking lot. There was a public dance and it was crowded with folks around town for the annual Indian Market. My son watched the dancers and began to move carefully from one foot to the next, his arms raised to mimic the spread of wings.

There are images that bless each poem, even from a very distant vantage. I count on them to see me through when I sit and apply myself to write. Sliding down a long dark tunnel, the image is the grapple. I am a poet drawn to dark corners, but my work is lit by the propulsive desire to hold an image of blazing joy at the center. Inside each poem my mind's eye turns to the south, watching a small figure in Northern New Mexico dancing like an eagle.

West

I have an affinity for concluding stanzas. Some poets like to listen at their readings for a laugh or a soft sigh, but I prefer a gasp. A strong ending is a salty baptism—it should burn through your lungs and make you glad for the land under your feet.

I wrote about a third of my last book of poetry hooked to blood cleaning machines. I was waiting for a transplant. If I allowed myself to become lost inside a flux of engagement with my own writing, I would be stunned by a blaze of pain when the session of dialysis ended. I needed to keep a finger on the off switch and my mind on the solutions floating in my body, not flitting around the intricacies of rhyme or line break. Those years were harsh, but they taught me not to trust the agency and inherent self-indulgence of a planned ending.

Seattle's Medical Hill lists on an incline between downtown's trickling into pools of Salish Sea and the arching eastward sprawl of residential neighborhoods. I like the feel of the name Medical Hill; it swirls around in my mind as a kind of counter-anachronism, both ancient and modern. Most folks don't call it that anymore, but when I want to call the place into my mind, that's the name I use.

When I remember the hospital, I can feel it most from the ankles, the deep stretch that entering it required and the vantage that changed so rapidly from the scale of the tilt. Driven over the city bridges on the very lick of midnight's leaving, I walked into the transplant wing as revelers sang for the end of the year. Five days later I was wheeled out in the rain. A steady breeze up from the bay smelled like salt and coffee. My feet no longer fit into my leather boots. I asked for my watch to assure myself that I was staying in a place where I might still need it. Braced and dazed, I bent my swollen fingers around a pencil—shaking and shaking, but poetry makes allowances for these vulnerabilities.

A map legend seeks to compress sensory encounters into comprehensible symbols. The ambiguity of hometown becomes an opaque dot, river is rendered into placid blue threads, and the miles of a life's peregrinations shrink into fingernail scale.

I earned perspective when I was sewn back into the city. The sun never departs; the western edge of Seattle is simply the most auspicious viewpoint to perceive the earth spinning. The page only ends its encounter to facilitate the turning.

Blackfish State[1]

1.

My son points up to the
ship's name—The Kaleetan.

Arrow, I say
in Salish.

A breeze tweezes a flight
of my hair with his,

so tonally similar
our locks

are inseparable—
murky raspberry brunette

in the softly drunken
beforehand light.

---

1. "Blackfish State" was first published in *Moss. A Journal of the Pacific Northwest*, https://mosslit.com/.

2.

Once I dipped
into the cove
on a dare.
    Dumbstruck—
cold water in my ears,
blanket of silt
resting on the starfish
so thick on the rocks
that I couldn't help
balancing myself
two fingers
on a bright magenta tentacle.
Shivering up the beach
I lobbed a dirt clod
at a faded church billboard
asking me if I had
    a God shaped hole.

There was a pod of orcas
visible from the ship home,
rippling neat and frisky
as a row of dominoes
toppling in perfect order.

The woman next to me
gripped the guardrail
with such frenetic thrill
her false fingernails
popped off one by one.
    A bright coral ellipsis
    gliding into the wake.

Past tense—
a sleek hole inside me,
moving in the shape
of a blackfish.

3.

One hand to steady
the mild June currents underfoot,

it feels off to clasp my son
to my left hip, but my right
abdomen is a swollen coil of dialysis tubing.
I shade his forehead from the rain
with a brochure
for a bed and breakfast
and register
the avid track of his eyes
taking in the water's blurred end-line,
the flicker of recognition
at the island's
   hump-backed breech.

Subtitles for a Film Never Seen: Writing "The Angel of History"

Carolyn Forché

> "The renunciation of the first-person subject is not a voluntary renunciation, nor, thus, is it an involuntary abdication. When the subject becomes absence, then the absence of a subject, or dying as subject, subverts the whole sequence of existence, causes time to take leave of its order, opens life to its passivity, exposing it to the unknown, to the stranger—to the friendship that is never declared."
>
> —Maurice Blanchot, *Writing the Disaster*

> "In the night-vaulted corridors of the Hôtel-Dieu, a sleepless woman pushes her stretcher along the corridors of the past. *Bonjour, madame. Je m'appelle Ellie.*"
>
> —*The Angel of History*

In the late spring of 1986, I was taken by taxi at night in the company of my husband, to the urgent care of Hôtel-Dieu de Paris on the Place du Parvis Notre Dame. Our son had been born by caesarean a week or so earlier, and I would be found to be suffering from septicemia, possibly as a consequence of the surgery. The hospital was chosen by the taxi driver, as the nearest to us with an open urgent care. It was raining and windy I remember, and the lights of Boulevard St. Germain blurred then jeweled in the back and forth of the windshield wiper as we entered Boulevard St. Michele and crossed the Petit Pont to Ile de la Cité. The driver pointed to the entrance for "urgencies" and he said something like *oui, this is God's hotel.*

Emergency was dimly lit and calm, as was the rest of the hospital, which seemed to have in residence many insomniacs, such as the woman with whom I would shortly share a room. They walked along the corridors, rolling their bottle trees, holding their gowns closed behind them. Windowless arches opened onto the courtyard below and the wet night. These patients, mostly men, nodded to us and to each other as they passed, and gathered here and there to smoke cigarettes. The nurses wore white starched caps and uniforms which I thought had vanished years ago, and much of the equipment, syringes and such, were made of glass, which altogether made it seem as if this hospital wasn't real, but a hospital from a war film, a distant memory or a dream, and as such was a place for ghosts to be care-taken. The poet Rainer Marie Rilke had been a patient here in the earliest decade of the century, but before knowing this I sensed that much had happened in this place, and many of those who died here might still be walking the halls. In my fever, I remember thinking that they weren't insomniacs—they were ghosts.

The nurses lifted me onto an ice-bed to bring the fever down. I was floating on my back in a cold lake, looking up not at passing clouds but passing ceiling tiles. These nurses were like those with whom I worked as a young nurses' aid during high school. Somehow they had returned, bringing quietness, an apothecary lined with amber bottles, glass ampoules and cloth bandages. Was I delirious? No. I saw very clearly the bottle of silver light and felt precisely the needle entering the vein. Are there ghosts here? I asked, and a nurse laughed and said perhaps, some people say so. There has always been a hospital here, since the seventh century, not this building of course, but always a hospital on this very ground, so why not? You seem to be feeling better. We'll soon take you up to your room.

They advised my husband to take my purse home with him, but before leaving, he placed my small notebook and a pen under my hand.

My roommate was awake when they wheeled me in, sitting on the edge of her bed, rubbing her forearms vigorously, rocking back and forth, her feet hanging slipper-less over the edge, her legs thin and red beneath her child-sized hospital gown.

And what are you? she asked. Not who, but what. Was it still night? Morning? *Bonjour? Bonsoir?*

I'm a poet, I said, surprising myself because I almost never tell anyone this, especially in the beginning.

And I am also a poet. And I don't speak any languages fluently, she said in strangely accented French. No language? I had not heard anyone say this before—surely everyone has at least one language—

Mesdames, the nurse sang out, *bonne nuit*. It is time for you to be asleep.

And I don't sleep, the woman whispered, rocking again, now rubbing her face. I saw that she had some kind of rash all over her body, and a few open sores. The nurse tucked the crisp sheets around me, put the call button on my pillow, and the pen and notebook on the bedside table along with a water pitcher, emesis basin, and a thermometer which was to be my own, and then she switched off the lamp and again said good night.

English? the woman whispered. You are English? American. Ah. It would be better if you were English. England is the enemy of France, you see. Or it was, long ago. But at least you aren't French. I couldn't have shared my room with a French woman. And you're a poet? I asked, hoping to befriend her, or at least to keep her from having the same contempt for me as she bore toward the French. Of course I am a poet. What else? And I loathe Paris, I will tell you that.

It was the second strange thing she said to me: she spoke no language fluently and she hated Paris. I suppose it's possible to hate any city, but this one? With its twenty-three bridges, cathedral and catacombs, its lamplight, its cemeteries? I felt myself fortunate to have arrived in Paris in time for the birth of our son, Sean. We thought, in some way, that if he were born in Paris, he would have the city's protection for the rest of his life. As Ernest Hemingway wrote in *A Moveable Feast,* in a passage I copied into Sean's birth album: *if you are lucky enough to have lived in Paris as a young man—.*[1]

I begged pardon of her, and wanted to ask why she hated this city, but she had lain down on her side and seemed asleep. The starched nurse arrived again, padding across the floor on her rubber-soled shoes to pull the rail up on the side of the woman's bed and to cover her with a blanket. She looked at me, and walked out, shaking her head.

I lay awake for what seemed hours, missing my infant son whom I knew was safely asleep in a basket beside his father. The fever that wracked me a few hours earlier, that made me feel impossibly cold,

---

1. "Foreword" by Patrick Hemingway. *A Moveable Feast: The Restored Edition*. Scribner, 2009. p. XII.

had abated. As many others do who are tethered to an IV, I watched the fluid drip down the tube, and into my arm. As many others, I wanted to yank it out, get dressed, and go home. I needed an antibiotic. I didn't need anything for pain or sleep. I didn't need whatever was sending me floating over an orchard in winter.

When I opened my eyes, the hospital was awake, the door open, and the woman was again sitting on the edge of her bed. A new nurse came.

Bonjour Mesdames, avez-vous bien dormi? She carried one then another tray of croissants and café au lait, a folded newspaper, not *Le Monde,* and vases filled with violets. She cranked my bed until I was sitting up, set the tray on a rolling cart beside me, took the empty IV. bottle from its hook and replaced it, did the same for my roommate, then left us alone.

Her name was Ellie she told me, and once again she'd found herself, *malheureusement,* hospitalized for an outbreak of St. Anthony's Fire, a disease common in the Middle Ages. She seemed to have forgotten that I told her I was an American, nor did she remember anything about the previous night, insisting that it was impossible that she'd ever said she was a poet.

Did I say that? No. I could not have said it. But the nurses say I'm sometimes out of my head.

The two books of poetry I had published by that time were collections of first-person, free-verse lyric-narratives that depended on the constructed illusion of a speaking voice, recounting lived or remembered experience. There were a few prose poems among them, and the others could have been prose as well, I suppose, had they not been lineated more or less syllabically, with attention to the drama of enjambment. They resembled dramatic monologues, but with a speaker corresponding to the poet's self, and expressive of her experience, sensibility, and consciousness. The confessional poets had strongly influenced my poetic formation, as they were the dominant school in the academy during my coming of age, although I had the good fortune to be introduced by a mentor to the work of the Black Mountain poets, and recall being mesmerized by the voice of Denise Levertov on a reel-to-reel recording played in a long-ago seminar room. The work of the Objectivists also interested me, particularly the poetry of George Oppen, but I belonged to no school or movement, and came to be most strongly influenced by the translated works of European and Latin American poets. While my first two books differed in subject matter, these differences had to do with the circumstances of my life rather than a shift in my poetics. In the first collection, I was an American poet of an old-world, Central European upbringing, inclined toward exploration of the wilderness; the second was written in the aftermath of becoming a translator of the poet Claribel Alegría, and a witness to repression in El Salvador, where she had spent her childhood. After the second book's publication, and for reasons having as much to do with social consciousness as poetics, I was restless, and wishing to break the constraint of writing poems in the first person. To get out from under the "I" that made such claims for itself, and to write as "an I without I." (Blanchot)

During the previous eight years, my life had been one of continuous upheaval, wherein I lived and traveled in many countries, some of them at war, and the pace was such that there wasn't time to reflect, to order the disparate moments into a coherent narrative. I experienced memory as kaleidoscopic and sound as an echo chamber; one world resembled another, one violence another.

Tracing my steps back along the path taken toward the writing of the ruptured, polyphonic sequences of *The Angel of History*, the book I would write in the aftermath of my stay in Hôtel-Dieu, I would find markers in my reading of the poetry of Edmond Jabès, particularly *The Book of Questions*, a four-volume dialogic reflection on the Holocaust, translated by Rosmarie Waldrop, and also the text of Claude Lanzmann's epic documentary on the Shoah, with brief forays into the filmscripts of Marguerite Duras. I imagined writing the subtitles for a film never seen, and had a very provisional sense of the form this would take. But if I go all the way back to the moment when the shift in my poetics began, I would find myself in that room in Hôtel-Dieu with Ellie, who spoke no languages fluently and who seemed not to know the difference between day and night.

Ellie was a German Jew who had hid during the Shoah, first in Germany and then in France, along with her two young sons, at least one of whom apparently did not survive this hiding. Her story emerged brokenly over the course of the week we stayed together in a room filled with light, with windows open to the spring air. My husband visited every day, but couldn't bring our son with him, as the nurses informed us of some possible contagion on the ward. At certain times, a group of men in hospital gowns gathered in the hall near our door. Smoke from their Gauloises rose about them, and if I took my bottle tree out to the hall for air, they would always offer me a cigarette. There were jonquils blooming down in the courtyard among the manicured hedges, and one early morning, a dust of snow covered the flower beds.

In German, in French, in broken English and a Slavic language that may have been Polish, Ellie let fall the pieces of her history, pausing to stare at the wall for long moments or to fall asleep. On waking, she would forget where she'd left off, at times repeating herself, at others leaping forward months or years, with brief returns to the present in her hospital room, or to describe the apartment where she lived on the third floor in the third arrondissement, always alone. If I seemed not to understand, particularly when she slipped into Polish, she would grow frustrated and try a different language or throw up her hands. More than once, a nurse in the room caught my eye and touched her finger to her head to signal that Ellie was not well in her mind. At first I thought they may be right, but after some hours, I realized that this fragile woman whose skin was on fire was attempting to transmit, with unbearable lucidity, in signals of ruptured utterance, through the prism of her several languages, a truth from the horrors of the near past to the obliviousness of the present. I picked up my pen and began transcribing her offerings, one upon another, into the notebook. If this was her court of last resort, I was her stenographer. When she saw that I was writing, her voice became more insistent. It was my impression that she recognized the possibility that her testimony might escape the confines of the room and of our time together. Something might come of this. Thereafter, she slept less, still oscillating among languages, her simple declarative sentences grouted with silence. Questions were intrusive; I served her best by listening intently, by remaining in a receptive state. She was willing to repeat herself until she felt that I understood. I kept the French in French, the English in English. Whatever she said in

German or Polish was mostly lost, marking in the notebook an interval of absence that I notated: GERMAN or POLISH. When she slept, I read back through my partially illegible script, repairing the cursive, but not attempting to re-order the text nor impose an interpretive supplement. What I saw on the page resembled subtitles to a film never shown, narrated by trauma "in different voices." During those seemingly rare moments when she realized that she had made herself understood, she held my gaze and allowed herself a moment of tranquility.

By the time I was well enough to go home, there were no pages left. We didn't exchange telephone numbers and I never learned her address in the third arrondissement. In Hôtel Dieu we had been sequestered from the city, the world, our lives beyond its walls. I wasn't to recognize what my encounter with her would mean to my work until two years later, when I was living in an off-season rental in Provincetown's East End, facing the waters of the bay. My son was by this time a toddler. My husband was temporarily working in another city and drove north every weekend to be with us. During the week, I devoted myself to child care and housekeeping, and took walks through the dunes and the beech forest. At night I read and wrote notes *toward* poems, as I imagined at the time, but these "notes" suggested the form of the work I would soon undertake.

My closest friend, the poet Daniel Simko, held a fellowship that year at the Fine Arts Work Center, and lived in an apartment on the West End. He had fled with his family as a young man from former Czechoslovakia after the Warsaw Pact invasion of 1968. My father's family, like Daniel's, was from eastern Slovakia, so we felt affinities beyond poetry. He became like a brother to me. That winter, he was worried that I hadn't yet returned to my own poetry, that the silence that followed the publication of my second book had gone on too long. It was time. He offered to take Sean for two hours each afternoon provided I write while they were away, and he wanted to see the fruits of my labors. It was difficult at first to return to that state of meditative expectancy before the page that allowed the flow of language. The silence of the house in Sean's absence, the lapping sound of the water against the pilings, the crying gulls all kept me alert to the world about me. The window framed a greying deck and a stretch of kelp piles, where a small wooden boat, painted blue, was overturned. When I set my hands on the keys of an old, heavy typewriter, a line longer than breath went to the page, not lyric but utterance. Someone not myself was speaking. Someone not myself answered. A third voice made a statement about the world. The first voice answered. It was Ellie.

As if someone not alive were watching:

> *Bonsoir. Est-ce que je vous dérange?*

For the past two years I had thought of her, or rather, she had visited my thoughts both waking and sleeping, a revenant recounting the smell of hay in a barn loft, of sleeping in the barn with pigs and goats, of the German patrol as it passed, of another barn locked and set on fire with people inside, burning in their striped pajamas, and nevertheless spring came and the crops once again rose out of the earth, and the forty-four children hidden in the farmhouse in Izieu were discovered and taken away to the camps.

> *Comment me vint l'ecriture? Comme un duvet d'oiseau sur ma vitre, en hiver.*
> In every window a blank photograph of their internment.
>
> Within the house, the silence of God. Forty-four bedrolls, forty-four metal cups.
> And *the silence of God is God.*

The line "How did writing come to me? Like birds" down on the glass in winter" was not Ellie or myself speaking, but René Char, from his poem "La bibliothèque est en feu." Others also came, and I told myself to let anyone in who arrives, wishing to converse as Jabès's rabbis conversed in "The Book of Questions." After all, that work begins with this admission: *You are the one who writes and the one who is written.*[2] He imagines the narrating self as not *in* the book, but at its threshold, never arriving in the person of himself, but in a doorway through which others enter. I wanted to emulate his comportment toward these others. However, I did not want to assemble an impenetrable text, so I allowed the poem to be guided by the advice of Theodor Adorno in his *Minima Moralia:*

---

2. Edmond Jabès, *The Book of Questions, Vol. I,* translated by Rosmarie Waldrop. Wesleyan University Press, 1972, p. 11.

> "Properly written texts are like spiders' webs: tight, concentric, transparent, well-spun and firm. They draw into themselves all the creatures of the air. Metaphors flitting hastily through them become their nourishing prey. Subject matter comes winging toward them. The soundness of a conception can be judged by whether it causes one quotation to summon another."[3]

The title poem in *The Angel of History* belongs to Ellie: a récit éclaté transcribed in a hospital room. It is not, for the most part, written in lines, but rather in fragments of dialogue and the declarative language of notebook entries. I inhabit the first-person "I" only three times: *When my son was born I became mortal* and *Eight years later in France I opened your letter* and *She touched the window as I passed.*

Ellie's poem begins in the fictional town of Cape Enrage, my pseudonym for Provincetown. The poem remembers, in the beginning, living in Paris. It remembers our time in Beirut two years earlier. The one writing this poem becomes *a woman broken into many women.* It opens in the April of Sean's birth, and a few days later, the April of the death of our neighbor, Simone de Beauvoir. The month of "The Waste Land." But it moves very soon to Hôtel-Dieu. Ellie tells me her name. She tells the story of Izieu, and of the camps in occupied France. She is silent between the lines, but attributes this silence to the being of God, a claim I would later read in Elie Wiesel's *And the Sea is Never Full: Memoirs 1969*—in which he refers to a cantata called "A Song For Hope."[4] In Ellie's poem, Gershom Scholem also sings, just as Ellie sang in German after confessing: *I am Jewish. Do you understand? Alone in a small room, always alone. To remain sane, I sing librettos to myself, and German lullabies, can you imagine?*

The poem's structure is cantilevered from her story of flight and hiding, of her husband's work in the Resistance, and of losing him after the war, but the bridge she builds is from the past to the present: the hospital, where *We must wear our slippers and not smoke. We must not go further than the sign* NO ADMITTANCE. The poem, too, works toward the present, to Cape Enrage, only to be told: *You should return to El-*

3. Theodor Adorno, *Minima Moralia*. Translated by E.F.N. Jephcott.Verso, 1974, p. 87.

4. Elie Wiesel, *And the Sea is Never Full: Memoirs 1969—*. Schocken, 2000. n.p.

lie. You mustn't leave her alone. Here the poem invites our neighbor to be present:

> Simone was alive. Twice her hand reached to fold the blue
> shutters back over the windows, and once she
> touched the window as I passed.

Simone died while I was still in the hospital, following the caesarean birth. Her atelier was identical to ours. We lived at 11 rue Schoelcher, and she at 11 bis. Parisians in mourning confused them, tossing bouquets of roses intended for her through my windows, so I filled the baby's carriage with these flowers, and wheeled them to her grave in Cimitière Montparnasse, across the street. A hillock of roses. When she appeared at the threshold of the poem, she was admitted.

Not so many years before this, my husband and I had been in El Salvador, not together yet, although we did meet once there. As not much time had passed, we hadn't yet exhausted all we could confide about that time. He stands at the threshold of the poem, then enters:

> *But when I came back from the border something odd happened.*
> *It had been more than seventy days and I weighed nothing.*
> *My bags were no heavier than usual but I couldn't lift them.*
> *After a drink and some talk I went for a rest.*
> *When I woke my room was filled with vultures.*
> *They were hopping about the room, belching and vomiting flesh,*
> *as you saw them at Puerto Diablo and El Playon.*
> *Exactly as you saw them.*

A dear Salvadoran friend appears, Margarita Herrera, and she too speaks, first from a nightmare and then from the pages of a letter. In the last passage of the poem, a military helicopter is lifting from the deck of a ship in the Mediterranean off the coast of Beirut. Ellie tells me her name again, and asks again if I am disturbing her. The poem is now on the deck of the ship and in the distance, *white phosphorous bombs plumed into the air like ostrich feathers of light.* Ellie and Beirut are all at once. *And it went on like that all night, questions in French, and it went on, radiant white feathers along the coast of Lebanon, until Ellie slept.*

When I first showed Daniel Simko the pages I had completed while he and Sean were away, I didn't want him to read them, believing it possible that once again, I was writing only notes toward poems, and when the poems finally came, they would resemble my earlier work: poems in a singular voice I would recognize, in a familiar form on the page, meditative free verse propelled toward an epiphany. Finally, I relented and let him read what I had written, provided that he understood that I considered this work to be something other than poetry. He carried the pages outside and sat facing the water for a long time, longer than it should have taken. When he came back inside, he told me that he thought I was wrong. These were not notes. You have done something new, he said, and you must bring it to fruition.

As a poem such as "The Angel of History" cannot come to an end, but suspends itself in the impossibility of resolution, the last line is a question: *And what did she say?*

It is the poem itself that constitutes the response.

Where the Line Breaks

David Herd

My understanding of what was necessary in poetry altered in October 2009. I have a bad memory so I don't recall much about the season except for the fact that we were preparing to move, from Whitstable, where our children had been born and where we had lived for eleven years, happily for the most part, to Canterbury. Kent isn't what people think. I don't remember particular sensations. I do remember that I was caught up in what I had started to read. I had read Charles Olson before, but never with more than a passing interest; I hadn't registered in his writing its historically lived experience. In 2009, when I started again, something in the violence and the drive to openness seemed current, his question, in "The Kingfishers':

> What stalks
> This silence[1]

But it wasn't a text, either poetry or poetics, that altered my understanding, albeit Olson stirred the ground. What caused the change was a building, or more precisely an assemblage of buildings, looking out towards Calais from Dover's cliffs.

The site in question had had many incarnations. Originally, and still visibly, it had been a Napoleonic-era fort, built to repel an invasion that never happened. The principal evidence of this function was the ditch that ran star-shaped around the perimeter, approximately a hundred-foot deep and laced continuously with barbed wired. It was a cold place to approach because of the way the wind blew up from the Channel. To enter the building, you parked your car on land owned in trust by English Heritage.

Before I heard about the building, which had been a borstal in the 1970s, and from which you can see Dover Castle, I was unaware that the UK detained people indefinitely under immigration rules. I was

1. Charles Olson, *The Collected Poems of Charles Olson (Excluding The Maximus Poems)*, ed. George Butterick. University of California Press, 1987, p. 92.

hardly alone in that fact; it was, at that time, a very well-kept secret. Just as it was that, in detaining people indefinitely, the UK was alone in Europe. The way the secret was kept was relatively simple. It involved what in the present moment we might call a lockdown. When you entered the building, which you could under the auspices of an NGO, you were required to hand over your belongings including, notably, pen and paper. This gesture was unnerving in itself, situating the building beyond inscription; all the more so when, as one investigated, it became clear the prohibition was systematic. For the men detained, for example, were they to have a hearing in the name of the UK's Asylum and Immigration Tribunal, that hearing—whether to secure bail or to appeal against deportation—would not constitute a court of record. Nobody was documenting; nobody was writing everything down. There was to be no trace of the voice of the person the tribunal called "the appellant," though that appellant was somebody who had sought asylum and who one day, perhaps years later, might be granted leave to remain. The reason I hadn't heard that the UK detained people indefinitely was because it did so in silence. The people housed on the cliffs at Dover might as well not have been there.

Olson's question is this, carefully and brutally calibrated:

> with what violence benevolence is bought
> what cost in gesture justice brings
> what wrongs domestic rights involve
> what stalks
> this silence[2]

It was this question I took to the building, and though it could have been otherwise it was through this question, or set of questions—which are posed also as statements in "The Kingfishers'—that the building came to make a kind of sense. As structure, it was a silence. The building contained silence. It silenced those within it and it was silent on the question of what it meant. Giorgio Agamben had started to find the terms. He called such a situation a state of exception; where the law was in force but where it might not be appealed to. Legally-politically, outwith the edge.

---

2. Charles Olson, *The Collected Poems of Charles Olson (Excluding The Maximus Poems)*, ed. George Butterick. University of California Press, 1987, p. 92.

But as much as the building was shaped by silence, so at the same time it was unusually eloquent. There is no topographical feature—name me a topographical feature—more expressive of Englishness than the white cliffs. It is here, if anywhere, the nation starts and ends. As such, and by any measure, the setting is singular. There are not so many global locations that fold culture so readily into geopolitics, where an accident of geography carries such an intensified cultural charge. One way to say it is as synecdoche, a "simultaneous understanding." Another way to say it is that if you had to concentrate a nation in a particular setting, if one location had to do all that geocultural work, it would very likely be at that edge, where all the meaning congregates, and where the State, as an assertion of sovereignty, had installed silence.

The poet who had identified Dover as beginning and end was Matthew Arnold. Think of his speaker looking out from that shingled beach. It was through Olson, however, that I approached the building. What he said in his set of questions, which I take to be at the origin of open field poetics, in his intimately folding, chiasmatic language, was that domestic rights incorporate wrongs, that the gesture of justice internalizes cost, that aurally and actually benevolence is threaded with violence.

That these conditions obtain, that the State's virtues coil so intimately around its brutalities, was a function, as Olson understood it, of political expulsion. He had trained himself in what that meant, reading deep into the consequences of mid-century states of exception, and he knew that where sovereignty asserted itself then human expulsion was both the condition and the result. It was this that drove "Projective Verse" and its radical image of opening, the animating principle of which, as "The Kingfishers" sought to embody, was that nothing and nobody might fall outside.

What I encountered at the building—referred to on the map as The Citadel, after its original designation, but specified as you approached as the Dover Immigration Removal Centre—was the reality of contemporary sovereign power. What ultimately that entailed was not just a separating out, a removing of persons, but a site, in its silencing, in which personhood was denied. For citizenship, in all the force of its privileges, to be maintained, there had to be—as the building said—people who were not.

All of which makes the encounter sound more coherent than it was. What in fact I experienced in October 2009 was shock. I think I am not entirely politically naïve; my politics was formed through protest in the 1980s. Still, in 2009 I was not aware that the UK had come to detain people arbitrarily and indefinitely, that people who were released were routinely re-detained. More than that, I didn't know it was happening in such proximity, that it was integral to where and how I lived. The exception was in plain sight. They hadn't even troubled to put it elsewhere. The silence, as Olson said it would be, was in our midst.

What I did understand, as anybody else would have understood, is that this setting was the darkest of political signs. What followed was a politically brutal decade in which personhood, and the rights underpinning it, were ruthlessly shut down, when expulsion became the conspicuous basis of national identity, a decade characterized by its explicit political construction, in the UK, of a "hostile environment." It was all there, in that site, in the logic that had allowed it, in the political disregard for bare life. What was there also, therefore, was a poetic demand; a demand on the poem that it register the expulsion, the silence on which the culture had established its ground.

How to acknowledge such a demand, how to take it into one's practice, must be an ongoing question. Form is not, as I understand it in practice, an extension of content. Form, as I understand it, is a constant act of negotiation, a means of bringing aspects of reality towards the light. What always the poem has to do, the poem that has been alerted to the silencing—to the intense efforts the cultural apparatus goes to in order to stop people and practices being heard —is to register the fact that all the time we are using this language we are using it is being rendered violent, it is being orchestrated to keep people out. That's what has to be grasped; that knife edge of violence. The poem in its desire for connection must seek forms of solidarity. It must draw on the languages of friendship and intimacy that are intrinsic to its backstory, to the history of lyric in which another's presence, or the fact of their absence, is brought to the fore. But if it is to be at all real, if it is at all to approximate to the real, it must register the fact that always the language is forcing people out. The poem catches itself in the act of trying to establish human connection, in a context where routinely and systematically the State is working, in the name of the language, to break those connections up.

In certain respects, of course, these tensions play out at the level of vocabulary. If the aim of the poem is to be creating a space of human relationality where the possibilities of that relationality are constantly being foreclosed, then the different vocabularies should be present and should be made present to one another. The language of the poem must hear the language of the law and the law must hear the poem speaking back. At the level of the line, and the line's expression, in other words, it must be acknowledged that our vocabularies have done this to us; that politically and culturally we have allowed the language to become organized around terms whose function is to establish citizenship by holding people out.

But if the poem's way of meaning, its way of bringing relationalities to light, could be said to settle anywhere, it is where, formally speaking, it is most itself. What matters in the poem is the break, the end of the line, that moment when sense might be suspended or where it might carry on. There, emblematically, the poem is always negotiating connection, where the decision is always being made—by both poet and reader—whether what has been established is continuity or separation. The end of the line is crucial, therefore, in a poetry that looks to register the political production of absences, because it is at the end of the line that the need to hold everything together is brought constantly into view. But if the line break is crucial, for the simple fact that it distinguishes poetry from prose, so its dramatization of suspension and continuity carries right through the poem. The quality of the line ending, this is to say, resonates across the syntax, where—if the poem is going well—the continuities are strongly felt, but where always it is being understood that they might be broken. What the line break introduces into poetry, in other words, is a defining vulnerability, where always the connection is having to be made. The poem, this is to say, knows that continuity is always at issue, that always, at any moment, the communication might break.

None of which is intended as a description, exactly, of poetic practice. What I am trying to indicate are some of the considerations that are brought to be bear on the poem. How those considerations formed, how they came into view, goes back to the site at Dover, that setting where political silencing was being installed. What that site called for was an opening out, a kind of urgently extended listening, an intimacy where otherwise a propensity to expulsion would stalk. As I write, we are in lockdown. It is unclear what kind of politics we will emerge into. The poem must open where the silence forms.

Wild Strawberries

Paul Hoover

At the age of eleven, I left the dentist office in Mount Vernon, Ohio, and had a couple of hours to spend before my parents could pick me up, so I peeked into a movie theater across the street. There was no ticket taker. After waiting a while, I just walked in after parting a curtain. Only two others were present, sitting together in the last row, their faces half-lighted. I chose a seat a few rows down, and the black and white movie began. Its title was *Wild Strawberries* and the director was Ingmar Bergman. It was about the life of an old man who had once been in love, but it had not worked out because his beloved married his brother instead. This was the second film I can remember seeing. The first had starred the cowboy, Hopalong Cassidy, so I was astonished when, in *Wild Strawberries*, the old man had a terrible dream. The clock on the wall had no hands, and some people were carrying a casket down the street. When one of them tripped under the load, the casket fell to the ground and burst open, causing an arm to flop out. We discover the corpse was the old man himself. What did I know of Ingmar Bergman and art film? I was in grade school. But I'll never forget the dark theater, the dead arm, the timeless clock, and the two young women seated in back. The theater, itself a kind of camera, contained three innocent souls and the ephemeral images projected upon our faces. I don't recall telling my parents anything about the movie. We drove to our house in Danville, a village of a few hundred people in Knox County. The area was entirely rural, the "gateway to Amish country," so why were they showing Bergman films in Mount Vernon? I later realized the answer. It was because Kenyon College was located in the nearby academic village of Gambier, which was even smaller than Danville. I played little league baseball against Gambier team. The popular singer and TV star, Ricky Nelson, had attended Kenyon. There was a local fable that a fraternity hazing cost the life of a freshman when they tied him to a railroad track, not realizing that trains were still running. It happened on Homecoming weekend, when his parents were there. People in the town spoke of the college as if it were a world entirely apart, not to be trusted.

Matters of town and gown are essential to poetics. With William Carlos Williams, the "town" of the poem, reality, is the dominant. The poem's "gown" is visible in its formal considerations, such as the triadic line. There was also the possibility that, being so direct, it was not poetry at all. So much depends / upon // a red wheel / barrow // glazed with rain / water // beside the white / chickens.[1] Language poetry possesses a lot of gown, because its grist is theory. On the other hand, a real-world innocence does exist in its language realism, a belief that the poem might name and limn it all, in New Sentence fragments. This explains their penchant for long poems. They are painting the town with words.

My poem "Driver's Song" is more or less "town" poetics:

> I shall never reach Danville, Ohio,
> Danville, distant and lonely
>
> Black car, small moon,
> in the back seat beer.
> Because I've forgotten the roads
> I shall never reach Danville, Ohio.
>
> Over the plains, through Indiana,
> where I was lonely also.
> Black car, yellow moon.
> My dead father keeps watch over me
> from an upstairs window.
>
> What a long way from California
> and in what a fast car—
> invisible to the soul.
>
> Ahead I see death moving slowly on the road.
> I know I will touch her clothing
> before I ever reach Danville, Ohio.
>
> Danville, distant and lonely.[2]

The "gown" of the poem is the reader's recognition that the work is a lyrical parody of "Black Rider's Song" by Federico García Lorca.

1. William Carlos Williams. *Spring and All, XXII, Imaginations*, ed. Webster Schott. New Directions Publishing, 1970, p. 136.

2. Paul Hoover. *Poems in Spanish*. Omnidawn Publishing, 2006, p. 15.

Does that mean it is any less sincere? Is sincerity a reasonable standard for poetry? Is artifice more reliable?

Another important encounter was reading a poem by Wallace Stevens, "The Connoisseur of Chaos," with its philosophical assertion that:

> A. A violent order is disorder; and
> B. A great disorder is an order. These
> Two things are one.[3]

I didn't know who Marchand was, of whom the poem speaks, but I was shocked and delighted by lines like "The squirming facts exceed the squamous mind." I was in high school. I didn't understand completely what it meant, but I knew it was wonderful way to speak. Its charm, its seeming truth, and its crazy logic warmed me to poetry. When I started writing poetry at age twenty-five, during the Vietnam War, Stevens became a gatekeeper for me. When I am in doubt about the value of poetry, especially my own, I read a couple of the insurance lawyer's poems, even though what I have read about his life is sometimes unpleasant. The same is true of Vallejo's *Trilce* and *Sermon on Barbarism*, which are for me pure poetry. To keep my aesthetic balance, I like an equal dose of W. C. Williams, with a sidecar of Marianne Moore's "The Fish" and Gwendolyn Brooks's "We Real Cool," poems with exquisite proceduralist manners. Stevie Smith's poem "Pretty" is so truthful as to be lethal. It feels fresh every time I read it. Terrance Hayes's *Sonnets for my Past and Future Assassin* should be read aloud to the Senate every morning it convenes.

For the metaphysical, always a lure for me, I prefer Emily Dickinson's depth charges and George Herbert, whose formal inventiveness was astonishing. According to Hugh Kenner, of the hundreds of poems Herbert wrote, a great majority were each in a different poetic form. For verbal freedom and astonishing diction, I rely on Hart Crane, especially "O Carib Isle!":

> Under the Poinciana, of a noon or afternoon
> Let fiery blossoms clot the light, render my ghost

3. Wallace Stevens. *The Collected Poems*. Vintage Books, 1982, p. 215.

> Sieved upward, white and black along the air
> Until it meets the blue's comedian host.[4]

I feel the same about Gerard Manley Hopkins, whose excess proves that too much can be just enough. Say this quickly ten times: "I caught this morning morning's minion, kingdom of daylight's dauphin, dapple-dawn-drawn Falcon in his riding."[5] It is the first line of "The Windhover," and the sentence continues for four and a half more lines. This is madness of the good kind.

Another major encounter was the poetry of Friedrich Hölderlin. In the summer of 2006, Maxine Chernoff and I set out to translate a few of his poems. We did not know the extent of his work, just a few of the "night poems" like the one about the weather vane clattering. Working all day together at the dining table, two dictionaries at the ready, we discovered in the fall that we had translated over a hundred pages. We then realized we had to translate virtually all of his mature poetry, including those written in a state of insanity, the "späteste Gedichte," or last poems. W. H. Auden said that all poets should learn to cook and translate poetry. Both are hospitable acts, you are pleasing others. Writing poems is also hospitable, even if you are a poet of oblique and difficult measures. Translating Hölderlin, as well as writing *Poems in Spanish*, drew me toward lyricism and away from irony, though not all the way. Hölderlin's late work, much of it in fragments, teaches how powerful broken and incomplete phrases can be. It also teaches silence:

> To My Sister (An meine Schwester)
>
> I stayed overnight in the village
> Air of the Alb
> Down the street
> Home again. Sun of home.
> Canoe ride.
> Friends.   Men and mother.
> Slumber.[6]

---

4. Hart Crane. *The Complete Poems*, ed. Mark Simon. Liveright, 1986, p. 111.

5. Gerard Manley Hopkins. "The Windhover." *A Hopkins Reader*, ed. John Pick. A Doubleday Image Book, 1966, p. 50.

6. Friedrich Hölderlin. *Selected Poems*, ed. and trans. Maxine Chernoff and

One day as a teenager, I discovered a stack of *Writer* magazines in my mother's sewing room, which occupied an unused bedroom of the Church of the Brethren parsonage we lived in. The windows of the room were not curtained, so light splashed across the polished wooden floors as I sat in the corner reading them. They held interest for me, because they revealed a secret she was keeping, that she was a writer and wanted something beyond the daily life of being a mother and wife of a pastor, with its prayer meetings and potluck dinners. She achieved her goal when The Brethren Press of Elgin, Illinois, published *The Roads to Everywhere*, her first and only book, which dealt with the challenges of young people displaced by European wars.[7] This explained why she went to bed early, sitting up with a notebook, pen, and papers. I returned more than once to read additional issues. I had no ambition to write. It seemed a dry and distant occupation. I see now that my mother's desire to make something, to inhabit the imagination, influenced me very much.

It was from an upstairs window of our country house that I saw a fox cross the highway and enter the tall grass near the house. It is the fox that we recall, the sun-glaze of the floorboards, and the dusty scent of the attic where the books are stored, not the advice of *Writer* magazine. The actual speaks with great confidence, without words. In a poem, the actual benefits from the irrational.

Jean Cohen writes in *Structure du langage poétique*, "Poetry is the most passionate form of literature, the paroxysmic degree of style. Style is one. It comprises an infinite number of figures, always the same. From prose to poetry and from one state of poetry to another, the difference is only in the audacity with which language employs the processes virtually inscribed within its structure."[8] Poetry's range is great, but what most moves us is the oracle staggering from her cave, her mouth aflame.

Paul Hoover. Omnidawn Publishing, 2008, p. 451.

7. Opal Hoover. *The Roads to Everywhere*. The Brethren Press, 1959.

8. In *The American Prose Poem: Poetic Form and the Boundaries of Genre*, Michel Delville. University Press of Florida 1998, p. 149.

Swallows and Robins

Ger Killeen

I want to begin with an anecdote which is less an illustration than an attempt to find "a local habitation and a name" for a peculiar set of unresolvable contradictions which forms part of the matrix of my life and my writing life. But first, a bit of context. I was born and grew up in Limerick City, Ireland, but I've now lived more than half of my life outside of Ireland, mostly in Oregon. I grew up, unsurprisingly, in an English-speaking household, but because of certain nationalistic passions on the part of my father I was encouraged more than most of our neighbors' kids to "keep up with the Irish," packed off to the Irish-speaking area of Ballyferriter now and then, and was blessed with some outstanding teachers. One teacher in particular, at that crucial time in life of one's mid-teens, seemed to grasp that my interest in Irish and English literature came from more than just a desire to do well in the final exams. And he introduced me to the work of Seán Ó Ríordáin. "Léigh An Ríordánach," he said, "léigh *Eireball Spideoige*, 's feicfidh tú cumhacht filíocht na Gaelinne."[1] ("Read Ó Ríordáin, read *Robin's Tail*, and you'll see the power of poetry in Irish."). And so I read it, blithely unaware of the critical rancor surrounding that big little book, read it and found the language difficult, read it and found it philosophically demanding, if not overwhelming, read it and, quite unconsciously, found in it a model for poetry as self-examination, self-struggle. Simultaneously, though, I was reading the American poet Robert Lowell, and I was finding there an English utterly different from what we spoke at home, poems which were also philosophically demanding, and a persona constantly struggling with his own conscience. In my adolescent brain Ó Ríordáin and Lowell were always talking to each other, maybe talking past each other and their conversations were the stuff of the overheated poetry I was starting to attempt myself, in both jagged Irish and verbose, glowering English. You could keep your Celtic *Twilight*, the real stuff was like entering a confessional where you were your own absolver, and was it ever *dark*!

1.Seán Ó'Ríordán, "Adhlacadh Mo Mháthair." *Eireball Spideoige*. Sáirséal – Ó Marcaigh Tta., 1952, p. 56.

That's some context. And here's the anecdote that's maybe more than an anecdote:

I live in a coastal, rural area of Oregon and a couple of times a week I volunteer at a nearby wildlife refuge where my task is to check up and collect data on a widely dispersed series of wooden nest-boxes which are mainly occupied by Tree swallows. Every year around March, we set up the nest-boxes on poles designed to keep predators like raccoons, packrats, even coyotes away, and in April the swallows begin returning from Mexico to breed and start building their nests in the small cavities of dead trees and in our ample nest-boxes. You can open these boxes with minimal disturbance to their occupants and look inside to see what's going on: At first they're all empty, though swallows are usually in the vicinity, then gradually you discover the beginnings of nests—clumps of dried grass stalks which soon take on a bowl shape as they're arranged and woven together, and finally an incredibly soft lining of small feathers and down, much of them left behind by the overwintering Cackling geese which flew north to Alaska as the swallows started to arrive. Then you wait, a week, maybe two weeks, and sometime in early to mid-May you open a box and there it is—the first egg of the season, tiny and unbelievably white, soon to be followed by three or four more over the next few days. The eggs are often well hidden inside the thick lining of feathers, and sometimes the mother bird herself will simply not leave the nest when you open the box and you have to gently stick your hand underneath her and feel about carefully in the soft, warm bowl in order to count the eggs.

Every time I do this, especially when, after a time, there are not only eggs but small, pink, naked hatchlings in some of the nests, it's impossible not to be conscious of the fragility of origins: "Bíonn gach tosach lag" (every beginning is weak) as an Irish proverb says; but the fact that I'm intervening here in the natural process with my own agenda also brings up the notion of care and taking care. And as I observe these nests, for myself I cannot *not* hear the Irish-language poet Máirtín Ó Cadhain's statement that words ought to be handled as carefully as new-laid eggs, or, as Anne Sexton put it:

Words and eggs must be handled with care.
Once broken they are impossible
things to repair.[2]

Encompassing, but beyond this, though, I think there's a dimension of poetry which is rooted in the ground of its author's specific language and literary traditions, a distinctive mediation of a distinct life-world, which might give us the "local rows" of *The Odyssey*, *Táin Bó Cuailgne*, *Beowulf*, and *Y Gododdin;* or indeed, Eliot's *The Wasteland*, *Ó* Ríordáin's *Cnoc Mellerí*, and Bernstein's *The Lives of the Toll Takers*. Now, poets have always borrowed and stolen from each other across languages, eras, and cultures, but I have to wonder about what is unborrowable, unstealable, even, dare I say it, untranslatable. Many things, undoubtedly, issuing from the fact that different languages are only partly mappable onto each other, get in the way of ready understanding, even when the speakers are of equal competence and similar background:

Sprache
abgehetzt
mit dem müden Mund
auf dem endlosen Weg
zum Hause des Nachbarn

"Language/ exhausted/ with the tired mouth/ on the endless path/ to the neighbour's house"[3], as the great Baltic poet Johannes Bobrowski writes in one of his many poems about the difficulties of communicating when language wears down into bloodless generalities and cliché, which in an instant can turn the world bloody. He wrote from bitter experience.

I bring the issue up in this way because already I've used several words which, while perfectly comprehensible on one level, turn out, at least as far as a my writing life is concerned, to be serious troublemakers which I have to, in making my poems, take the trouble to handle with care.

2. Anne Sexton, "Words." *The Awful Rowing Toward God*. Houghton Mifflin, 1975, p. 70.

3. "Language" by Johannes Bobrowski from *Shadow Lands*, p. 167, translated by Ruth and Matthew Mead, New Directions 1984. Translation modified.

I used two words, two simple nouns, two simple animate nouns—"robin" and "swallow." Let me tease out why they're so problematic.

The other morning I was standing by my kitchen window waiting for the coffee to brew, looking out at the summer's unseasonable drizzle saving me from the task of watering the vegetable garden when I saw a robin going about its task of hunting for worms and other insects driven to the surface of the garden by the rain. Except it wasn't the kind of robin I grew up with: the American robin is actually a kind of thrush, *Turdus migratorius* to be exact, a far larger bird than the Irish robin, *Erithacus rubecula*, with a completely different song, a different shape, different colored eggs, a different range of associations. When the New England poet Mary Oliver writes at the beginning of her poem "Work, Sometimes":

> I was sad all day, and why not. There I was, books piled
> on both sides of the table, paper stacked up, words
> falling off my tongue.
>
> The robins had been a long time singing, and now it
> was beginning to rain . . .[4]

The poem works because these are American robins who have a forceful but aloof presence, an upright stance, and a complex caroling song, an indifference to rain or sun, all of which the poet can set against the melancholy self-absorption of an overly intellectualized orientation towards the world. If you were to imagine an Irish robin in these circumstances the poem would lose the kind of physical assertiveness on which its structuring contrast depends.

But now think of these lines by Seán Ó Ríordáin from "Adhlacadh Mo Mháhair" ("My Mother's Burial"):

> "Bhí m'aigne á sciúirseadh féin ag iarraidh
> An t-adhlacadh a bhlaiseadh go hiomlán,
> Nuair a d'eitil tríd an gciúnas bán go míonla
> Spideog a bhí gan mhearbhall gan scáth :
> Agus d'fhan os cionn na huaighe fé mar go mb'eol di
> Go raibh an toisc a thug í ceilte ar chách
> Ach an té a bhí ag feitheamh ins an gcomhrainn,

---

4. *New and Selected Poems*, vol. 2 by Mary Oliver, p.6, Beacon Press, 2007.

Is do rinneas éad fén gcaidreamh neamhghnách."[5]

(My mind was scourging itself trying
To taste the burial completely,
When there flew gently through the white silence
A robin, unflustered, unafraid,
And stayed above the grave as though she knew
Her reason for being there was invisible to all
Except the one waiting in the coffin,
And I envied their extraordinary intimacy.)

This robin, this *spideog*, is small and bold, curious and hard to scare off, and in the poem it comes trailing a host of otherworldly, folkloric associations ingrained in traditional Irish culture in addition to physical attributes: from the traditional Irish poetic trope of birds as supernatural messengers and harbingers, to the specific association of the robin's red breast with Christ's blood which spilled on the little creature as she attempted to pull the thorns from his head as he died on the cross. All of these associations work to give us "an blaiseadh," "the taste," that unmistakable connection to a life-world that's both sensuous and meaningful. For the poem to work you are required to *see and feel* the "robin-ness" of *this* robin.

And of course the same is true of the swallows I mentioned. The birds I work with are specifically *tree* swallows, *Tachycineta bicolor*, which are unknown in Ireland whose swallows "fáinleoga" are *barn* swallows, *Hirundo rustica*; though close to each other in some behaviors, their colors are different, their nesting locations and nesting materials are different, even their twittering is distinguishable. So, when Michael Davitt in his poem "Drécht a Trí de Bhrionglóid" ("Third Draft of a Dream') says:

"Ar maidin, fíagaí focal
Á phlúcáil as a chodladh
Ag spéirarm fáinleog..."[6]
(In the morning, a hunter of words
being plucked from his sleep
by a sky-army of swallows...)

5. "Eireaball Spideoige" by Seán Ó Ríordáin, Sáirséal Ó Marcaigh, 1986.

6. "Freacnairc Mhearcair: Rogha Dánta 1970-1998" by Michael Davitt, p.49, Cork University Press, 2000.

What do you hear as the sounds of *these* swallows waking you up on a summer morning? Are they the same or different from the sounds the swallow in Mary Oliver's prosepoem "June" might make:

> "The swallow climbs high into the air, blue shoulders pumping hard. Then it swings, glides, turns towards the sea, is gone."[7]

(My sense is that she's describing a cliff swallow, unknown in Ireland. The sounds would be different. It's from a different world.)

A couple of years after moving to the USA, working hard on putting together a collection of poems in English, I took a break from that and skipped to the Irish side of my Irish-American hyphenated existence for a short while to try my hand at some poems in Irish. With quite an amount of naïvete I thought it would be relatively straightforward, my main difficulties being to overcome a certain amount of rustiness which had crept into my language through lack of everyday conversation. What came out, fairly soon, was a poem called "Leigheas in Oregon" (Medicine in Oregon) which though a little clunky raised a version of the questions I've been circling around today. The first section reads

Ligeann fiach dubh racht
gáire as ó bharr giúise
's greamaíonn sé mise
le súil lonnrach, dhorcha.
Táimid tar *éis* titim
isteach i scéalta a chéile.
Cad tá uaim anseo
i mo shaol nua ach caoi
éisteachta a fhoghlaim, gan
focail agam le bronnadh
i m' thimpeall ar rudaí
nach bhfuil Gaeilge orthu?
Caochann an t-*éan* an tsúil orm
's imíonn sé leis i measc na gcrann.[8]

(A raven's burst of laughter
from the top of a fir—

7. "White Pine," by Mary Oliver, Mariner Books, 1994.

8. "Lia a Léimfidh Thar Tonnta" by Ger Killeen, Trask House Books, 1999.

and I'm fixed in his shining,
dark eye. We have fallen
inside each other's stories.
What do I think I want
here in my new life but to learn
a way of listening, and not
have a single word to bestow
around me on everything
that doesn't exist in Irish?
The bird cocks his eye at me
and takes off among the trees.)

Things that don't exist in Irish? There were so many...kinds of trees, and shrubs, and plants, animals, and birds, and insects; character types, speech patterns and intonations and vocabulary, landscape features, kinds of weather, unspoken assumptions about work and life and God and culture and politics and poetry itself. In a way I was in heaven! So many new things to explore and think about and accept or reject. So many poems to feel my way into. In English, though. My Irish felt awfully inadequate, very artificial, very disconnected from my actual life, including the reading and writing life I was developing as a poet in the USA, in Oregon.

It strikes me now that as a poet I'm always suspiciously looking over my shoulder at my own language, my own English language, a patchwork of Irish, British and American influences. Though Irish still accompanies me as a kind of unconscious linguistic matrix in my life-world, I write now almost exclusively in English; but, in a sense, when working and reworking a poem I always feel a translator's struggle with myself and my own English. My struggles with Irish have deepened my sense of how a good poem can be a kind of protective integument for the words of which it itself is made, each word capable of holding up not just to intense interpretive pressure but acting as an implicit warning about the consequences of a widespread media environment where meaning is less important than functionality, where words are like Kleenex: picked up, used only half-thinkingly, thrown away. Beyond care with diction, beyond the attempt at precise denotation, beyond the exploration of connotation and the marvels of syntax and line, my sense of myself as always translating helps me be alert to the socio-political power-struggles behind the evolution of the meanings of words. Or:

> The world wakes
> in your usual reach
> exceeding, as usual,
> your reflexive grasp:
> scraps and pieces of hairy triton,
> crab carapaces,
> at play in the void
> of the names
> you deploy, as if
> you know more
> than nothing.
> As if you.

That's how I might translate all that into part of a poem.

You See the Snow-White through the White of Frost

L. S. Klatt

For much of my writing career, Robert Frost, the transparent Frost and the opaque one, has lived in me melting, an iceberg endangered, imposing.

In 1983, I purchased *The Poetry of Robert Frost* from my college bookstore, the Holt, Rinehart, and Winston edition, the price stamped in charcoal on the first blank page, a photograph of trees in evening light laid out on the dust jacket.

There at hand was his life's work, Frost epitomized, eleven books in one volume, hardbound.

For an oral report, I read through the entirety and got it into my head that during the presentation I needed to intone the old man's voice. It was juvenile to act him out, histrionic, but that was the hold he had on me.

Some twenty years after his death, there I was entertaining classmates with my warped rendition of the poet and rehearsing poems of his I valued but dimly comprehended. Faux Frosts. False Frosts.

Perhaps even to himself the man was an imposter—a native San Franciscan not a Vermonter—writer pretending to be farmer.

The New England transplant idled away his days mostly failing as a dairyman. Lost children tragically to diseases, depression. Lost his best friend, Edward Thomas, to gunfire during the first world war. It makes sense that a poem for him was a momentary stay against confusion.

A poem, he said, needs a theme to steady itself down. So did I.

I wasn't a serious poet in college, barely an enthusiast. But Frost blew me away with the formal sophistication of his sound effects. What he conjured surprised, as if glitter bombs or weather events. Yet his lines, laced with sonic opiates, also could sedate.

The woods are lovely, dark, and deep.
But I have promises to keep.[1]

It's not just the music that captivated me. A scene like this one, stripped of landmarks, comes across as archetypal. The speaker, ambivalent about leaving behind a snowscape impenetrable and alluring, invites identification. Who could resist lagging with him at the edge of storybook forest?

Here and elsewhere, I have felt when reading Frost a fairy tale enchantment, an atmospheric Snow Whiteness complete with magic mirror, poison apple, glass coffin. Innocent, yes, yet foreboding. The region the poet points to is not really geographic-specific Vermont or New Hampshire but somewhere imaginary I wandered as a child. *Snow falling and night falling fast, oh fast/ In a field I looked into going past.*[2]

These snowscapes turn out to be surface. Yet under the shine—and this is what I wanted—thought in its highest abstraction. Frostbitten.

In the thick of a teeming snowfall
I saw my shadow on snow.
I turned and looked back up at the sky,
Where we still look to ask the why
Of everything below.[3]

Yvor Winters once described Frost as refugee from faith and reason, a "spiritual drifter," the right road lost.

The Frost persona seeks but refuses answers, at least orthodox ones, preferring to tramp in a *selva oscura* painted with rime until, absorbed in contemplation, he finds it impossible to move; Frost, as it were, spellbound, snow blind, in a granite state.

A blanker whiteness of benighted snow
With no expression, nothing to express.[4]

What but design of darkness to appall?[5]

1. Robert Frost, "Stopping by Woods on a Snowy Evening." *The Poetry of Robert Frost. The Collected Poems, Complete and Unabridged.* Edited by Edward Connery Lathem. Holt, Rinehart and Winston, 1979, pp. 224–25.

2. Frost, "Desert Places." Ibid., p. 296.

3. Frost, "Desert Places." Ibid., p. 296.

4. Frost, "Desert Places." Ibid., p. 29

5. Frost, "Design." Ibid., p. 302.

For all his talk of spring flowers and mowing, there is an obsession with oblivion in Frost brought on by snowflakes. The momentum is downward. The effect, whiteout.

Frost appears to be imagining whiteness darkly the way Melville did in *Moby Dick*.

> Is it that by its indefiniteness it shadows forth the heartless voids and immensities of the universe, and thus stabs us from behind with the thought of annihilation, when beholding the white depths of the milky way? Or is it, that as in essence whiteness is not so much a color as the visible absence of color, and at the same time the concrete of all colors; is it for these reasons there is such a dumb blankness, full of meaning, in a wide landscape of snows—a colorless, all-color of atheism from which we shrink?[6]

As grandiose as this passage is, I have felt that threat when reading "Stopping by the Woods on a Snowy Evening." Others have experienced in the same poem a menace altogether different.

Thylias Moss, for example, finds in Frost not winter wonderland, not even metaphysical wasteland, but a white supremacy she has had to cast off. How else can a poet of color discover who she is when whiteness (white authorship) dominates the landscape? *A young black girl stopped by the woods,/ so young she knew only one man: Jim Crow/ but she wasn't allowed to call him Mister.*[7]

That's legit.

I've had a dissimilar (whiter) kind of trouble with monoliths Americans admire, their stature not their ethnicity or gender. I recognize the genius; no doubt I've been overpowered by them; but I rebel.

Robert Frost, however, has composed a likeness of himself difficult for me to deface. Bluff. Monumental. Like greeting cards, his lyrics tend to jingle and ingratiate, but they also open the mind to a vast,

6. Herman Melville, *Moby Dick or The Whale*, The Modern Library, Random House, 1930, p. 282

7. Thylias Moss, "Interpretation of a Poem by Frost," Poetry Foundation (lines 1-3).

overwhelming emptiness. It's understandable, retreating from a Frost poem, that one can sometimes feel diminished or, worse, obliterated.

When I was in second grade, before ever setting out to become a poet, I collected fossils, read about dinosaurs, and pronounced myself a paleontologist. Well, Frost was my first Rex.

Every bit of the universe, according to the poet, wants to tear us limb from limb. Even the leaves.

> All summer long I thought I heard them threatening under their breath.
> And when they came it seemed with a will to carry me with them to death.[8]

Frost, the nature poet. Yet what is natural about these lines?

I don't know if one gets over a versifier like Frost, the singsong and the void; the woods filling up with snow; the leaves shocked by winter, still green in a hard, cold glittering.

When Frost said in "Design" that the spider carries the wings of the moth like a paper kite, that's not kid stuff; run for your life on this planet patterned by predation.

Terror, Lionel Trilling claimed, was the real hallmark of Frost's poems. Not a criticism. Anxiety and panic are justifiable—in fact, instinctive—responses to a cosmos that extinguishes everything it ignites.

It might be that a benign creator is, for Frost, simplistic, a bygone figment. Or that St. Aquinas and his argument from design are recast in the poet's own fugitive image. I'm thinking of the Frost poem "To a Moth Seen in Winter," where the hand the speaker offers to the moth cannot really touch it, "much less can save."

> And now pray tell what lured you with false hope
> To make the venture of eternity
> And seek the love of kind in wintertime?[9]

There's something deeply felt in the predicament he exposits. And ponderous. The Frost of these poems is a man out of season.

---

8. Frost, "A Leaf-Treader." Ibid., p. 297.

9. Frost, "To a Moth Seen in Winter." Ibid., p. 356.

A hundred years later, I end up voicing a similar, though perhaps more radical, alienation. While Frost is aware of the gulf between human and creature, I feel a personal responsibility for the rift.

> I found an octopus in the snow.
> And not knowing what it was or why it was there, I gutted it
> as if a hunter.
>
> To me, up to my elbows in bladder, the ink was a surprise.
> I wore it like opera gloves in the moonlight.[10]

Frost helped me to see myself in nature, friend as well as foe. I don't know that my own poems, thus burdened, will ever be able to stand up straight again.

I guess that's the deformity of influence. Or the beauty.

Frost's contemporary Wallace Stevens observed that "One must have a mind of winter" and "have been cold a long time/ To behold the junipers shagged with ice,/ The spruces rough in the distant glitter// Of the January sun; and not to think/ Of any misery in the sound of the wind."[11]

A mind of winter may seem anachronistic today, out of step. The buttoned-up bitterness of 1920 strikes a different tone from the emotive *milk and honey* of 2020, as in Rupi Kaur, social media sensation. But though they flirt with pessimism, I don't think Stevens or Frost recommend it. To wax exclusively dark does not jive with swingers of birches and emperors of ice cream.

Anyway, the mind of winter belongs to "The Snow Man" who, inanimate as he is, feels nothing, whereas the sentient feel everything. Better to be human.

I came of age in the era of other Frosts, *Frosty the Snowman* and Kellogg's Frosted Flakes®; these chorus lightheartedly, trivially, in my consciousness to this day, having visited me a lifetime ago via television in the service of profits and advertisements. I still feel cocooned

10. L.S. Klatt, "Liquefaction." *Cloud of Ink*. University of Iowa Press. p. 3.

11. Wallace Stevens, "The Snow Man." *Collected Poetry and Prose*, edited by Frank Kermode and Joan Richardson. The Library of America, 1997, p.8.

thinking of them, though it might be, as with heavier frost, a kind of freezing to death.

My more recent reckonings with the poet have to do with his sentences, which he delivers affected yet plainspoken, running down a hillside stop-start over rhymes, conversational, burbling. Not stream of consciousness. Directed. Allowed to brook, eddy. Every gush a different sentence sound, or so he claimed.

> I shall be telling this with a sigh
> Somewhere ages and ages hence:
> Two roads diverged in a wood, and I—
> I took the one less traveled by
> And that has made all the difference.[12]

Such pronouncements have not aged well. Anyone listening to an old recording of Frost reading the poem knows it reeks of "poesy," the practiced, orotund rhetoric of some thespian bard, so easy to lampoon, especially those first two lines. And yet . . .

this stanza lives forever hardwired in my musical register, its phrasings so charismatic that despite my attraction to a more disjunctive poetics—L=A=N=G=U=A=G=E poetry, the New York School—I can't shake them.

The magnetic pull of Frost's lines I find puzzling. Rhyming the end words "sigh," "I," and "by" seems facile, an uninspiring sonic arrangement, but the harmonies the poet devises find a way to defeat monotony. How?

Essentially, he mismatches rhyme and accent at crucial turns in the stanza, creating a hermaphrodite rhyme between "hence" and "difference" so that the "ence" we expect to chime lacks emphasis, as does "by," even though paired with "I," because Frost jiggers the rhythm.

Add to this the repetition of the pronoun "I" at the end of one line and at the beginning of the next, which generates an unexpected fusion that, once heard, is difficult to unhear.

12. Frost, "The Road Not Taken." Ibid., p. 105.

With the sound signature alone, Frost leaves his mark; but the paradox he inscribes (one road can't be "less traveled by" if "the passing there/ Had worn [both roads] really the same") also lingers.

From the outset of my career, I've been intrigued by the way Frost, in poems like this one, was able to engage simultaneously two distinct audiences—those for whom poetry is all sweetness and light and those who want complication.

I've sought to satisfy both types of readers with my own sentence sounds, but, instead, more often than not, I baffle, whereas Frost prevails.

His poetry has an ease about it; the secret, he said, is in letting a poem run its course. *Like a piece of ice on a hot stove, the poem must ride on its own melting.*[13] As if the energy comes from poem not poet, the writer having little to do with it.

Is this disingenuous? Did verses simply fall out of his mouth, the right words in the right order?

Yes and no. A poem, he insists, "may be worked" but not "worried into being." Frost, the technician, wants us to believe that it was the labor he invested that made the poem seem effortless. First, the work, then the letting go. But not quite.

Beginning, middle, and end, a poem remains wild, a "wild tune," independent of its author; it exists primarily as a feeling, an outburst, somewhat reluctantly put into words.

> Just as the first mystery was how a poem could have a tune in such straightness as meter, so the second mystery is how a poem can have wildness and at the same time a subject that shall be fulfilled.[14]

So says Frost, making peace with enthusiasm. The music of poetry lives because it is feral; but it survives and is remembered because it is captured. Yawps, howls, won't do if not eventually tranquilized by motive and meter.

13. Robert Frost. "The Figure A Poems Makes."*Collected Poems, Prose, and Plays*. The Library of America, 1981, p. 778.

14. Ibid., p. 776.

I'm sympathetic; I feel in my bones the alchemic impulse to spin the world into golden utterances. But that strategy is no longer available. For if the poet's business is to traffic in wisdom, what wisdom? Whose?

I don't buy the quaint wit Frost recycled from his neighbors, nor am I particularly impressed by personal revelations in poetry. Invariably, they come off contrived, self-serving.

Emily Dickinson's self-disclosures are an exception—verses to which Frost was attuned. I feel in her poems, as Frost felt, a real threat of anomie. Perhaps heresy. A willingness to say the impermissible and to say it neither plainly nor veiled but sideways, askew.

While Frost preferred a prosody that retained the precisely ruled measurements of Greek and Latin, Dickinson packed her explosives in little boxes that had a tendency to become unglued.

Even so, Frost recognized in her erratic cadence a companion soul. A sibyl who would probe and probe.

Frost's cold intellect was no less renegade or empirical. Maybe more so. The heavens are not home for him, nor are they divine in any religious sense; they consist mostly of "empty spaces/ Between stars—on stars where no human race is."

Yet strangely, alone in the universe, Frost is anything but disenchanted. As long as he remains earthbound.

> When stiff and sore and scarred
> I take away my hand/ From leaning on it hard
> In grass and sand,
>
> The hurt is not enough:
> I long for weight and strength
> To feel the earth as rough
> To all my length.[15]

For most poets of Frost's generation, and beyond, this world may not be charged with the grandeur of God, as it was for Hopkins, but it is charged. And it is reassuringly substantial.

---

15. Frost, "To Earthward." Ibid., p. 227.

I keep hearing from the cellar bin
The rumbling sound
Of load on load of apples coming in.[16]

The ladder Frost climbs points "heavenward," albeit that's not where the poet dwells; the earth calls him back down to "Essence of winter" and "winter sleep."

I cannot rub the strangeness from my sight
I got from looking through a pane of glass
I skimmed this morning from the drinking trough
And held against the world of hoary grass.
It melted, and I let it fall and break.
But I was well
Upon my way to sleep before it fell,
And I could tell
What form my dreaming was about to take.[17]

As I have tried to make sense of my relationship with Robert Frost, I have had to admit that our aesthetics are at odds. He writes representational poems of New England farm life, lucid and comprehensible; my poems, for all their grit, favor abstract clouds of ink.

But the way he practiced his art persistently occupies my headspace, and we have met, demiurges, in a darkroom flickering with afterimages, *carrying out some intention more felt than thought.*[18]

Retrieved by the imagination, concrete memories, such as Frost's apple-picking, are not as definite as they seem. *Magnified apples appear and disappear./ Stem end and blossom end,/ and every fleck of russet showing clear.*[19]

The fruit, in this quasi-state, is transparent enough to look through; on the other hand, a "piece of ice" becomes a "pane of glass" that distorts the "world." *I cannot rub the strangeness from my sight.*

---

16. Frost, "After Apple-Picking." Ibid., p. 69.

17. Frost, "After Apple-Picking." Ibid., p. 68.

18. "The Art of Poetry, No. 2," interviewed by Robert Poirer, *The Paris Review, Issue*, vol. 24, Summer-Fall 1960.

19. Frost, "After Apple-Picking." Ibid., p. 68.

Frost sees with a mind of winter; he sees through a glass darkly. The piece of ice is first and foremost a piece of ice, but it also operates as a looking glass that melts what is into what seems.

In my own poems, I have tried to hold the image meditatively, as Frost held it, but it's slippery.

Years removed from my first encounters with Frost, years of reading and being swayed by different poets, poetics, I can identify other strategies for expressiveness that have energized my writing besides the image.

But my apprenticeship to Frost and his long list of descendants (Stafford, Ammons, Kinnell, Heaney, Walcott, Graham, Glück) has showed me that figuration is the primary labor. A poet like Frost figures sentences under the restraint of meter and renders his thoughts into patterns.

My lineation is looser than Frost's, but I find his verse-making appealing, and perhaps for this reason I return often to the couplet. Frost didn't write couplets, as it were, but his stanzas rely on seeing lines as pairs, one line in relation to the other.

The couplet is basic to formal English poetry, and as such, is a tradition difficult to erase. There are other, more modern, takes on prosody that seem almost allergic to coupling; they unlock the handcuffs of rhyme and meter to create paragraphs that look—and sound—indistinguishable from prose. Frost, like his contemporaries Pound and Eliot, solved the problem by resorting to blank verse. In unrhymed iambic pentameter, he found he could marry the finesse of poetry with the freedom of prose.

In my latest manuscript, I've been fiddling with ten-syllable lines spliced into muted pairs. These are not iambic, per se, but, to my ear, they bear a sonic resemblance to Frost's matter-of-fact rhythms.

however

I am snow without direction; havoc
ensues when I essay. How can I face

the world snow destroys after I blow it,
measure who I am, right violence? For whom

is snow innocent? A comfort my death
with the help of metamorphoses. I melt.

Get lighter. Preserve the lime twig, devoted
to what it needs. My issue is doubtless,

and together snow and I will be
respectful, if also unpredictable.

My poetics deviate from Frost's template and tone. On the other hand, it might be fair to say I shadow the man through blizzards and desolate places.

In this regard, my captivation with troubled white landscapes (*For whom// is snow innocent?*) may belie a race anxiety that Toni Morrison claims haunts American writers, great and small. That is, the conflict between races is forever showing up in our literature, sometimes intentionally, sometimes subconsciously.

As one example, I think of the poet Kevin Young's fabulist dream, titled "Negative," where the speaker views the American social scene in reverse:

Wake to find everything black
what was white, all the vice/ versa—white maids on TV, black

sitcoms that star white dwarfs
cute as pearl buttons. Black Presidents,
Black Houses. White Horse

candidates.[20]

Published in 2001, "Negative" is utopian and at the same time prescient, anticipating the election of a black head of state while also challenging the root of the problem, prejudice fed by greed, which brought about racial inequities in the first place.

Is this what we've wanted

---

20. Kevin Young, "Negative." *To Repel Ghosts*. Zoland Books, 2001, p. 69.

& waited for? to see snow
covering everything black
as Christmas, dark pages written

white upon? . . . .

Only money keeps
green, still grows & burns like grass
under dark daylight.[21]

Progress, Young suggests, requires deeper changes than wordplay or imagination can effect. Then again, soul-searching thought experiments like "Negative" are not inconsequential.

As far as I can tell, aside from an evocative passage in an early poem "The Black Cottage," Frost rarely turned his attention to racial matters. White and male, his position in twentieth-century American society was artificially elevated, out-of-touch with the budding Civil Rights movement. While his New England pastorals were not provincial in terms of themes and introspection, they ignored what many of his generation viewed as urban—or perhaps, Southern—problems.

It's an uncomfortable fact, though not determinative, that Frost's father was a Confederate sympathizer who named his son after Rebel hero Robert E. Lee. It's possible that the prejudice handed down to him was eventually educated out of him, or, fed up with the legacy, he rejected it wholesale. Hard to say. But overt racism wasn't characteristic of the man, at least not the poems.

Reckoning with the influence of Frost on my process makes me examine anew what social responsibility has to do with poetic practice. How can one go on writing snowscapes when the streets call for protest?

By temperament, Frost refused the role of activist. Disappointments and personal trauma drove him to a life versed in country things, which he felt could salve if not remove psychic pain. Even the Great War that snuffed out his friend Thomas didn't generate as much poetry as daily walks through fields and pastures.

21. Young, Ibid., p. 69.

In a more critical mood, it would be easy to dismiss Frost's verses as escapist. But considering him generously, as a man of his time, a case can be made that he retreated to nature in order to confront his place in the cosmos or, expanded, the human predicament entire. As Joseph Brodsky once observed, Frost disappeared in the woods to look not out but in, and looking inward he discovered, "It was dark inside."[22]

I needed, and probably will always need, Frost's cosmic imagination. But to genuinely understand race, the wound that for Americans won't heal, I've had to turn elsewhere, away from the monochromatic.

Still, "Pod of the Milkweed," the opening poem of Frost's final book published in the last year of his life, may be a sign that a diverse America was not far from his mind. The poem envisions, however faintly, the milkweed as a site of riotous "peace and war," where (biologists tell us) swallowtails, admirals, hairstreaks, fritillaries, coppers, sphinxes, tussocks, and monarchs compete for territory. Admittedly, Frost gives us more of a "restless dream" than a reckoning, but, in the full bloom of summer, whiteness suffers by comparison.

"Pod of the Milkweed" is an invocation, "Calling all butterflies of every race" to come to the flower and "with their color compensate/ For what the drab weed lacks of the ornate."[23]

> And yes, although it is a flower that flows
> With milk and honey, it is bitter milk,
> As anyone who ever broke its stem
> And dared to taste the wound a little knows.[24]

These lines were published in 1962, the year I was born. It's also the year that Dr. Martin Luther King, Jr. gave an early version of his "I Have a Dream" speech to high school students in North Carolina. Two different dreams. Two different dreamers.

---

22. Joseph Brodsky, "On Grief and Reason," *Homage to Robert Frost, Joseph Brodsky, Seamus Heaney, Derek Walcott*. Farrar, Straus and Giroux, 1996, p. 12.

23. Frost, Ibid., p. 411.

24. Frost, "Pod of the Milkweed." Ibid., p. 411.

It's taken my generation a lifetime to fully appreciate that for every white dream there is a black dream waiting to be expressed. And behind that dream, another. And another.

In the late nineties, I studied with Kevin Young at the University of Georgia. During that period, Young launched his anthology *Giant Steps: The New Generation of African-American Writers.* At that time, he also described to me his own formation as a poet in The Dark Room Collective, a group of creative insurgents seeking to honor and extend the tradition of black experimentation in the arts.

Young championed Langston Hughes in classes and introduced students to *Montage of a Dream Deferred* (1951), a radical improvisational book-length poem in the manner of jazz, swing, ragtime, bebop, blues, and boogie-woogie.

Hughes, according to critic W. Jason Miller, was the muse for King's "I Have a Dream." Though a leading figure of the Harlem Renaissance, Hughes did not enjoy Frost's broad popularity, in part, because of his skin color, in part, because of his ties to Communism. It was Robert Frost, not Hughes, John F. Kennedy would select to read a poem at his inauguration.

But when preparing the "I Have a Dream" speech, Martin Luther King, Jr. preferred Hughes. His poem "Mother to Son" gave King the language and the rhythms of dissent.

I am rehearsing this bit of literary history because I'm trying to make sense of why Frost's poetic strategy—what Lawrence Raab called "playful concealment"—has appealed more to me in my own poetics than the outspokenness of Langston Hughes.[25]

Perhaps, like many Americans, I feel that my ethnicity has been homogenized and suburbanized right out of me. Thanks to the melting pot, I don't have much of a specific ethnic heritage to draw on other than the white man's, and as a member (unwilling but a member nonetheless) of that tribe I don't have the right or the credibility to speak out the way Hughes did, though I can certainly speak out.

25. Lawrence Raab: On "Mending Wall," *Touchstones: American Poets on a Favorite Poem*. Edited by Robert Pack and Jay Parini. University Press of New England, 1996, n.p.

Silence is not an option, but neither is presumption. Then there's the fact that some of my ancestors were part of causes that were not so noble.

When Hughes sang the self and declared it beautiful, democracy was activated for blacks. Whitman (white men) had announced the possibility; Hughes made it factual. He really was, like Phillis Wheatley and Gwendolyn Brooks, an unacknowledged legislator of the world.

Was Frost?

If not intentionally political, it turns out that Frost's poetry could at least be appropriated for political purposes. The story goes that, when surveying the barrier between West and East Berlin, President Kennedy lobbed a line from a Frost poem at the Soviets. "Something there is that doesn't love a wall."

As much as the poet felt an affinity for Kennedy, as much as he himself entangled the poem in Cold War rhetoric when he was sent, late in life, on a diplomatic mission to Russia, Frost had deep misgivings about poetry used as propaganda. Lawrence Raab notes that Frost believed the complexity of a work of art like "Mending Wall" was "spoiled," by being reduced and "applied," even if he himself was the one doing the applying![26]

Later, reflecting on this in a letter, Frost said that a poem should "suggest." It should "almost but not quite formulate."[27] Ambiguous, it opens up rather than closes down exploration.

As a poet, I believe in a generative ambiguity where the poem I write follows its own intuitive path. A path that leads somewhere I didn't know I knew. A better country where whiteness is a blank. Waiting to be inscribed again. Then erased.

---

26. Raab, Ibid.

27. Raab, Ibid.

Oh Dear, June Jordan: Gertrude Stein: Emily Dickinson: Phillis Wheatley

Éireann Lorsung

In the midst of writing there is merriment.

—Gertrude Stein

To write, and to adopt or have thrust upon me a posture of merriment: to *become merry.*[1] Dear Gertrude Stein, what do you mean that in writing's midst there is this other thing? And what is it to be merry? I sense that reading could be a kind of merry-making, as in, *I read this and even now, remembering reading it and re-reading it, I get a hollow, sparkling feeling in my chest and stomach*. But "merriment" is something one does with others, and so merriment, bursting on the scene of writing, seems to me an interruption of solitude and a demand that one recognize one's accompanists. In the midst of writing, I am not alone: I am with the texts that are there with me, with their makers, accompanied by others who also did not invent the alphabet we all share. Becoming aware of merriment puts me in awareness of relations, already in place, to others, also already in place. Like citation, merriment joins me in thinking what others have begun and will continue; it thickens the place of my writing. Like citation, the merriment in the midst of writing reminds me to leave behind the myth of the solitary genius.

Making merry, as at a party, I look across my glass to toast or meet the eye of the other in conversation. In any case merriment does not happen in a closed circuit or without resonance. It requires something *else* than my self; maybe that's writing (what I have written, or the ongoingness of writing itself) or maybe it's what's been written by others, or maybe it's others themselves. If I am not solitary, what is left to me? Only the midstness of merriment, where I run smack into relation in a field I had been taught to occupy alone.

---

1. An earlier version of this essay appeared in *No. 1 Gold,* https://no1gold.org/doing-things-with-books/seance-writing/spirit-letters/.

Dear Emily Dickinson, in your three-hundred-and-twentieth poem, you wrote that it is "internal difference—/ Where the Meanings, are."[2]What is not one is not one: and that is meaningful. Meanings arise at the point of internal difference, difference within something rather than difference pointed to across distance, as merriment in the midst of writing. And so maybe merriment is a place for Meanings.

Dear Gertrude Stein, you wrote that in the midst of writing there is merriment. Dear Emily Dickinson, you wrote that Meanings *are* in what leaves "no scar" but can nevertheless be recognized, internally, to be non-identical with itself or oneself. Let me follow you away from the isolated field.

* * *

Dear Éireann, name some (new) (possible) ways to be-reading and to be-read?

I have not been able to write, or wanted to write, for a few months. I read Twitter and feel more and more despair about extrajudicial killings and the disproportionate mortality rates of Black women in labor and the daily lessening, legal and cultural, of the value of trans people's and Black people's lives. But maybe my despair is a question of how to be with literature, or how to make it. How I could make it. *Who* makes it? Who I make it with, because of, and for. If I feel lonely in the writing, maybe I need to keep more company. Or realize the company I'm in.

What company makes me isolated in this field? And whose company might make a merry I, too, could join in making? How do I learn to see what is already here? How do I learn to be-with? How do I learn what the merriment in writing's midst could mean?

* * *

Here is a story I was told. Maybe you have been told this story, too. The "Writer" walks out of the house and says to the world, *look what I can do*, while, back in the house, meals are made and children are

2. Dickinson, Emily. Poem 258, "There's a certain Slant of light." *The Complete Poems of Emily Dickinson*. Edited by Thomas Johnson. Little, Brown & Co., 1960.

raised without fanfare: and neither become Culture. The garden is tended, the wash is done, and these, too, are not Culture.

This way of being "Writer," walking out of the house and into the World, leaving the family behind and standing alone, means for the most part being a white man, probably married to a woman, almost assuredly cisgender, probably of some means or supported by someone of means, and of a Christian background.

So: a narrow thing, being, in this sense, which was a sense I received and believed without thinking, for a long time.

There are cracks in this sense of being, though. One crack I sensed was the way that working in a garden, mending clothes, cooking food for others, caring for the sick, elderly, and young made meaning happen for me. Dear June Jordan: you call this work "the other things that have to be done" and you know that it is this work that makes the poem possible. I did this work because it made meaning for me, but I also learned to do and to expect to do this work because I am one *kind* of person to whom it has, historically, been relegated. Not the only kind of person: but my feminization and my class make it so.

This crack in my own knowledge of what work constituted writing was an internal difference, in Dickinson's words, or as she also says, "Heavenly hurt" of which nevertheless "We can find no scar." The hurt is a track, but unlocatable. It points me to where I might go; it is speculative, radical, open, and *other* to a closed-down history of literature which has already settled and established how and what thinking can be, and by whom and where it can be done. It was an opening. In addition, it allowed me to understand writing as ongoing: and the irruptions of cloth, soil, ceramic, soap, others' bodies to be part of the weave, not breakings of it. In turn I began to see that my work, too, could not be a breaking-with. It had to be a being-with. How and with whom did I have my being?

* * *

Dear Gertrude Stein, are there cracks in solid time?

I encounter Stein and think, *She has given up the decorative function and devoted herself to finding out what language* is. *I want* to poem *in her wake*. The difference of Stein's project is not *play*; it is the work of being-with, of irrupting as oneself-with-others within a field that would deny your being. Where the meanings are.

To poem is a question of being as being-with, despite a history in which being alone appeared to be the mode of the poet.

Stein gives me a glimpse of the cracks in the time-being of the (white) (male) poet wandering among the daffodils while his sister keeps house (invisibly) in the background. *Here is another possibility*.

One possibility she brings me is the suggestion that merriment bears relation to writing, while acknowledging a difference (an "internal" difference: merriment is "in the midst" of writing) between the two that might be tonal. "Writing" is not "merriment." (We know that because the two things have very different names. We also know this because of the way merriment happens in writing's midst. The location of merriment with relation to writing—in its midst—tells us they are not the same.) Writing might give us many things, including seriousness, self-seriousness, misery, gloominess, distress, heartbreak, melancholy, pleasure, joy . . . . *Nevertheless, nevertheless, nevertheless*, Stein proposes a break (both pause and rupture) in the midst of writing, which is gaiety, exuberance, cheer, festivity, pleasure, and togetherness. Merriment, unlike writing (verb), is shared. It is convivial. And whereas writing might seem just to appear (the verb and the noun can take the same form), *merriment* must be *made*. If merriment is laborious, it is not alienated from what it labors over or who has labored over it.

* * *

Dear poet-siblings,

I have been looking for a way to be in the world, as a writer, other than the way that means keeping time in that narrow, isolating way of the greater or lesser geniuses of the white Western canon. There has been enough wandering among daffodils while someone else, as June Jordan writes, "cleaned the house, washed the clothes, cooked the food, watched the children." (I am quoting from Jordan's essay "The Difficult Miracle of Black Poetry in America," which Jordan subtitles "Something like a sonnet" and dedicates to Phillis Wheatley.)[3] Let me be clear that I am in favor of daffodils, wandering, and solitude. I am also and no less in favor of the stockpot, the rough sound of the sponge against floorboards, and the weight of a child. But in the world Jordan writes about in her essay, the English world of the poets the young Phillis Wheatley would have read, it was daffodils, wandering, and solitude that formed the ground of poetry. I know that is a ground—a field—only granted naturally to some. I know my own poems have come from a different ground; I attended to that internal difference, but I needed a language for it. Stein gave me a direction, a kind of grammar.

Dear June Jordan: it was your essays that gave me language for this other ground. They showed me the conviviality of poets who already knew what it means to exist, in your words, "beyond and without those terms under consideration"[4]—terms, like "benighted" or "redemption" supplied to Wheatley *by* or *to the benefit of* white literature, white enslavers, white dominant culture. To both exist in language and to refuse the terms of that language; to know oneself as a rupture and point of reinvention; to understand with clarity the violence of the tradition, and its stipples of beauty.

Jordan writes, in the same essay, that Wheatley "created herself a poet, notwithstanding and in despite of everything around her."[5] The creation of the self-as-poet, when one is also self-as-Black-woman, or, as Wheatley was, self-as-enslaved-Black-woman is what Jordan names a "miracle."[6] Miracle, from, linguists postulate, a proto-Indo-European word meaning "to smile at." To *wonder* at. Probably, the dictionary says, "miracle" has a shared root with "merry." And miracle can be a verb as well as a noun: to miracle, meaning, to work a miracle on. Which is what the "difficult miracle" of

3. June Jordan, "The Difficult Miracle of Black Poetry in America or Something Like a Sonnet for Phillis Wheatley,"*Some of Us Did Not Die*. Basic Books, 2002, p. 177.

4. Jordan, Ibid., p. 178.

5. Jordan, Ibid., p. 177.

6. Jordan, Ibid., p. 174.

the poet and Black woman Phillis Wheatley, is and does: Wheatley *is a miracle*; she *miracles*. Because "she [. . .] created herself a poet, notwithstanding and in despite of everything around her." Yes. And Wheatley *miracles* the future (and her present) of poetry in the United States. She changes its course. She *is* its course. She renders it, in her having written, possible at all.

If merriment is both rupture ("internal difference" to the act and history of writing) and a site of togetherness (conviviality), then Wheatley's poems *make merry* the literature of her adopted country and language. Writing, Wheatley renders a conviviality possible, or even already achieved *by her having written at all*: *she* is the conviviality, the internal difference which indexes a relation that was *always* there (the relation of the one who prepares the meals or grows the crops to the one who, nourished and fed, can walk out into the world and transcribe it as *poem*). When Wheatley's writing enters the scene, there is *more* to writing, and to "Writer," than there was. "Following her "intrinsic ardor," and attuned to the core of her own person," Jordan writes of Wheatley, "this girl, the first Black poet in America, had dared to redefine herself from house slave to, possibly, an angel of the Almighty."[7] Such that I sit here, two decades into the twenty-first century, my being and my writing made possible by Wheatley's having written. And by Jordan having written about her.

* * *

Dear June Jordan,

I remember when you died. I was in my early twenties. I didn't understand who you were; I knew your name but I didn't realize your stature. Now, looking back, I am amazed that I lived in a world and time when you were alive and I didn't *know* what that meant. Where Gertrude Stein gave me a glimpse at the cracks in the solitary subject poet, you showed me how to be whole: not individual, but one (as C. D. Wright said) *with others*. You showed me the impossibility of poetry apart from politics, of art and literature ever being neutral. You taught me what it meant for me to have thought neutrality was

7. Jordan, Ibid., p. 178.

possible. I mean to say, your writing has contributed to the ground of my liberation (ongoing, unachieved).

I knew Phillis Wheatley's name then and I had read her poems, but came late to your essay-sonnet to her. For her. In which you mourn the loss of the poems of "Phillis the woman, [. . .] who had chosen herself, free, and brave to be free in a land of slavery,"[8] poems which were never published; which were lost. You identify one of the scars in this. You write, about Wheatley's second manuscript of poems, poems of her adulthood and her freedom, "I believe we would not have seen them, anyway. I believe no one would have published the poetry of Black Phillis Wheatley, that grown woman who stayed with her chosen Black man [. . .] an independent Black woman poet in America."[9] Dickinson writes of the "Heavenly Hurt" the light of winter afternoons gives, hurt that leaves no scar except "internal difference" and resultant "Meanings." To me that scar of internal difference is your knowledge of all that might have been in a world where Wheatley's poeming could have been prized, even as an adult, even as a married woman, even as a Black woman coming into her own power. It is not only your knowing (and valuing) of that possibility, but your knowing it and asserting its value against the reality of the violent whiteness of literature as field and institution. You write, "Can you imagine that [the publication of a free Black woman's poems], in 1775?" You write, "Can you imagine that, today?"[10]

My education, like, I imagine, the education of most white children and young adults in the U.S. in the 1980s and 1990s, had given me to understand an all-white history of literature as *naturally occurring*. Where Black writers and other writers of color appeared was a sort of scar. I do not recall being encouraged to trace that scar, to find the "Meanings" there. Black writers and writers of color appeared as blips on a homogeneous surface, a skin of writing which was otherwise white. I did not know how to see you or Wheatley as historical. I had not been taught to perceive your *lineage*. I had to learn this after my formal education ended, by following the lines, sometimes extremely subtle, of reference and allusion in the writings of Black

8. Jordan, Ibid., p. 183.

9. Jordan, Ibid., p. 184.

10. Jordan, Ibid., p. 184.

women whose work I had begun to read online. When I began to find you, I was shocked that we had not been given your work at the center of any of my degrees. Not even a class on you. Not even one poem.

I began to be able to see your work as a tributary to mine and valuable regardless of its relation to me. Valuable regardless of its relation to what I had been taught to call *the canon.* I had been educated without manners in some way: I was incapable of being convivial in a way which you and Wheatley had had no choice but to be. The pictures of literary life I had been given were images of solitude. I imagined, without even knowing I imagined, that I was alone in my field—poetry—which nevertheless and paradoxically extended all around me, covering the world. The field appeared to *be* the world. It had to: it was a field established as part of a project of dominance that began before me but extended through me. Writing with no merriment in its midst; writing only petulantly interrupted for care, relation, labor, world-making with anything other than the pen; writing by anyone other than those whose days have always been shared.

You have multiplied the world.

Dear June Jordan, you write about judging the Loft McKnight Awards in creative writing, awards administered by a literary organization in my home city, Minneapolis. "Last week [...] I read through sixteen manuscripts of rather fine poetry," you write. You go on to list "lexical items" you encountered in the poems—"Rock, moon, star, roses, chimney, Prague, elms, lilac, railroad tracks, lake, lilies, snow geese, crow, mountain, arrow feathers, ear of corn, marsh, sandstone, rabbit-bush, gulley, pumpkins, eagle, tundra, dwarf willow, dipper-bird, brown creek, lizards, sycamores, glacier, canteen, skate eggs, birch, spruce, pumphandle"—and to say that these "are the terms, the lexical items accurate to the specific white Minnesota daily life of those white poets."[11] These lexical items point away from a shared field. In that list, it might be possible to forget that the land on which the poets walk was stripped from its first occupants; that those occupants were forcibly separated from their languages, traditions, religion, families, homes. There are no corner stores, police, mortgages, funeral parlors, asphalt trucks, sewing machines, or pigeons in that list. These words form a lexicon of what is accept-

11. Jordan, Ibid., p. 184.

ed as unmarked in (white) English-language poetry, and among the unmarked things are structures of power that supersede individual talent, goodwill, or ambition. This is the same unmarkedness of the poet wandering among the daffodils. It is the unmarkedness of a writing life that can think of itself as unattached to a political being; that can think of itself as *merely* being.

Dear June Jordan, I realize from reading you that a poem, a field, in which only urns and willows, streams, the Classical features of a marble girl appear is a field that is insufficient for our shared life. To cultivate such a field would rely on my disregard for you.

A poetry of "internal difference" is a poetry of the many, multiple: a poetrys. A poetry in the midst of which is "merriment" is a poetry of non-assimilation and of being-together. When you write that the poems you read for the McKnight awards are "accurate to the specific white Minnesota daily life" of their writers, I see an extension of recognition that is not extended, as you write, to Black poets who "have been rejected and [. . .] frequently dismissed as "political" or "topical" or "sloganeering" and "crude" and "insignificant" because, like Phillis Wheatley, we have persisted for freedom."[12] Your ability to see the *both* of poetry (its capacity for persisting for freedom *enlarging* its historical sphere of the personal, the lyric, the pastoral, rather than "sullying" these) is an index of your vision. Your own capacity. Your merriment, the miracle of Wheatley and indeed the way you yourself miracle our shared literature.

* * *

Who am I with?

Who is with me?

"It was not natural," Jordan writes, and "she was the first."[13]

In 1775, she was the first. Not the first to think, sing, want, dream, poem. But the first we know of to write, whose writings were cared for and kept.

12. Jordan, Ibid., p. 184–85.

13. Jordan, Ibid., p. 185.

"And she was the first."

Can I join in? I will stand in the kitchen, fill glasses and plates, wash dishes and do laundry. These are the ground of poetry, too. Shared work in a field we also share, the dishes and the sewing irrupt into the field of the poem. Because I encountered you I understand my life can be one whole thing, not broken into fragments. Because I encountered you I know this work of wholeness is not only to do with my being a woman but to do with the social power of my whiteness; I know it is not only a matter of making a space for myself in the shape of myself but of refusing any part of me that imagines any other person or their work as not part of the field we all already share.

In our language and culture, light is a metaphor for knowledge, so when in Dickinson's poem the winter light slants into the room I cannot divorce it from a shared history of revelation and enlightenment. It is that arriving light that hurts without visible scar and that establishes "internal difference." Knowing changes a person. Dear June Jordan, your essay is a scar indexing "internal difference" and also "Meanings" for me. As "merriment" breaks through "writing," it breaks through me, and there is a trace of it left once I finish reading. As a white poet and one of your readers I am asked to awaken to the relationship I have always *already* been in *to* Wheatley, *to* you, and *to* a history, lineage, and ongoing genealogy of Black poets and writers and artists who have "persisted for freedom," theirs *and* mine. Your conviviality pre-exists me. It has made everything possible: has been what makes my writing "about wild geese flying over Prague" as well as about migration, white dominance, nuclear devastation, and world war possible.

Dear Éireann, do you not owe what courage you have to the example of poets like Wheatley, like Jordan, who in writing "of the terror and the hungering and the quandaries of [their] lives on this North American soil" have refused to be subsumed into similarity and invisibility, who have been the "miracle" and the "merriment," the irruption and the "Meanings," without whom you could in fact never have written at all, could not have learned to write at all?

Given in the Folding

Farid Matuk

> "You slavers will know what its/ Like to be a slave/ Slave to your mind/ Slave to your race/ You won't go to heaven/ You won't go to hell/ You remain in your graves"
>
> —Exuma, covered by Nina Simone

> "love precedes us to the grave and follows us into it"
>
> —Etel Adnan

It is 1994, or 1995, sometime between Reginald Denny and George W. Bush, and I am driving to catch a view. I am poor, barely documented by the amnesty calculated into an immigration reform law, fatherless. I sleep in a small room in my mother's mobile home, and she cries each time a doctor pushes free samples into her palm so she can save on prescriptions. I feel a sticky weirdness layer on our things on the rare occasion Americans visit our home. I know we aren't right, and that derision I think is taste. I have some college credits, I've read some Pascal, some Duras; I have a copy of Elias Khoury's *Little Mountain* in my bag. Most things outside—glass-front office parks, palm lined blocks, arching overpasses—look curated, and their habit of rolling off my windshield has me thinking it doesn't matter I was never meant to be their audience because I'm still driving and I'm still looking.

And if I feel smug, if I should push my little Honda to lurch through a long turn, and if my stomach should lift and my eyes narrow, I'll steer toward downtown Long Beach where Lindon lives in a building half gentrified into lofts, its upper floors still scaffolds and unfinished walls, missing windows. The light comes down honeyed through the methane and carbon monoxide. I can't really know, but I want to be covered under a man's more than human form. I can't really say, but I want eyes that melt every white face they reach.

every place my breath doesn't reach . . .

It is 2020, and this year I will be as old as Lindon was when he died. But when we were close, he was around 35 and I was 21. He was a professor at my school, and though I was never on his roster, he made me want to think my way out of what passed for life. We had sex but we weren't lovers. We were friends but we weren't equals. Years into our time together he took my asking about his exact age as the reason to stop speaking with me. I held on to that hurt for too long and then one day in 2008 he was dead.

Testimonials to Lindon Barrett's life online and in print focus on the ways his work was among the first to pursue critical theory and African-American studies as mutually constitutive, and they focus on the joy he infused into his classroom, into his studies, and into his dance parties, the respect and love with which he mentored students. Sometimes, those testifying allow themselves an oblique nod to what they take for Lindon's mercurial nature, but he was not volatile. He minded particular fault lines. In the life Lindon made, categories and the stories they supply were shelters built on the shakiest ground.

My people are Andean mestizos and white Christian Arabs from Syria. Before US Americans learn my name, I'm taken for white, or white enough to think hard about how I write of a black friend, one born in British Guyana and raised in Canada, about his body, his sex, his listening, and his death. My encounter with him is still happening in my body, in its sex, and in its listening. But I don't know how much our bodies should be here. Lindon would have laughed. He made space for me to come into the body I've been given, to feel and to theorize there, and to not believe too much in any self that would claim that body by presenting a deed. But this is an essay, not the life to which he showed me a body could be dedicated.

I think he would have understood my discretion as a way to care for us, to draw something round us while still giving us over to the conveyance of this page. But he would have laughed because that kind of care risks setting categories and the power differentials between them as a point of arrival. To Lindon, categories were sometimes things to occupy, but mostly they were best left behind. He was committed to lingering outside, and it was any attempt to shelter him elsewhere that he took as betrayal.

I need to start with betrayal because that's how he comes back to me. There's no need to arrange the words into a picture, but a few nights ago I was masturbating alone, and after my orgasm I dropped back into a body gripped tight from within and I realized I wasn't breathing. Those mechanics are familiar enough, but this time the gripping was total, each cell tightening around the space where oxygen would have been. When I could feel anything again, I was scared. My body had never choked itself; I don't know why it did that night, but my next thought was of Lindon, the way he was found naked on his bed, a shoelace tight around his neck. There were no signs of forced entry. A few days later cops arrested a young man who was in possession of Lindon's car. I remember from the local papers that his name was Marlon Martinez. Within days Marlon was found dead in the jail where he awaited his arraignment. I found one story with a single sentence that stated Marlon had reported abuses by the guards a day before dying. No one ordered an autopsy and no one reported a reason for the boy's death. I can't find that report any more.

The betrayals layer. In the introduction to Lindon's posthumous second book the editors—well-meaning colleagues and friends—place his death in a line of black queer intellectuals whose choices created the conditions for their tragic, violent ends. This is a cliché, a mutual friend tells me, and he's right. I can't know how Marlon contributed to Lindon's death. Still, I know that Lindon could look the tragedy of everyday whiteness in the eye so routinely, with such fortitude, that I can't imagine he needed to invite chaos into his bed. It's not that I can't imagine Lindon was fallible or that his ferocity exacted compensating tolls in private parts of his life. Lindon hurt like anyone, or he hurt like anyone with a habit of separating life from the coagulant of whiteness. But it's just as likely as not that Lindon and Marlon were friends, something like Lindon and I had been friends.

Marlon could have taken Lindon's car not as a thief but as a scared kid who didn't have his own means of getting far away from a mistake he never wanted to make. Erotic asphyxiation, or breath play, was never part of the sex Lindon and I had, but maybe it was a pleasure Lindon had come to explore in the years after we stopped talking. Maybe Lindon asked Marlon to tighten his grip a little more because it felt good and he wanted it to feel better. Lindon could have died the way I remember him living, not happy, exactly, but unashamed that his imagination should range, vagrant, but always away from whiteness, not the racial category but the mistake that confuses being with self-possession.

Self-possessed, one could claim rights, imagine an ethic and enjoy freedom. Lindon didn't deny the power of those terms, their tactical value in the project of survival, but he did not believe in them. He knew whiteness to be more pervasive than white people, more foundational than racial orders, since it promises lifetime employment in the maintenance of one's boundaries. I mean, how do you find the world treats you now that it has promoted you to the management of your own integrity? Lindon was not "a black body," but he lived in a body so marked. I used to think he lived in that racialized body always at escape velocity and that on his last night he did not stop. Now I think he understood he was never admitted into the fantasy of boundaries in the first place, and to survive that sustained exile he didn't need to practice escaping, he needed to practice pleasure.

I don't mean despairing or nihilistic hedonism. I mean pleasure. And I don't mean nihilism by means of pleasure; I mean pleasure. Orgasm's moment of blankness, it's small suspension, always seemed secondary to him. How do I explain this? We hung out a lot, so I saw him grieve, and rage, and feel hollowed out with sadness. I came to understand that the senior white colleague who capped a faculty meeting by suggesting Lindon "go back to the ghetto" and the campus cop who escalated Lindon's parking ticket into an arrest were at once wholly mundane, wholly unwelcomed, and wholly intertwined characters in a black intellectual's story. And as good queer, immigrant sons, we grieved together our estrangement from our immigrant moms. I've no doubt Lindon brought his complex mourning to his sex and sensuality like anyone might. But he wasn't trying to get blank. Sex with Lindon as I knew it was never sticky with despair, it was never a stage for baroque power plays, it was never a site where old traumas could find enough soil to generate new ones. He had the lightest touch, so this year, when my body chokes itself hard, resisting the sluicing from one realm to another that sex can be, I think that of course Lindon had to ask someone else to choke him, because on its own his body would never be so committed to its own dominion.

I'm coming to understand the pleasure Lindon cared about realized itself as a simplicity of feeling. In *The Fire Next Time*, James Baldwin knows that to write about pleasure and beauty he has to rescue sensuality from anti-blackness, arguing for a sensuality that is "much simpler and much less fanciful" than "the quivering dusky maidens or priapic black studs"[1] he worries the word, when coming from his racialized mouth, might conjure for readers—white or otherwise—who are bound to a tradition of smearing simultaneously excessive and diminished sensuality onto black bodies. Against this tradition, Baldwin doubles-down on the centrality and power of sensuality itself. "To be sensual," he submits, "is to respect and rejoice in the force of life, of life itself, and to be *present* in all that one does, from the effort of loving to the breaking of bread."

That emphasis on the word "present" is Baldwin's, and I'm embarrassed by it. It conjures for me caricatures of self-indulgence, seekers borrowing from whatever practice of joy is at hand in order to lose nothing but their anxiety. A lot of thinkers, including Baldwin, have made the point that to adjust oneself to Western culture requires contortions that, from a global perspective, maybe don't deserve much sympathy, but are nonetheless psychically brutal. And we know that psychic survival, like anything in a caste society, takes on the particular exigencies of one's place in those intersecting but hierarchical castes. I can't dismiss anyone trying to get calm when I remember all that. But what if the presence Baldwin imagines requires us to give up even the self that would be improved by evading anxiety? Calm or not, a self can't even take shape without traveling along various frenzied circuits of value, circuits like the one that trades emergent aspects in exchange for layers of self-awareness that promise to ossify, stabilize.

Maybe I have dismissive laughter at the ready because I'm rooted in the order that would be threatened by what Baldwin imagines. How could I not be, particularly as a white-proximate person of color, which is to say as someone tempted to dream aspirational white dreams? My education has been content to stop at the idea that bodies don't just enter systems of oppression, but that they are wrapped in layers of debased similitude, layers of coerced consent, layers of

1. Baldwin, James. *Collected Essays*. Library of America, 1998: 311.

satirical recursion, layers of reactionary vigilance. I've been told socially dominant bodies are wrapped in layers too, though layers that train the fascia to affect different reflexes. Or as Claudia Rankine writes, "words encoding the bodies they cover. And despite everything the body remains."[2] But what if that layering is only half the problem? The layered figure requires that we imagine a recess where something primary—the body—remains, waiting to be coded otherwise, a recess where another, healthier call can lodge itself as the longed-for authentic thing in the frenzied thing. When I think of Lindon, I can more fully sense the kind of presence Baldwin recognized as an unashamed and vital aspect, and I think such presence can be dangerous not because it might lead to canned ideas like "a life well lived," but because it revises the whole topology the call relies on.

I know the sex Lindon and I had was simpler and less fanciful than the fetishized roles assigned us by white fantasies, but it was also simpler and less fanciful than the normative enough roles of lover or romantic partner, boyfriend or fuck buddy. We didn't take on the daddy/son or mentor/mentee role play that men sometimes use to organize cross-generational intimacies, even though we attended to something like the emotional needs those roles sometimes help convey. Our relationship was one of the undetermined but real things queerness is always producing without bothering to codify or represent. I know we never kissed, not a real kiss that might lead to something promised. I could count on one hand the number of times we partnered as two bodies in intercourse. We saw beauty in each other, but were not one another's objects of desire. Time with Lindon had sex in the air, a diffuse and social potential, and no one we hung out with needed to condense it into narratives. A drive to the beach could pass reading poems or absently masturbating. A dinner party could morph into a casual, lazy kind of orgy, though dinner was just as likely to lead to a study group or a dance party.

Whatever happenings our sensuality made, listening was there. We could spend a whole night sitting in front of the stereo, listening and analyzing, improvising figures for what we heard, which I eventually understood was a way of joining the band. Lindon showed me sen-

2. Rankine, Claudia. *Citizen: An American Lyric*. Graywolf Press, 2014, p. 69.

suality is always a practice involving others, or their traces. We tended to audible traces on vinyl, or to fugitive traces novelists grazed with the figures of their language only to let them settle back into the necessarily unsaid, or to traces of ancestors, their routine witnessing and bearing of their lives, their smallest unheroic gestures, "heard" or echoed in our routine witnessing and bearing of our lives. I think what Lindon was practicing was a listening with an ear so sensitive that it was ready to admit and somehow to enter at once. To enfold, I want to say, in order to rethink the topology of self and "the body's" place in it. Anne Cheng has written about something like this in the work of Theresa Hak Kyung Cha. "Since listening," she writes, "remains one of the only physical activities of the human body that occurs simultaneously inside and outside the body, we might understand listening here to be initiating a boundary contestation. . . . There is no speaking subject," she continues, "that is not already an echo."[3]

The sensuality Lindon practiced coursed inside and outside the body at once, but what if the speaking and listening entailed in that sensuality might be unmoored from so-called subjects? Maybe the most often cited formulation Lindon offered us is the "sly alterity of the singing voice" (58) from his first book, *Blackness and Value: Seeing Double*[4], in which he reads narratives of escaped slaves against the tendency to take these as barely mediated objective accounts of suffering. The linguistic play and aporias in the literary craft of the writers he studied indexed authorial power and subjectivity, but they also opened as portals for Lindon onto the conceptual violence that slides a narrow kind of literacy into whiteness and whiteness into subjectivity. Seeking to think of literacy beyond the page, Lindon wrote of the "sly alterity of the singing voice" as a way of naming an expansive range of vocalization that calls attention to the material reality of the body's interaction with breath. The body orchestrates bellows and force, producing an array of sonic counterpoints that can signify against demeaning lyrics and against white conceptions of voice that would foreclose the improvisatory, wayward possibil-

3. Cheng, Anne. "History in/against the fragment: Theresa Hak Kyung Cha." *The Melancholy of Race*. Oxford UP, 2000, p. 161–62.

4. Barrett, Lindon. *Blackness and Value: Seeing Double*. Cambridge UP, 1999, p. 58–93.

ities of black vocalization. And against nineteenth century white commentators who received communal black song only as body, only as a tumultuous derangement of sense, Lindon read the physicality of body and breath in relation to patterns of call and response and to the interplay between lead and background vocalists as generators of meaning.

Whose desire is it, though, that would find in Lindon's ideas of sly signification a petition toward earnest signification? Despite finding authority in the literary artifice of ex-slaves' narratives, despite finding meaning in the structures of song and in the situations these realized, in less cited passages Lindon also figured his ideas about value, voice, and song in ways that displace listening, singing, and blackness from subjectivity. Thinking through commentaries on black singing by Frederick Douglass and Alice Walker, Lindon wrote of the singing voice as a "standard of an African American present absence." Thinking through Edmund Husserl's wish for voice and speech to offer coincidences of unmediated presence, Lindon pushes Derrida's critical take on Husserl, arguing that the embodied materiality of speech and song, specifically in African-American practice, "emphasize the *infinitude* of "unmeaning" that presupposes and inaugurates signification" (emphasis in the original, 84). Taking up historian Nell Irvin Painter's injunction to trouble the figurative nature of money with the fact of African American enslavement as "embodied currency and labor force," Lindon concludes that "African-Americans and their self-performances prove crucial sites at which valueless-ness and value conflate" (93). Present as absence, valued yet valueless, signifying yet anterior and causal to signification as such, these formulations resist any understanding of sly signification as something for which African-Americans had to settle. Lindon's thought swerved any trajectory that would deliver sly signification in black song onto an idealized, fully self-same signification where intention and expression coincide with one another, and with enfranchisement into subjectivity.

I don't have the training as a theorist or scholar that would help me dare anything conclusive about Lindon's work. But I can read that his thinking encompassed both claims to dignity that make possible political strategies for social advancement and the contention that blackness is excised from the possibility of subject formation, and in fact that blackness occupies the position against which subject formation is at all, and always secondarily, reactively possible. In other words, Lindon's thought swam in currents that characterized an earlier institutionalized African-American Studies as much as in currents that now run through what we've come to call Black Pessimism. What I know is that while he mourned and raged against the routine and compulsive ways whiteness relitigates the exile of blackness from civil society, he did not cling to mourning or rage as shelter or hammer. What I know is that his living was given to him in a continual practice of being present, at the edges of all his senses, exactly in that absence that's without origin and before origin.

Maybe what I mean is that the way Lindon listened let him improvise with listening itself. Rather than forming his subjectivity—perpetually or at all—as a psychoanalytic baby always in reaction against his permeability, Lindon listened for expansions of his permeability. I remember the night, a year or two after I'd graduated, that *Blackness and Value* arrived from Cambridge University Press. He had to explain to me what that meant, how the prestige of the publisher would help make his tenure case unassailable. We opened 40oz beers to celebrate and sat on the ground on either side of the massive cardboard box. We took out copies of the hardcover edition and he showed me where I was included in the acknowledgments, thanked for my "earnest interest in the life of the mind." It was a partial truth, a dodge from the conflated everything that we practiced and a concession to institutional propriety. When we were good and drunk, he threw the copy he'd been holding across the loft. It flew out, pages fanning, cover spreading toward the north facing windows and caught the glance of the moon peering through them. I was young and proud to see my name in print. I was proud of his achievement and that I was an incidental witness to it. Driving over freeways enraged by my susceptibility to exploitations I couldn't understand, yet trusting in a fundamental arousal of my body's susceptibility, I'd enjoyed months of refuge in Lindon's loft. Without invitation I would show up and he would let me watch his gay porn VHS tapes, masturbating openly on his couch while in my periphery he sat at his desk, deep in composition of his manuscript. I was so proud that my friend, through some interplay of intellectual power and career maneuvering I could hardly conceive of, had rendered that manuscript into an actual book that would live in libraries and in grad students' bags. It was his achievement, but it was also the closest I'd gotten to an imagined professional future for myself. So, when he threw the book away from us, it hurt.

He said he wasn't ashamed or angry, he wasn't disavowing all that work. He just didn't want to believe in a book. He said something about how the book was an artefact of institutional disciplining more than a record of study, that it could only ever be a reduction of life. I remember we ended that night naked in the top-most floor of his building where there was nothing yet but scaffolding. We stood at the edge looking west over Long Beach toward the Pacific. Lindon was to my right, our dicks simple as any part of the surfaces that surrounded us. It was late enough that we were no longer drunk. I think we left a pulsing impression in the fabric because I can close my eyes now and step into that outline and the streets below, their distance and lights, the people stirring, the water pulsing beyond, my friend's easy presence, all gather to touch me. I didn't understand it then, but that night of flinging the book and standing exposed is now twinned in my mind with an afternoon when I was on his bed. He came out of the shower and lingered at the door of the bathroom and just stood there, looking down at his half hard cock. I reached for it, but he asked me to hold back. It wasn't a teasing pause in a longer seduction; he just wanted to look at it, himself. Hadn't I ever looked at my body without using it, he asked. I can hear it now as an invitation not to dissociation but to the gesture of flinging, flinging the phallus off a dick like flinging the book off a life.

I think now that these least sexualized gestures were the most erotic gestures, delivering Lindon onto permeability, affectability, but not to an original recess that was hiding underneath waiting for its covers to be flung off. Fred Moten has talked[5] about musician Rahsaan Roland Kirk's performance of the song "The Business Ain't Nothing but the Blues,"[6] the way Roland Kirk blows across the aperture of his flute while simultaneously humming. It's a way to figure a fugi-

5. Hartman, Saidiya & Moten, Fred. "Fugitivity & Waywardness" (presentation). *Arika*, 2014, arika.org.uk/archive.

6. Roland Kirk, Rahsaan. *Rahsaan: The Complete Mercury Recordings of Roland Kirk*. Polygram Records, 1991.

tivity that, whether running from danger or sitting safe, nonetheless splits from itself, what Moten calls a cascading fugitivity. This cascade helps me think that we might gesture at flinging off, but as in listening, we occur and remain at once inside and out, and so this flinging doesn't expel so much as it opens up slack in what we thought were boundaries of self and body, delivering these toward a general displacement. But this is where I want to imagine enfolding. I don't want to think of the fold as the baroque covering of drapery in painting or intricate façades on buildings that offer themselves to a stable viewer as some kind of dimensional mystery. The cascading motion of fugitivity maybe doesn't peel off strands of difference into nothingness, and maybe the most interesting potential in the cascade is not in the splitting but in the ways the peels can enfold, returning all of the something into which, with which they are flung. I want to think of enfolding as multi-directional traversal, but also as ontology, as the sub-atomic matter that has already displaced viewers and viewed, here and there, into one another such that one and the other can only be place holders, poor signs for the way atoms already attest to the unaccountable means by which they touch across estranged distances, which is to say across time. That transiting emerges from and adds to a space that's replete with traces of languages, memories, viruses, attentions, wishes, and ghosts, their rage and love. It's not art, only sensate living to be fibers in that fabric, but I think it's the kind of presence Baldwin was pointing to, a kind of presence that also invites a revision of any distinction between art and life.

In this sense I have to think of Baldwin along with Lindon and the both them along with Alice Notley. Notley has written that our work is "hearing & saying/ at the double edge of body &/ breath,"[7] and I believe her. Hearing and saying at this double edge can be one technology for working *with* while remaining *of* that dense weave, pleating and slacking and pleating again. This complex topography is of the body and of its beyond, its Möbius-like double edge entangling far and near, inside and out, present and past. And this always doubled edge may be the finest instrument verse can use to reimagine its own etymology in turning. At the double edge of body and breath contact with the outside is inevitable and no longer relevant since every turn-

7. Notley, Alice. *Grave of Light: New & Selected Poems 1970–2005*. Wesleyan UP, 2006, p. 172.

ing out is also an enfolding return. It's how I've come to think of rhyme, to pick only one aspect of verse. Rhyme, whether internal to the line or at line's end, whether perfect or near, doesn't reconcile a preceding sound in its second instance; instead, a sound's repetition welcomes its initial iteration and all the difference that iteration grazed across the syllables it traveled to meet its rhyme. Robert Duncan's visionary aspect rendered such a folding in "Often I am Permitted to Return to a Meadow,"[8] for example. The poem offers the seeming contradiction of an expanse, an "eternal pasture," that is "folded in all thought" and this folding gives cause to the existence of "a hall therein." How could an expanse be folded and therein contain a throughway? But Duncan may not be offering us a poem about misprision as compensation for the onrush of a present in excess of our sensory apparatus. A "property of mind," yes. An "omen," which is to say a stand-in for a return, yes. But for Duncan the referent is no less than "what is," folding us back again to presence in living.

The fold allows a rejection of nothingness, a rejection of evacuated space. It's a way to think of quantum entanglement that resists the habit of mistaking even this drastic conception of matter for more familiar binaries of foreground and backdrop, living energy and dead things. These familiar spatial concepts from Cartesian coordinate mapping deserve some critical pressure for the way they exert a lasting influence on the way we think of poems too. Advancing, ongoing, in love with the power to generate next designs, are all things we might say of "innovative" poems, things we'd say if we were committed to an expansionist relation to the assumption of empty space, with all the plunder this implies. Or, in a more optimistic cast, these are things to say about poems for those committed to a poetics that resists closure to allow for possibility, a truism of various strains of the U.S. avant-garde. But this commitment to indeterminacy forecloses on the emergent possibilities it would celebrate by remaining bound to a conception of space as empty expanse. The trace of this retrenchment is legible in every plaudit piled on the singular self, the artist, brave enough to face the edge of nothingness and from it steal the new. Beyond the conventions of textual poesis,

8. Duncan, Robert. *Selected Poems*. Ed. Robert J. Bertholf. New Directions Books, 1993, p. 44.

thinking space "thickly" in terms of the fold also allows us to recast the practice of everyday life away from conceptions of subjectivity as individuated, atomized self-possession. Michel de Certeau[9] sought a sociology of everyday life in which the individual claims, customizes, perverts, repurposes, the commodities, habits, and ideologies of mass appeal toward unexpected ends, thereby finding the individual's autonomy beyond conformity's reach. Lindon didn't want to be any system's agent and he wouldn't suffer any abdication of the power of critical analysis to cut a path that backs out of ideologies. But that path leaves one alone in an infinite regress, always taking a step back from ideology into ever more radical positions of self-awareness, crowned with the righteous isolation of the exceptional thinker. Lindon showed me that if my critical analysis gets me out of something, I can then turn and there risk critical creation with others who surely preceded me. I'm here for any art, any aesthetic, any everyday practice that will fling slack across the entangled fibers where the disaggregated can stretch out, disperse, and gather again as constituent parts, changed and differentiated, in echoes and rhymes, in lovers and ancestors, at once bearing and borne.

Hard questions, though, come to a crisis for me at the gathering points of the fold. Folks wanting to challenge the impulse to get down under self-possessed individuation point to the dangers of collectives. If capitalists favor organizing people into masses by reductive traits for easy marketing, fascists would organize a national collective whose glamour of stylized uniforms and stylized gestures stokes a desire to belong that dampens defiant or deviant impulses. The difficulty for me isn't in being left to commit to a good collective over a bad one. What's difficult is safety, or rather the risk to safety that enfolded entanglement requires. Fascists give over individuation to the collective because a paternalistic state promises to ensure the integrity and consistency of that collective's boundaries: blood and soil. Defense at the boundary, guaranteed, symbolically and materially by the state, reconstitutes the collective as another singularity, albeit one with internal, if dampened, difference, kind of like the individuated subject. Maybe, then, at least structurally, every citizen of any nation is a fascist.

---

9. Certeau, De Michel, and Steven Rendall. *The Practice of Everyday Life*. Third ed. U of California P, 2011.

Lindon never dampened the differences between us, yet he continually listened for moments where he could make a presence in his vulnerability. Refusing the policing of his own boundaries meant inviting me, and others, into that gesture of flinging that opened critical displacements and into the enfolded gathering those displacements made possible. In some ways that is the most perverse lesson he offered, the one I benefit from even as I fail to enact it. Amidst a well-intentioned zeitgeist of minding one's position in structures of power, Lindon said come stand with me, come lay here in my social death, come dance our way through it. But when he flung the book off his life or the phallus off his flesh, he pitched weights that were particular to him. Lindon flung a book about black people authoring their ways into (and beyond) the category of the human with his own authoring black hand. He looked past his dick as likeness—a likeness compulsively atomized, feared, desired, and viciously committed to light in keepsake lynching photographs,[10] pornography, and high art compositions[11]—from within a black body committed to living in and through blackness. I came across the stray porn film offering exoticized scenes of Southwest Arab/North African (SWANA) or Latinx people, but those were rare encounters, dismaying oddities, not a norm I had to survive in the work of articulating my own desires. I wasn't forced to contend with representations of demeaned nudity that implicated my body until the spring of 2004 when Iraqi men, men who could have been my cousins, appeared naked and tortured in souvenir photographs taken by U.S. soldiers assigned as guards to Abu Ghraib prison. The body where my life happens and the sex that gets made there were always simpler and less fanciful than the codes and materials given to Lindon. The poet Harmony Holiday has written about the way her white mother's life-long love of black men that began with Holiday's father was also a quest to love both blackness and herself unequivocally and simply, without imposed fancy. Still, both her mother and her mother's lovers had to contend with "America's haunted love affair with

---

10. *Without Sanctuary: Photographs and Postcards of Lynchings in America,* withoutsanctuary.org/

11. Mercer, Kobena. "Reading racial fetishism: the photographs of Robert Mapplethorpe" *Welcome to the Jungle: New Positions in Black Cultural Studies.* Routledge, 1994.

blackness, its desire to be reborn in a kind of noir armor . . . ."[12] That's the mistake of non-black people, I think, to regard blackness as another skin, its seeming redundancy making it available as armor we could inhabit as loving, desirous parasites.

Lindon himself told me to go read Hortense Spillers, but I didn't really pay attention until years later Fred Moten and Stefano Harney talked[13] about her foundational essay, "Mama's Baby, Papa's Maybe, An American Grammar Book."[14] There, Spillers traces the profound dispossession that seemingly creates the category of blackness. Before bondage nullified patrilineal or matrilineal claims to children in favor of a master's property claims, there was the middle passage. Before the middle passage left the enslaved "culturally "unmade," thrown in the midst of a figurative darkness that exposed their destinies to an unknown course" (215), there was theft from one's name and from one's indigenous land. Stolen from names and from lands, enslaved people were forced, it would seem, into a generic blackness manifested as a displacement of "other human and cultural features and relations, including the displacement of the genitalia, the female's and the male's desire that engenders future" (217). Unmoored from generational ordering, ungendered, excised from civil society, and suspended outside of time, blackness in this scheme is more wound or raw flesh than it is skin. Divided from skin and left with flesh, Spillers argues, enslaved people marked as black "lose any hint or suggestion of a dimension of ethics, of relatedness between human personality and its anatomical features, between one human personality and another, between human personality and cultural institutions. To that extent, the procedures adopted for the captive flesh demarcate a total objectification" (208). Following the way Spillers details this descent into objectification, it's tempting to assume that such dispossession creates the space of blackness and

12. Holiday, Harmony. "Mama Looks for Melanin." *Longreads*, June, 2019, longreads.com/2019/06/05/mama-looks-for-melanin/

13. Harney, Stefano, and Fred Moten. "'Give Away Your Home, Constantly' —Fred Moten and Stefano Harney Revisit The Undercommons In A Time of Pandemic and Rebellion" (podcast). *Millennials Are Killing Capitalism*, July, 2019, millennialsarekillingcapitalism.libsyn.com/.

14. Spillers, Hortense J. *Black, White, and in Color: Essays on American Literature and Culture*. U Chicago P, 2003.

that one should resist remaining consigned to those depths by citing historical narratives of changing nuance and circumstance. In the U.S. context we could keep faith with the idea of historical responsibility by pointing to African-American votes cast, real-estate owned, political offices occupied, acknowledging that while those activities may be under constant threat of diminishment, they point to ways black people are no longer bound to "total objectification." One could counter that dispossession is ongoing and that it continues to create blackness from which no one so marked emerges by pointing to the efficacy of those threats of diminishment, to the ways carceral capitalism reconstitutes enslavement's commitment to extracting value from black bodies, and to the compulsive, almost ritualistic violence perpetrated on black people by inescapable agents of the state and by sidewalk vigilantes.

What Lindon learned from Spillers, and Moten and Harney did too, is that there is nowhere to escape to. Or as Spillers herself wrote, ". . . the liberational urge for freed persons is not so much the right to achieve the nuclear family as it is the wish to rescue African-Americans from flight, to arrest their wandering away from . . .—essentially, to bring the *present* into view . . . " (249). Substitute any of the categories that accrue to the self—gender, generation, individuality, civil society, or citizenship—for "nuclear family" in that formulation and Spillers still brings us to the same proposition: we bring the present into view, indeed, we enter the present, by understanding the problem is not dispossession but possession. In the same podcast conversation between Moten and Harney where I was reminded of Spillers's essay, Harney says it this way: "So much of the march of the modern bourgeois subject is . . . the closing off of what Denise Ferreira da Silva calls "affectability." It's the insistence that my feelings are generated by me and out of me, that there's not someone else working in me, that my reason and my body, these are sovereign." If self-possessed individuation is the way to ensure one's integrity and safety, this is only so because it is also the most reliable generator of violence that would be imposed on others. This is the case, Harney suggests, because "the only way to insist on any of that [sovereignty] is to act out the most brutal forms of access imaginable, and we can only imagine them because they fucking did them and are still doing them in the name of an idea that we are self-determined." It's possible to imagine, then, that selfhood is not the privileged space from which others are barred. Selfhood might instead be a condition developed as a means to survive the radical vulnerability of being given in the fold. If selfhood is a reaction formation that attempts to order and discipline the entangled folding, then the horrible fact of the present, and of presence, is that we access it not by running away to some place where we might be afforded the right to own it, and to own ourselves; we find ourselves already given in presence, instead, by continually corrupting our ability to make presence private. The opposite of forcing one's access into others is giving away access to what passes as oneself.

Moten and Harney and others argue this originary dispossession is what blackness is. And if this is so, what, as a non-black person of color, should my orientation toward blackness be if not to take up the work of destroying the world order and my place in it by dispossessing myself of myself? What this also means—and I recoil as I type this because I've so internalized the imperative to imagine an ethic as a prophylactic between so-called identities—is that blackness is not limited to bodies so marked, blackness is fundamentally accessible by any body, even as violence levied on bodies marked black is the pervasive means by which whiteness consolidates its categorical stability and systemic power. Lindon's response to that pervasive violence was not to try to cover the flesh with skin. Lindon flung open the doors of his own practice of black and queer life—around his stereo, in his study, in his bed, at the club—and let me in. Or he didn't let me in, he dismantled the structures that would contain those practices and exited their ruins in order to give those practices away. Nothing makes this okay. I mean, I can't dampen that kind of vulnerability into something comforting. Lindon could try to ward off chaos, but his openness, or his folding, might have gathered anything back. Maybe Marlon was, in fact, a murderer. Maybe I was both a friend and, in some calculation, a parasite on his blackness, and maybe now my well-fed living haunts his ghost.

And, though the intensities and resonance of our age difference and of our positions in the university don't match that of our racial difference, how do I account for my vulnerable place in those coordinates? Access without consent or by means of coerced consent in any context is not only an obvious evil, but as Spillers and Harney and

Moten and others indicate, it's a foundational evil because it is the means by which whiteness, possession, and subjectivity find themselves in confluence. Lindon never pressured me toward any psychic or sexual intimacy. Though we carried plenty for one another, he never tried to make me an emotional crutch for burdens that were beyond my age or understanding. Mostly he gave me space. I was too uncertain to become a regular at gay clubs, I was still figuring out how to make space for my simultaneous attraction to men and women, masc and femme, and I wondered if my desire for cis women disqualified me from queer spaces. Antiretroviral therapy for HIV/AIDS emerged at this time, but it was too new to clear the stigma of early death, so I couldn't quite imagine casual sex with strangers or new acquaintances. Before hook-up apps and before on-demand porn on smartphones, Lindon gave me a safe place to hang out, to explore all kinds of sensualities, and to be cared for in a decidedly black and queer space. For all of this wholesomeness that imbued our transgressions and intimacies, I don't know what to make of the fact that I was a student where he was employed as a professor. I work as a university professor now, and I don't make myself available to sexual or intimate relationships with students. I've counseled students who've shared their discomfort with another instructor's unwanted advances or with another instructor's oblique or brazen ways of sexualizing class discussions. I've also come to understand that sexual contact and intimate relationships across power differentials, even when they're saturated with consent, still risk the less empowered person in the dynamic in ways that are unforeseeable. And such intimacies risk spilling toxicity beyond those who consent to participate in them. Cross-positional relationships in universities can corrode the experience of a student cohort, for example, by muddling institutional processes that should be transparent and fair with anxieties about favoritism, about discretion, about retaliation. Setting aside possibilities of intimate relations, teaching as such is an exercise in domination, at least to the extent that teachers are responsible for assigning value, determining disciplinary boundaries, policing learning behaviors, and translating study into accreditation. I still feel shame when I think of the end of one semester when a trans woman student sat me down, with generosity I hadn't earned, to share with me the ways my transmisogyny had spilled out through my attempts to discipline their way of being in the classroom, their way of challenging texts and ideas.

I try to keep faith with that particular shame by developing a critical understanding of my access to harmful systems. I make this part of my intellectual, creative, and pedagogical work. If I don't, I know unexamined scripts of systemic harm will be there to help me exert control over my students again. I stay vigilant about power relations in the classroom by inviting students into critiques of the procedures, assumptions, and hopes for our shared work. I have clear policies that define harassing behaviors, and I list official channels for redressing concerns. And because institutions routinely compound relational injuries with procedural ones, I also work with colleagues to devise new committees and create alternate chains of communication, reporting, and accountability so that students have an array of differently positioned people to go to if they feel threatened or extorted or disrespected by peers, instructors, or advisors.

The power of these boundaries to reduce harm forecloses on the possibility that I might one day reprise the role Lindon played in my life with a student. Yet I wouldn't trade Lindon's influence on me, which was nothing less than a practice toward presence, for anything. I can't reconcile those two things. How could Lindon and I know we had leveled power between us? Or did we offer what we each had to make an unequal trade, to give naked and unafraid, drunk vomiting unafraid, dancing in the living room unafraid, to let me into the black church, queer church unafraid, to let him, unafraid, into my living attention after his death, giving what can't be taken. I want to say my whole life has been a double gesture in the wake of Lindon's living: to tie myself to any boundary or structure that could stand the wind of just going, of displacing one's skin in favor of one's flesh the way he did, yet trying somehow to let that wind still move through me. Or, more simply, was Lindon so pure, so disinterested in advantage, that his giving neutralized the structures in which we met?

What I do know is that Lindon's giving was not sacrificial in a way that would aggrandize his singularity, nor did it leave him bereft in isolation. It left him held in dispossession. Moten and Harney often say we should read Spillers on flesh alongside Baby Suggs's sermon in Toni Morrison's *Beloved*.[15] Baby Suggs names her congregants as flesh and directs them to love that flesh: "Here," she said, "in this here place, we flesh; flesh that weeps, laughs; . . . Yonder they do not love your flesh. They despise it . . . Love your hands! Love them! Raise them up and kiss them. Touch others with them. . . . You got to love it, you!'" It's important to me that this "you" is a collective, it's a congregation, but I also read Baby Suggs's words as a translation of a fact that has already occurred into an exhorting charm that hopes to stretch that occurrence into a future. And the words can only become charm, I think, because they emerge from an interplay between pastor and congregants where each role emerges from the other without separation. The passage begins with Baby Suggs inviting folks to cry "for the living and the dead." In response and "without covering their eyes the women let loose. It started that way: laughing children, dancing men, crying women and then it got mixed up. Women stopped crying and danced; men sat down and cried; children danced, women laughed, children cried until, exhausted and riven, all and each lay about the clearing damp and gasping for breath." The love of flesh Baby Suggs urges in words already happened in that enfolding of tears and sounds, emanations of wind and water from within and across the material of flesh. And the silence the folding opens is the space into which Baby Suggs can speak her exhortation. Speech becomes charm when the silence not only receives but takes in, enfolds those words into a weave that waits to be stretched, and that unfolding inaugurates what we might call a future but is only one more ply in the living presence. When that presence gathers it also holds up. Baby Suggs addressed herself to "Feet that need to rest and to dance; backs that need support" and, after her sermon leaves its own silence, the congregation once again answers with a singing voice that isn't sly but does carry its own alterity. Like Moten's cascading fugitivity, that singing voice in "four-part harmony" gathers up again the stretched-out silence into folds that can hold "their deeply loved flesh" as much as their hands did, offering rest from carrying a pair of feet or a back as if they were parts of a single body.

It matters, too, that the women in the congregation were the first to let loose their cries. May proximity to the fold be our gender. And

15. Morrison, Toni. *Beloved*. Vintage Books, 1987, p. 103–04.

may the idea of gender be given to new shapes in the folding. This is how Lindon was committed to living "outside" of sheltering categories. For him, as much as for Baby Suggs and the congregants, flesh is not recess, or freedom, it's the folding, filled space where the markers of singular being dissolve into lingering as something at once possible and other, into the living presence toward which and with which we are flung. And it's in life, and toward life, this double-edged feeling, that oriented Lindon's miraculous arrival in the flesh, in material that includes in its weave the immaterial, the sensate and senseless. Dispossession proves the surest way to be with one another, to be given in one another, where one another includes the earth's materials in such a way that we'd layer no world atop it because we're already in and through earth, crossing and returned.

In the work of writing I've asked how a topology of the fold might shape poems. I have practiced forms and grammars that might enact giving oneself over in the fold. Anacoluthon, for example, that allows for a sentence to alter grammar or tense midstream, something like articulations of the fold. I've shaped text in syntax where a phrase can simultaneously modify the preceding and subsequent parts of a sentence to maybe enact the idea of entanglement where pieces exist in and for one another, available in multiple ways at the same time. Writing sonnet in series has let me draw containers of single poems that hold difference and also let that difference spill out and double back across the sequence. I've noticed, too, that keeping an ear out for the percussive force of consonance and for the gathering points of the fold that internal rhymes can be creates effects in performing and listening bodies. Those tools are interesting to me for the particular stimuli they produce, but we don't need prescriptions for poetry. We don't need anything that would foreclose the real time of both composition and performance as improvisation, which is the closest term of artistic practice I can find for being given in the folding.

Poetry in a general sense concerns me more, or returning any practice on the page to the space of ritual and charm where Baby Suggs and her congregants co-create. More relevant for this than any method or poetics is the fact that there's an impression of Lindon's loft that I can step into in the same way that I can step into the outline we left when we stood naked on the unfinished edge of the building where he lived. I can walk into that loft now and I'm not scared. The light in the north facing windows, the expanse of the kitchen counter, the pot on the range, the crumbs on the counter, the space on the floor where we sat around the box of his books, the large painted portrait of Diana Ross, the stereo system below it, they are all there, on loan to me. The space isn't mine, certainly, but it's there for me to be with. To receive impressions and to travel back to them, or to gather them closer to what seems like my present tense, to leave words in plies whose unfolding will make a future.

"You know, in language we inherit the voices of the dead,"[16] Nathanial Mackey has said. I've no reason to doubt him, but as much as I listen for them, I don't hear voices. In the folding Lindon left me traces that are lighter; they're echoes of jokes, traces of excesses, both private and public, they're moments of intentional and inadvertent revelation, intentional and inadvertent pleasures that emerged in being together and paying attention to our thinking and feeling, to what our thinking and feeling couldn't anticipate. I'm shy to demand much of ancestors, to ask them to be as reliable, locatable as their graves. The Bahamian artist Macfarlane Mackey, who performed under the name Exuma, made music that drew on a system of healing and spiritual justice sometimes called Obeah. He calls on the creation loa of the Haitian Vodou tradition, Dambala, in a song by the same name, to help him draw for slavers the form of their reckoning. I came to know the song in Nina Simone's version, with her piano rolling beneath the words like the work of tides. Nina and Exuma sing, "You slavers will know what it's/ Like to be a slave/ Slave to your mind/ Slave to your race/ You won't go to heaven/ You won't go to hell/ You remain in your graves."[17] I think that's right. Practicing ownership of ourselves in life, of our minds and of our race, guaranteeing that deed by cultivating unfettered access to others, either directly or through proxies like agents of the state, will leave us holding on to our graves.

---

16. Cole, Norma. "Start Singing." *To Be at Music: Essays and Talks*. Omnidawn Publishing, 2007, p. 46.

17. Exuma. *Dambala*. Mercury Records, 1970.

But I think it's also true what poet and painter Etel Adnan promised, that "love precedes us to the grave and follows us into it."[18] If love precedes and follows, then it can be another way of understanding the fabric of the folding. Gathering that love closer can be a way to help the dead out of the holes to which habits of ownership called honor would consign them. Lindon found a way to stop running and give himself over to presence, a way of staying outside that doubles back in, but he never confused staying in the gathering and loosening of the fold with a place to stay. He never talked about wanting a partner either, he hardly talked about romantic love, maybe because, rightly or wrongly, he saw it as a kind of shelter where he didn't want to remain. Our friendship was never the same after our falling out. But we got to talking again a bit before he died. The last thing he told me was that he met a friend, an athlete who was black, lighthearted, and beautiful, who had a way of swooping behind Lindon to lift him onto his broad shoulders and carry him as far as he could until they both tired of laughing. That's one of the moments I gather near, his telling of it. I won't let this text or my memory of him be another shelter or grave where a parade of mourners I might join would come to lay their claims. But I want to gather the love that precedes and follows, folding not him but his bearing closer to my bearing, to attend and receive and release in the midst of that routine, unheroic witnessing in a way that might join all those who carry him as he carried me. I want this to be what the word "ancestor" means. To ancestor, as a verb. Let it be what I do. Though still breathing, people die in the work of being people. Lindon managed to live despite being a person; he doesn't need one more name.

18. Adnan, Etel. *Sea and Fog*. Nightboat Books, 2012. p. 73.

a series of directions none abandoned (Agnes Martin's "untitled")

Rusty Morrison

I'm walking toward an Agnes Martin canvas. Pausing in front of it, I realize that I haven't been giving full attention to anything in this museum, that much of my attention has been running feral, following thoughts just below my awareness. What's in the series of feelings accompanying those thoughts? Too many feelings, it seems, too subtle, too hidden, to register. How often does this happens to me, and not only in museum? How many feelings disperse before I ever recognize them?

Those busy questions thin before Agnes Martin's canvas, as it wakes me to a focus that is enthralled by the painting, and then I wake from *that sensation of waking* to a color within the canvas's hue, a color which is as much a feeling of loss as it is a color, longer than memory. My mind has been running feral for so long (years?) that recognizing this change engulfs my perception of anything in the painting with the *sensation of recognition,* how powerful a change it might bring. But I'm already using it, seeing through it, not only to the painting's color, but to what seem to be hand-drawn lines, exquisitely poised, which I imagine to be a communion of what are now invisible points, fused. I feel them, sharp, under my skin, along the backs of my arms, around the base of my skull.

All are prickling along an edge I don't want to recognize: the edge of a choice to discern in the painting whoever I am, in this instant of viewing it, which is a different "I" from an instant ago, and will be again in the next, just as these lines of Martin's are subtly different from each other, reiterating infinitesimal differences I rarely see. It's an edge that Martin offers me, offers anyone.

I sense how Martin's lines, which are now my attention's focus, as well as the color below them—that all of what I see in the painting is fragrant with whatever fallacy I devise for it.

I take my eyes off the lines, look again between them, and I find that I'm watching myself typing on keys here at this keyboard, as letters form on my laptop's screen. As I revise and revise again what it is that I see in Agnes Martin's canvas, so as to name, to describe what a color with lines across it is seeming to ask me to recognize—all that rises up from the residue of thoughts and feelings I've ignored, sediment from fallacies I've chosen to believe.

Around me is stillness; it has its own scent, which I want to breathe in deeply, which I need to remember. The "need to remember" in me draws another and then another increasingly apprehensive breath—even as the stillness may be my own awareness, my own insight that Martin's art is deathly calm. And death is kind of breathing that might be a centuries-long decomposition of color. This is the color of Martin's background.

Deftly, each of Martin's precise hand-drawn lines on this canvas is traveling above that breathing, riding all that is below, rising from, then falling back into the painting. Can I hear how the lines themselves are an emphasis of each breath?

But what I hear is actually beside me—it's only a child's nasal breathing. She has allergies or a cold. She is looking at the Agnes Martin, not seeing me, nor is she listening to the slightly stooped, brightly-dressed older woman, probably her grandmother, directing her to come see a painting in the next room. Her grandmother must've been smoking outside. Her odor is talcum and tobacco, and I sneeze. The little girl looks up at me, but doesn't return the smile I wear like a helmet with full face-guard. She doesn't assume, yet, that she needs one. Her eyes are intent on what I realize is a line passing from her to me, that I imagine she has drawn up from Martin's canvas.

The girl watches, in a way that I can't, as the line passes through me. She seems to see where it's going. The line passes beyond the instant that I believe I am, but to where, I don't know.

The feeling of being intersected is overwhelming, yet the sensations I have are sensations I don't want to control, though they frighten me. Agnes Martin has created in this canvas the illusion of a surface of pure sensations. Any one of them, I realize I could simply follow, as I follow a line.

As I type, I begin a line, hand-drawn.

Here on this page I've just typed the word "begin," as if I haven't already been hand-drawing a line since the moment when I first paused before Martin's lines—drawing one precise, precarious line from that moment to this one, a line which rides across all that is unrecognized within these moments of my awareness. And then another line. Just as Agnes Martin's lines cross above a background I can't see to its end.

I describe the time that I spent before Martin's canvas as if it ended, but it actually extended in a way I hadn't expected, or previously understood, as a breath might, with practice, for who knows how long. I do know that it's here, now, and I'm watching, in that few instances of time, what I hadn't watched closely in the museum—how decidedly the girl chooses to bide her time, looking a little longer at Agnes Martin's canvas, before following her grandmother into the next room. I find her eyes in these words, as some of what they mean to me dilate into what might be the expanding life-lines of any instant, which I might glimpse, and record on this laptop screen, as I'm able, biding my time.

CODA

What I saw in Agnes Martin's painting, and what I saw in the girl, these create two points of energy. Sometimes, what I understand about my ways making-meaning-out-of words-on-a-page (my ever-evolving approach to my writing practice) becomes a third point. All three (if I perceive them as focal points of energies that continue to bear examination) become three points that connect, and a triangle forms—a triangle that is a frame with an empty center of open space. Into that opening might come an unexpected, ungoverned, improbable visitation, which then has a place from which to rise, become language about anything (my past, the future, the image of an object with an inscrutable center. . .), which may be instilled with the essence, the scent, of all three. Nothing remains for long. I type swiftly, or any given visitation will be gone. I do have faith, born of experience, that another will arrive, but the last one never returns. I've come to recognize, too, that what's true about how I perceive

Agnes Martin's painting, and the girl's demeanor, and my current ways of approaching writing, is true about these arisings—there is no single direction that any given arising provides for my writing to take. There is no single way for me to perceive the energy of any given visitation, or any single way for it to leave me changed.

I Am Thinking about Will Alexander

Sawako Nakayasu

I am thinking about Will Alexander.[1] I wonder if it has anything to do with the fact that I am thinking about Cecilia Vicuña. I am thinking of poets and the universe. Will Alexander got me young, perhaps age twenty-one or so. Something shimmered in a dark cavity of my being. I was surrounded by typical canonical texts and those who professed of them, and yet somewhere not far away, George Lewis was waving his arms. Somewhere also not far away, Jack Halberstam was Judith Halberstam. I didn't feel pulled immediately, at that moment, but there were forces that were willing to transform me, the same force that moved me like a little piece atop a Ouija board, from Chemistry to Music. Will you let me in? I asked.

* * *

There was a surrounding confusion through which I listened, sympathetic strings, their melodics more profound and originating from some other law. I needed it for survival. I had not known that I needed it for survival. It was a language and it was a language I did not know but I understood it immediately, then gradually, then quietly. It was verbal, it was trombone, it was dance that centered the head and the tail. Sometimes I asked how old they were. I wanted to know how long it took to own that language.

When it was not verbal it was something to point two fingers at: deep in the neck. The trombone provided continuum. But language was an advantage, joy, current. I listened to my cells—did I listen to my cells. Could I?

It is hard to live up to the notion of teaching poetry, when the ways in which I had been taught poetry are so luminous, incendiary, fresh blazes, Amiri Baraka when not feeling too happy or calm—I only write poetry when I am down, he says.

---

1. This essay first appeared on *Harriet*, the blog for the Poetry Foundation.

* * *

Will Alexander as a teacher, the imaginative wild diurnal poetic prophet blowing through the desert.

* * *

Will Alexander is everywhere. There are suitable religions for this. The time I have spent with him is not terribly long, but he is everywhere, including some of the outermost cells. When I say that I feel free and that the cells have been unlocked and that it is in relation to my engagement with art, it has something to do with having exchanged molecules with certain people at certain moments. I am not typically in the habit of discussing the exchanging of molecules with poets. In fact this makes me feel skeptical. The fact that I feel skeptical interests me, because of the very thing that has transcended this skepticism being a real thing. As real as I am typing these words into a computer, the same one I use all the time for all kinds of spiritual and non-spiritual tasks. I do not care to discuss the spirituality of tasks.

* * *

But I didn't come back here to sit back and quietly join this status quo or that status quo. There are too many, to be frank. I came back to survive, to find newer and better and more pleasurable ways to survive and assist in the survival of others. Ongoing, as ever.

I am small in physical stature, but my willingness to fight the quotidian carnivore is great.

The fire at this level prepares me for the larger burn. Over any number of life years accumulated, one hopes for a greater capacity for heat. Both to generate and to withstand.

A magnetic breath. I practice some kind of kinetics. Some people are willing to teach you twenty years after the fact, my hats go flying off at the soft curling recall of such memory, still circulating my neurals.

* * * * *

I start over with realia, delight, an understanding that the real study is over there. Some use their own homes, I try the palm of my hand —not to read, nor sharpen, more a warm, flat, open plain. Take some money, just enough, then go on the real hunt. Excise the tumor: the block in the stairwell, the faulty sentiment that allows the mere threat of heat to grow in the mind into something larger and more menacing.

I peer into a screen and see the partial bodies of Nam June Paik, of Jacolby Satterwhite. The writhing mass of Carolee Schneeman takes over. All this. Until Gabrielle Civil steps over and forward out of the screen, into this physical space which I will, for now, call a remote voyage of the sumptuous imagination. This is a poetics. Not *the*, not *my*, but *a* as in, this is it right now. For the right now. A moment of restlessness with which to apprehend the ongoing terror.

On the other side of town, a Book Club repeats itself and repeats itself.

* * *

The ceaselessness of Will Alexander is a line of music. He is a tonic chord of anti-hegemonic harmonics, sympathetic compressions of image into anima, edges of the animorose, it sounds itself underneath the overtures and I strip off one identity layer after another until I am untraceable, maybe just an echo, knock on that wall and listen. Will Alexander is the higher intelligence that poetry patiently listens to; Cecilia Vicuña's voice goes lower than I had imagined. I had not listened to a single recording before seeing her in real life. Not technically true, but spiritually.

I open up Will Alexander's book; the one in physical proximity is *The Sri Lankan Loxodrome*. I debate whether or not to look up the word loxodrome again. I angle myself appropriately and continue, look for my own breathing.

* * *

This is the moment where I sunken myself down.

Knock on my wall if you would like to be helpful. Density is random at times, but even a vastness such as Southern California can, at times, have the right kind of density. I say thank you to my timing and I say thank you to my teachers, and to the ghosts of my teachers, them too.

I refuse, however, to continue in the language they spiral around me, a web of repeated insistence, tone of comfortable inertia, it is as simple as refusing to abandon the metric system. My dates, though, are Western—a tiny gesture against the timings of Imperial Japan.

* * *

Allen Ginsberg died when I was a student. Some fellow students came over. Rae Armantrout came to my crappy suburban apartment with a six-pack of beer. We read Allen Ginsberg poems.

And now, two students walk into my head. I sign myself up for penultimate wretched antiblasphemous flow. Two more get their head done. I sign up for interiority literary law. I wave my arms at Butch Morris. I lose count. Let the stars erupt. Duck for tumescence when the moment is ripe. I walk out of my own class and hurry to open up the Will Alexander vein in my neck. This has everything to do with how to teach poetry—the neck, the hurry, the walking out.

How to build an institution within each mind.

That was surreal. What was. No, it was not. The price of freedom in different currencies. I walk around the room and tap each person where I think it is most needed. Whisper, then ask for recall. Hum, burn. My exposed bone for what cause.

The blank page constellates its shadows like a blanket, spreads gentle creases over every potential line of thought. Crawl in, crawl in. The white page is not the same thing as a white person. Both safety and violence in a blank white page. How do you choose to inhabit that, dear you.

* * * * *

In search of an exit, I flip around. Over. When the planet is done with us, Will Alexander will have established means for other conscious beings to speak on our behalf. That language. I tell you to aim for that language. Your anti-failure, or completion if you will, or abandonment if you prefer, is not in the arrival but in that attempt. In the post-present infinite configuration of expansive sonic awareness, only some creatures will have sustained their claim to language. The rest of us will trace the black shadows, cooing and lolling.

* * *

I press the clock. It does not yield. In an imaginative breach, I leap back anyway, to a time predating Imperial Japan. I wish to do that in spite of myself. Earlier still, when the language was oral. Leap forward. What kind of thanks is that, for the gift of written language. Whenever I press towards the collective, there are always some who will hate it. I am one of them. What am I doing.

I wonder if surviving in a place like this is akin to a return to a particularity in language. Or can I insist on continuing to exist like this. The labor of returning. The implosion of a disappearing species is a labor articulated by not me, but Will Alexander. This is a particular instance of labor, mine is unsteady though passionate. I distribute animal sounds, hide into a written voice, detonate the bags under my eyes earned by the lateness of the moment. I female some moments, retract my nails. Blaze, spread the heat. I open my hand to you, here is a small mound of heat for you to take, just take it.

* * * * *

Postscript: I am asked to articulate more specifically the ways in which Will Alexander has shaped me as a poet. After all this time, it is still not possible for me to point to such elements at the level of the word, line, or poem, but I can say that there are several books of mine that were written, more or less, in this *mode* – from deep in the neck—it is my first book, *So we have been given time Or* (Wave, 2004), and my most recently written book, *Pink Waves* (Omnidawn, 2021).

Melancholia

Eric Pankey

I must have been eleven years old, old enough to convince my father to drop me off at the Nelson-Atkins Museum to spend a few hours, while he went into his office on a Saturday morning in downtown Kansas City to catch up on work or get an edge on the week to come.

I remember entering an ill-lit gallery, and across of the room's dim distance, as if its own source of light, the figure of John the Baptist loomed: brooding, melancholic. Life-sized, the seated figure appeared larger than life to me: his head lowered, his eyes shadow-cast. His starkly lit, mostly naked body broke through the membrane of darkness as if at a moment of birth. If there was another painting in the room, I did not see it, transfixed as I was by the dramatic chiaroscuro of the figure.

When I visited the painting again last year, fifty years later, the gallery label read:

> "Set against a dark wilderness composed of oak trees, a young man with dark ruffled hair sits with head downcast and wears a fur-lined loincloth and scarlet cloak. He holds a reed cross in his right hand while his left arm is folded across his body, the hand resting under his right elbow. Two leafy green plants can be seen near his feet."
>
> Michelangelo Merisi, called Caravaggio Italian (Lombard, Roman), 1571–1610. *Saint John the Baptist in the Wilderness*, 1604–1605. Oil on canvas

At eleven years old, I was still a year from getting much-needed glasses, thus the oak trees that composed the "dark wilderness" were lost to me. The black behind the figure gave back no light, no detail, and no reflection. It absorbed, to my eyes, all light that fell upon it. Poems, I noticed, when I first began reading them with urgency and hunger at about this same time in my life, emerged surprisingly out of a silence, not unlike the way this figure of John the Baptist emanated from a depthless dark. I had been to the museum many times before this and yet this is the day I associate with *seeing* art for the first time. What about Caravaggio's John the Baptist held me spellbound, transfixed, and enthralled?

John the Baptist in the wilderness, although an infrequent subject in contemporaneous painting, is the subject of eight Caravaggio paintings. Three other paintings by Caravaggio depict two other narrative moments in John's short life: one of his execution and two of Salome featuring John's lopped-off head. The biblical source of the painting, *Saint John the Baptist in the Wilderness,* is Matthew 3:4, which reads *"And the same John had his raiment of camel's hair, and a leathern girdle about his loins; and his meat was locusts and wild honey."* The "raiment" in the painting is a draped, buckled skin, hide side out, with a bit of the fur side slung over the young man's right shoulder loosely. How might the garment have been attached? Where, one might rightly wonder, did this rustic come by yards and yards of tight-woven, brightly died red cloth to both cover his left leg (and perhaps his "leathern girdle") and to cloak the rock he leans upon? One could almost suspect that this is the shepherd boy, soon to be king, David, were it not for the attributes of the reed cross and camel skin garment. These were not, of course, the questions I was asking at that moment fifty years ago when I first came upon the painting, when I felt what I would describe now as *awe*, that common side effect of a confrontation with the sublime.

On the Nelson-Atkins Museum's website one finds this useful and well-written description of the painting and its history:

> This masterpiece, one of the Museum's greatest treasures, is one of only a few original works by Caravaggio in American collections. Although he never accepted pupils, Caravaggio's enormous influence on other artists (including many represented in this gallery) played a vital role in the development of the Italian Baroque. In this *Saint John the Baptist,* Caravaggio has traded idealism for what oftentimes became in his own time a controversial realism. He has literally stripped the Baptist of nearly all traditional attributes (halo, lamb and banderole inscribed *Ecce Agnus Dei* or Behold the Lamb of God) leaving the brooding intensity of the saint's emotional state as the subject of the painting. Saint John's solemn pensiveness is reinforced by a Caravaggio

> trademark: the dramatic contrast of deep, opaque shadows, playing across his body and shrouding the sockets of his eyes, with a bright light that illuminates the Baptist from above and to his right. This stark contrast of light and darkness, the brilliant scarlet of the saint's cloak and Caravaggio's placement of him in the foreground, close to our own space, all contribute to the dramatic impact of the painting. Evidence of Caravaggio's working method, in which he incised lines into the gesso ground to guide his hand while painting, can be easily seen along the sitter's left leg in the right corner. Caravaggio most likely borrowed the Baptist's pose from one of Michelangelo's seated prophets and sibyls on the ceiling of the Sistine Chapel in the Vatican, Rome.[1]

Caravaggio's *Saint John the Baptist* was commissioned by a Roman banker, Ottavio Costa, for a small, private chapel on his estate near Genoa. The saint's brooding melancholy surely inspired silence and introspection in those who visited the chapel, an effect recorded in a guidebook of 1624:

> Before ascending to the . . . church, in the narrow but fruitful valley, one comes upon a small, holy oratory . . . formerly the parish church, restored in the modern style in honor of that mysterious nightingale who announces the coming of Christ, St. John the Baptist. The image of him in the desert, mourning human miseries, was painted by the famous Michelangelo Caravaggio, and it moves not only the brothers but also visitors to penitence.[2]

In 1994, on a summer grant from Washington University in St. Louis, I stumbled by chance upon an art exhibition in the Museo Correr in Venice, called *"Preferierie di no": Cinque stanze tra arte e depression,* which translates to *"I would prefer not to": Five rooms about art and depression,* an exhibition of art over five centuries that has as its subject and source depression and melancholy. Although the show included no Caravaggio, the works displayed much of what had attracted me to *John the Baptist in the Wilder-*

1. https://art.nelson-atkins.org/objects/1130/saint-john-the-baptist-in-the-wilderness.

2. Mina Gregor, *The Age of Caravaggio, 1590-1610*. The Metropolitan Musuem of Art, Electa International, 1985, p. 303.

ness, what I have described as the *brooding*, the *melancholic*, and what the sources noted above call the "intensity of the saint's emotional state as the subject of the painting," the saint's "solemn pensiveness," "downcast"-ness, "silence and introspection." In a review of the Museo Correr exhibit in the *New York Times*, art critic Ken Schulman, quotes the exhibit's curator, Bonito Oliva, who says "I began thinking about the rapport between art and depression . . .when I was writing about the Mannerists. I realized that the Mannerists' style was the response of a depressed mind confronted with the discomfort of living in a chaotic and disorganized world."[3]

Each of the five rooms was organized by one of five archetypes of artists associated with depression. In my notebook from the time, I jotted these five kinds of artists: 1) *The arranger: whose desire is to preserve the world without transformative logic.* 2) *The collector: whose desire is the obsessive iteration of the object.* 3) *The observer: whose desire is burdened by the impossibility of the artist to intervene in the world's transformations, amplifying the artist's role as privileged, but impotent observer.* 4) *The destroyer: whose desire is to incessantly build to destroy to rebuild.* 5) *The embracer: whose desire is to open into circles of segregation and inclusion.*

Although I did not know it then, I was in a depression that would grow steadily deeper and darker over the next three years until at last in order to keep going I had to admit to it and get therapy and medication. Since then, more often than not, I have kept a step ahead of my depression, kept it at bay, or at least manageable. Since then I have recognized several of these artistic archetypes in myself as a mask, mode and model of creation. At work in 1994 on my fourth collection of poetry, which would become *The Late Romances*, I felt as if everything I needed to know about the poet I was becoming was here before me in the exhibit's five rooms. I could not help but recall my earlier encounter with John the Baptist. In the painting, he is a mere boy of seventeen or eighteen. At the same time, he is a prophet, a recluse in his wilderness exile; he foresees and foresuffers. He prepares a way, but is not the way. As if its own source of light, the figure of John the Baptist loomed. I saw then a reflection of my future self: brooding, melancholic.

3. Ken Shulman, "An Artistic Look at Depression," *International Herald Tribune*, June 18, 1994, n.p.

To Encounter

Carl Phillips

I came to poetry writing in what maybe seems a roundabout way, these days, but was the only way I knew: by reading books of poetry. I didn't know of the existence of writing programs. I was a high school Latin teacher with an interest in writing poetry for what felt mostly like fun but was also a survival mechanism, as I made my way closer to understanding my sexuality, something I wasn't quite ready to understand in a more conscious way. So I wrote poems, but without any real idea of contemporary poetry. Instead, I'd studied classics, so I knew Virgil, Homer, Sappho—for example—and I'd grown up reading older English poetry like Tennyson and Wordsworth, Housman probably being the most contemporary. Around 1987, I "discovered" William Carlos Williams, whose poems showed me that it was possible to write about seemingly ordinary things—a woman eating plums, say. But while I'd made it to the twentieth century, in terms of my poetry reading, I had a lot, still, to learn.

In 1988, while prowling around my favorite bookstore at the time—the Market Bookshop, in Falmouth, Massachusetts (sadly gone, after all these years)—I came across a book of poetry just published that year, Marie Howe's *The Good Thief*. And it changed my entire understanding of what a poem might be. I bought it immediately, and spent a good year studying every single poem, trying to figure out exactly *how* the poems made me feel what I felt. I think I instinctively must have known that vision, though separate from technique, must have some relationship to it, and I wanted to understand that relationship.

The Good Thief opens with "Part of Eve's Discussion":

> It was like the moment when a bird decides not to eat from your hand,
> and flies, just before it flies, the moment the rivers seem to still
> and stop because a storm is coming, but there is no storm, as when
> a hundred starlings lift and bank together before they wheel and drop,
> very much like the moment, driving on bad ice, when it occurs to you
> your car could spin, just before it slowly begins to spin, like
> the moment just before you forgot what it was you were about to say,

it was like that, and after that, it was still like that, only
all the time.[1]

So much to say about this poem, starting with opening a book with it. I was a few years, still, from even thinking that I might put poems together into a book someday, but this seemed even to me a startling entry point. We aren't told what the "it" being described actually is, but it seems crucial for the speaker to be able to describe it. The title potentially points to the Eve of Genesis, and in that context the "it" could easily be the expulsion from Eden—or for that matter, could be the moment of tasting the forbidden apple on the Tree of Knowledge—but the more contemporary reference to driving and a car spinning on bad ice throw that off, a bit. Ultimately, the poem seems to say "there is something I can't—or won't—name, but which I feel I must describe, though it kept changing until it settled on being like one particular thing all the time, namely "like the moment just before you forgot what it was you were about to say,""—which is presumably the moment when you still *do* know what you want to say, yes? Only, what does *that* feel like?

It was maybe the first poem where I could find no clear argument; it's a poem as the gesture of thought, of trying to narrow down, via thought, how to identify a specific moment, and the more I read it, the more I saw that this gesture had been made palpable by at least two prosodic strategies. First, Howe's poem is an extended run-on sentence, which creates momentum; it's chief punctuation is the comma, which provides for a brief stall, but also by definition (as a marker of sequence) tells us to move forward, that there's more to come. Second, the sentence proceeds via a combination of correction ("like the moment when a bird . . . flies, just before it flies"), negation of what came before ("because a storm is coming, but there is no storm"), and finally corroboration "it was like that, and after that, it was still like that, only all the time"). And it does this in a patterned way, only arriving at the corroboration at the moment the poem ends, which is what makes it feel like closure, even though the ending remains open.

Another way the poem is structured: in terms of time. The phrase "just before" or "before" occurs fairly steadily throughout the poem,

1. Marie Howe, *The Good Thief*. Persea, 1988. p. 3

in lines 2, 4, 6, and 7—at which point the repetition ends, and we have "after that" in line 8 and "all the time" in line 9. One way to interpret this is that Howe's poem is not so much about an event as about how time changes *around* that event—it's a certain way before the event, another way afterwards, and the result is a release—if you want to call it that—from a constantly shifting world to a steadiness or stability. The world was constantly changing, then it wasn't—this could be a good thing, like the move from chaos to stability; or it could be less appealing, a move from variety to sameness. Howe doesn't say, and I think this is another part of the poem's power, its confident withholding of information—not only of the subject itself, but of how we are supposed to feel about it.

Reading Howe's book was the start of my understanding that free verse involved alternative structuring devices; repetition isn't new, of course, but the repetition of a phrase seemed a useful—and new, to me—alternative to the repetition of meter or rhyme. I also learned, from this poem and from all the rest in *The Good Thief*, that a sentence was potentially the truer source of power for a poem, rather than the line. Maybe I'd have learned this in a poetry workshop, or in a manual on prosody, but I didn't. I learned by reading poems and having no one to explain them to me—so I had to figure it out for myself, which has always seemed to me a more reliable way of learning about a thing, rather than academically, abstractly . . . Here, I learned that a run-on sentence was a valid one, and that it, like any sentence, could have what I'd later call muscularity, that quality that makes the poem's thinking feel almost palpable—in the case of "Part of Eve's Discussion," at least part of that effect is the result of the dynamic of correction, negation, and corroboration that I mentioned earlier. We feel pulled, as readers, in different directions, without let up, until the leveling out of time with which the poem ends. Because each of these moves seems akin to the different muscles required to perform a gesture like raising one's arm, I have come to call it muscularity. It's something I found in a very different opening sentence in Howe's book, the complete sentence that begins "From Nowhere":

> I think the sea is a useless teacher, pitching and falling
> no matter the weather, when our lives are rather lakes

unlocking in a constant and bewildering spring.[2]

The sentence begins with a declaration—"I think the sea is a useless teacher"—that could be a sentence on its own. But it is then followed by a participial phrase ("pitching and falling") which is then itself characterized by an adverbial phrase ("no matter the weather"); the effect is of corkscrewing deeper, from noun to participle that describes the noun, to adverb that describes the adjective. But the sentence isn't over. There's no the counterbalance to the initial declaration: "our lives are rather lakes," whose development parallels the development of the earlier declaration; the noun of lakes is followed by a participle describing the lakes, and the participle is further defined by the prepositional phrase that serves as an adverb. That is a lot to be going on in a single sentence! That's muscularity!

This sentence also taught me that authority can be gained simply by assuming it—I don't know that it's absolutely true, what Howe says, but the certainty with which she says it stops me from questioning it, and she's already got my attention. *How* she says it was the other valuable lesson of this sentence, namely, her casualness, all of which is contained in a word that I can imagine a workshop finding unnecessary: "rather," which I find essential, not just for suggesting casualness, but for what it suggests about the speaker's sensibility: I get the sense of a speaker who thinks what she thinks because of things that she just assumes we all agree are true, in this case that our lives are lakes—not *like* lakes, notice, but actual lakes, which reinforces the authority, none of the tentativeness that always somewhere attaches to simile, but the assured equation of metaphor.

One other note on how authority is gained here. Though I wouldn't know for years how to put it, I now understand that authority almost always requires vulnerability, if it's to be convincing. Howe achieves this by including the first two words of the sentence, "I think." She could easily have said "The sea is a useless teacher, etc." But by opening as she does, Howe undercuts any heavy-handedness, saying that the statement is only what *I* happen to think, and I only *think* it, which is different from *knowing* it. In a sense, the sentence gains authority by a combination of certainty and doubt, which makes the resulting authority feel like the result of trial and error, which is to say, it's

2. Marie Howe, Ibid., p. 11.

been tested, which is tantamount to proof. Or to put it another way, the sentence feels like the mind making its way from thought and possibility to resolution and fact.

I've already said a lot here, and that's just from looking at parts of two poems. *The Good Thief* was a book that unlocked poetry for me, by containing poems that made me want to look closer, to understand why I couldn't *stop* looking closer. What I didn't understand was resonance—a word that meant nothing to me back then, in terms of poetry; *The Good Thief* was an essential catalyst for that understanding.

I should mention that Howe's book was one of three that I discovered in that same year of 1988. For the purposes of length, I've limited my discussion to Howe's book, but I also bought, that same year, the debut books by Lucie Brock-Broido and Brigit Pegeen Kelly, *A Hunger* and *To the Place of Trumpets*, respectively. Together, they were all I knew of contemporary American poetry, and between them I learned almost everything I know when it comes to writing poems. But Howe's was the first.

Encounters. A couple of years later, I brought poems of my own to my very first workshop, taught by Alan Dugan during the summers at the Castle Hill Center for the Arts in Truro, Massachusetts. (This, too, was the result of a chance encounter, when the poet Martín Espada visited the high school where I taught, looked at a poem I wrote for a 20-minute free write he had organized, and afterwards told me to apply for a state arts grant, which I ended up winning. With the money, I paid for the workshop in Truro, along with my very first computer.) At the end of that summer, Dugan organized a public reading where each of us students would present a handful of poems at the town library. I'd never read my poems in public, and I'm sure my nervousness showed. After the reading ended, a woman started to approach me. As she got closer, I realized she was speaking, but it took me a minute to understand that she was reciting some lines that I had read earlier. She repeated them. And then "Where have you been hiding," she asked, "you are a poet, you know that, right?—Oh, I'm sorry," she said, "Listen," extending her hand, "I'm Marie Howe. Can we talk?"

The Swaddling-Pages: An Evening with Bill Knott

Donald Revell

A perfected and necessary legend.

("The University Abandoned Overnight")

In the winter of 1972–1973, as a sophomore at Binghamton University in upstate New York, I was awaiting my draft notice. Nixon had abolished student deferments by then, and I'd drawn a very low number in that year's lottery. Across the various scenarios, from Vietnam to prison to Canadian exile, I was considering options, but only considering. Each shone with the lustre unique to its perfection—heroism, martyrdom, the expatriate adventure. (*Exile's Return* by Malcolm Cowley was holy writ to me back then.) But each was also darkened by all-too obvious and scarifying imperfections. I could not choose. At a loss for will, I was likewise at a loss for words.

For three years I'd been reading poetry with an all-exclusive, deepening pleasure. And I'd been making poems of my own for nearly as long, continuously but without anything worthwhile to show. I had a model, a hero—Hart Crane—whose poems I'd had the motion picture serendipity of first reading on the subway, Brooklyn Bridge to Pelham Bay line, having just purchased the Doubleday Anchor paperback *Complete Poems*.[1] It was the watercolor bridge on the cover that decided me. But Crane proved to be a difficult model for a young man impatient for perfection. His intricate, home-made dialect of American English was inimitable, and his every project seemed to thrive and to radiate its unique glamor only by foundering, only by disappearing below the horizon of its utterance. My own attempts at poetry had no trouble at all foundering or failing; but as to anything like a radiant glamor, they hadn't a clue. I couldn't make a way, as Crane nearly always does, through a scherzo of idioms to plain truth. I couldn't account for such stanzas as

O brilliant kids, frisk with your dog,
Fondle your shells and sticks, bleached

1. Hart Crane. *The Complete Poems of Hart Crane*. Doubleday Anchor Books, 1958.

By time and the elements; but there is a line
You must not cross nor ever trust beyond it
Spry cordage of your bodies to caresses
Too lichen-faithful from too wide a breast,
The bottom of the sea is cruel.[2]

Somewhere between the colloquial of "brilliant kids" and the metaphysics of "lichen-faithful" I'd lose track and falter, forced to conclude that my intense pleasure in the poem was, finally, somehow objectively mistaken. To lose all trust in an essential pleasure is paralyzing. I was getting nowhere because I could see no way to navigate that strange region of absolute subjectivity in which the ruin or vanishing of one idiom illumines the truth of the next: the region of true poetry. (You might say I was trapped inside that most sophomoric of conundrums: the *poete maudit,* the aesthetic option of no options.) And, of course, moving on from early Crane and into the monumentality of *The Bridge,* I found a perfect ruin whose perfections I could not compass. Its strange coherence I could not make cohere. Its subjectivities prorogued mine. My impossible, impassable model modeled nothing of my own. I needed options.

One afternoon of that dismal winter, my girlfriend came by to tell me about a poetry reading that coming evening at the university art gallery. Maybe it would lift me out of my funk a little, maybe even inspire me? I'd never attended a reading. Auden was right, I think, when he said that every young poet, busy emulating the dead, believes himself the only poet living *now*. I'd never heard of Bill Knott, but my girlfriend was sweetly persistent, and the prospect of ample wine and cheese made a trip out to campus, across the icebound Susquehanna, worth the while.

We reached the gallery just in time. The introductions had ended and Knott had taken his position on a little raised platform in yellowish spotlight. With no lectern to stand behind and no book in his hand, he looked misplaced. He was wearing an ankle-length overcoat, although the room was quite warm, and he never removed it once throughout the course of the evening. Directly behind him hung an

2. Hart Crane. "Voyages I," *The Complete Poems and Selected Letters and Prose of Hart Crane*, edited by Brom Weber. Liveright, 1966, p. 35.

enormous female nude, and his spectacled face seemed afloat in its pelvis. After some silence, he reached into one of his coat pockets, fetched out a piece of paper—a poem—and began to read aloud. Some ten or twenty lines in, he crumpled the paper and let it fall to the ground, unfinished, discarded. He took another out of a different pocket and began again. Again, unfinished, it was crumpled and dropped. A third poem he read all the way through, returning it to a pocket when it was done. And that was the rhythm of the evening: one poem finished for every two or three begun. By the end of the reading, Knott was standing at the center of a little heap of crumpled pages, smiling into applause. Now here is the odd, the wonderful, remarkable thing. Not once had anyone laughed or groaned. No one had left. Knott's absolute sincerity, his unassailable, absolutely subjective judgment delivered over his poems conjured only awe and then, most miraculously, understanding. Some of the poems (I would later track them down in *The Naomi Poems, Auto-Necrophilia,* and *Nights of Naomi*) raged poignantly against the war in Vietnam. The audience, myself surely, welcomed them. Rage, however briefly, drives out fear. Other poems spoke from deep inside a hermetic, immeasurably passionate intimacy. Of these, our understanding was an act of faith made effortless by Knott's singular presentation, devoid of all irony. All told, over the course of that hour, he'd accomplished a poetic authority I might never have known, save for that hour, save for him. His stance among the discards was the furthest thing in the world from abjection or martyrdom. He was no *maudit* and nothing in his "performance" relied upon pathos. Rather, what shone visibly through the applause was Love standing upright in the debris of pathos. His words upon the air were the vivid substance of a project hovering above the ruins of that project, entirely intact. Later that night, back in my rooms (#6 North Street, apartment C), I had a new mind to bring into the paperback Hart Crane at the bedside and into the stack of spiral notebooks underneath the bed.

> (And they fall into bed with us)
> (And the bed flexes its shooting stars)
> (Stars in front of which your face rockets)
> (Destination: beautiful)[3]

---

3. Bill Knott. "Monster from the World's End." *Selected and Collected Poems.* Sun, 1977. p. 53.

A separate peace was cobbled together, and the draft was suspended a week or so before I was due to be called up into the Army. My girlfriend and I were at a Neil Young concert when we (along with some thousands of others) got the news. The air filled with a snowfall of torn apart draft cards as Neil Young launched into "Southern Man." And the image of Bill Knott standing inside that circle of crumpled pages, of poems discarded en route to Poetry, which is the resurrection of Love out of the ruins of pathos, which is the triumph of Form over the shadow of personal intention, moved me, and continues to move me, even more than that blessed image in Madison Square Garden that returned my youth into my keeping. Thanks to Knott, I could begin to understand the objective perfection of Hart Crane's most absolutely subjective passage:

> And so it was I entered the broken world
> To trace the visionary company of love, its voice
> An instant in the wind (I know not whither hurled)
> But not for long to hold each desperate choice.[4]

One evening, Bill Knott taught me, embodied for me, a guiding principle. Only when subjectivity becomes absolute and only when the poem is valued not by any previously understood or intended measure of perfection (such measures arise from pathos), but rather by the objective new-found Form, perhaps disguised as ruin at first, does Poetry, like warm love, enter in. That Hart Crane, in his very last poem, with the monumentally perfected ruin of *The Bridge* behind him and suicide on the horizon, could articulate and treasure "each desperate choice," knowing that desperation and freedom ("freedom is choice" as Milton's angel said) are the proper lineaments of love, could instigate a "visionary company" has chastened and cheered me throughout my writing life. It helped me to learn invaluable lessons from the lithic desperation of Cesar Vallejo.

> When there is no longer space
> between your greatness and my last project,
> beloved,
> I will return to your stocking, you well kiss me,
> going down your repeated stocking,

---

4. Hart Crane. "The Broken Tower." *The Complete Poems and Selected Letters and Prose of Hart Crane*, edited by Brom Weber. Liveright, 1966, p. 193

your portable absent, tell him this way . . . [5]

And those lessons in turn helped me to make and to move my first book, *From the Abandoned Cities*, out of a paralyzing ideal I called "Christall" and into a real and beloved ruined city. Years later, when I felt that all my purposes and metaphors had disappeared into my sister's inexplicable early death, it helped me to learn the actually sacramental lessons of Mallarme's *A Tomb for Anatole*.

what!
to rejoice in
presence
and to forget him
when absent
—simply! ingratitude!
no—"hold" on
the life of the being
who was—absolute[6]

The grieving fragments culminate in a mysterious "perhaps." And from that "perhaps" I learned a new rite, leading me through my book *Arcady* (an elegy for my sister) and, indeed, through all the books I've written since. One evening in the winter of 1972–73, Bill Knott pocketed my future and left my first ambitions crumpled on the floor. I owe him much.

5. Cesar Vallejo, "Sweetness through heartsown sweetness!." *The Complete Posthumous Poetry*, translated by Clayton Eshleman and Jose Rubia Barcia. University of California Press, 1978, p. 59.

6. Stephane Mallarme. *A Tomb for Anatole*, translated by Paul Auster. North Point Press, 1983, p. 102.

Encountering

Peter Riley

Is it possible to speak of an "encounter" which is not with any singular or particular entity—poet, poem, book etc. —nor is it with any poetic condition—climate, currency, technique, belief , etc.— but which is something wrapped up in continuous experience and continuing work, and the "encounter" is the act of noticing it, which is a singular, personal and repeatable event, possibly slightly like a conversion.

"Influences" come and go. They take over but wear thin and need to be renewed or allowed to subside and fall out of sight, for the sake of originality or fidelity to experience. The encounter springs from that uncomfortable sense that there is more to it, there are further or greater possibilities than your language is reaching, which lie ahead and/or all round you. Language asks you to let it breathe, or involve it in a sense of purpose. It keeps having a go at you year after year and you begin to recognize it and expect it. It may be best not to think of it in terms of quality.

I had a periodic sense that there was a broken thread of unthought concession in what I was doing arising from the will to be no more than "modern" and certainly not anything so robotic as "experimental," but that even this modest sense of progression could, if not guarded, bring with it an underlying negativity like a flickering shadow on the final sum of the poem. Sometimes. It was fragmented and scattered but it was nevertheless a recurrent liability, and noticing it and feeling uneasy about it were manifestations of a contrary and singular encounter which persisted, pointing to the same lapse in other or not-yet-written work, as if seeking me through cracks in my language. It was an encounter with something tapping on the window in the middle of the night which might be no more ghostly than fresh air wanting to tell me I had forgotten something.

Negativity seems to have become a part and parcel of modernity. It is widely assumed that if you are engaged with perception of self and society in current conditions your task was inevitably one of critique, including that critique which consists of placing difficulties in the reader's path by distorting or completely wrecking the language. You feel the warmth of approval from an imaginary community of "advanced" poets at each negative stroke of the pen, whether cryptic-academic or long-haired dreamland or whatever.

But the problem was not with oppositional poetry, nor with "innovative." Some of Larkin's poems seem to have had a drastic encounter with positivism towards the end. The problem is with self-reinforcing assumptions which were never challenged, never confronted with the questioning encounter, and so that whatever the poem's general drift, whatever its mode, it is susceptible to a still small voice asking if it is really going to leave it at that. And however rightly fierce in opposition, the whole construct risks finally holding thought and act in a locked shell, denied width.

A decision made as a result of this familiar encounter affects a short prose poem of mine published in 1995 which goes from a sculptural "fallen warrior" image through images of light, serenity, clarity, to reach—

> . . . soft and caring words soaking through you, forgotten to, what happens to, as the rain continues to, fall, soft and caring words forgotten, to . . .

When the work was reprinted in 2004 that last "forgotten" became "remembered" as a direct result of my recognizing the gravitational pull down into gloom, the heavy thump at the end and the unwillingness to breach the poem's circularity. This encounter with positivity was a slight adjustment which changed the tone of the whole poem.[1]

It seems that to recognize the encounters you have to acknowledge currents and courses underneath the poem, sub-texts, which are not easily controllable and are a necessary enrichment of the medium, but which can also trip you up. Probably they especially need watching in a textuality such as that of *Excavation,* from which the above instance is taken, which is a deliberately modernistic work framed

1. The reference here is to *Distant Points* (1995) the upper poem on page 49 and *Excavations* (2004), the same poem, now numbered 83, on page 95.

to release the sub-texts into the open. It is a collection of 180 meditations among tombs which I've always thought of as light-hearted and positive, a mass of fragmentation and collage so that, hopefully, linguistic tokens of hope and comfort can escape though the cracks thereby opened, each poem a choric dance before the tableau of death, rejoicing in the natural obscurity of song. The words bounce off the gravestone and make games of the epitaphs. Entertaining, I thought.

This encounter with positivity, if that's what it is, can, and should, become like something implanted in the poet, which sets an alert against the thoughtless drift into gloom and frustration which tempts anybody. No more than an alert, a small-voiced question which can readily be denied. Despair may well be the necessary weight of a serious poem under political and social conditions which could not be worse. We have been saying since the 1960s that things could not get worse, and they have done nothing but get worse ever since, having reached a pitch now where the ways in which they may continue to get worse are worryingly clear, when the throat gets hoarse and the vocabulary shifts towards the military. Most poetry either fails to acknowledge this or retreats into fiercely guarded enclaves of privileged identity with prescriptions of guilt against all opposition. Is it the encounter with the remaining question which finds so much of this attractive and enterprising poetry inadequate in the long run, because it insistently closes on itself and treats its location as a field of action without an exterior?

Actually, I don't think it is possible to write coherently about this thing, this "encounter" or whatever it is, because it is disguised as everything else. It is essentially flimsy and transparent but merely to mention it as a possibility is to invite it to be understood as a large-scale condition or belief. You can only insist on what it is not; it is not optimism or quietude or subjective or objective or a compromise or any thematic position. But it is powerful, for it is not a doubt but a certainty which once caught (like an infection) can reach through your entire acquaintance with poetry and inform large-scale (but probably provisional) judgments and practices.

For example: was it this same little bug which made me recently notice after 40 years of acceptance, that T.S. Eliot's earlier poetry is through and through negative, inspired by, enjoying, propagating negativity at every stroke, from the horrible strangulated little *Preludes* right through to *The Waste Land* with its desperate attempts to escape into a global asylum? At which point (c. 1930) the entire enterprise was abandoned. It was a confrontation with the metropolis which seems to have been necessary in that decade and in his case was one of horror, disgust, and rejection. All those failed, trapped people, it was because of them, because of what they had allowed themselves to become.

And to notice that many others faced this confrontation, and met it with various forms of repulsion, especially by ignoring it. But that Ivor Gurney when he was in London faced the same condition with equanimity by recognizing that he was a part of it, that is, ordinary, and instead of leaping for the throne of poetical election, viewed the whole scene through a shared humanity—

> And yet I swear the costers and coal-heavers
> Have courage, Will-to-Life as high as any
> Dwellers by hills, valleys, or tiny rivers.

And Pound's answer to this suffocating quantity was critique. "You're doing do all wrong. I'll tell how to do it for the rest of my life." All these poets (and perhaps all poets) set up paradisal images to counter the overwhelming confrontation with the mass, of which Pound's was an unreachable garden of ancient beauty far from the earth, informed by wisdom and art. Eliot longed for any kind of definitive ending. Gurney's paradise was the Cotswolds and "The dearness of common things." [2]

---

2. The only specific references is to Ivor Gurney, "Town Thoughts from Severn" in *80 Poems or So* (1997), probably written about 1919. Gurney (1890-1937) was a poet and composer at first known as a war poet of 1914-18, but who afterwards was severely inflicted by what was probably paranoid schizophrenia and in 1922 entered an asylum from which he never came out. The bulk of his poetry was written there and not published until some time after his death. His allegiances poetically and musically were entirely with the English continuity, but his mental condition gave rise to unusual features in the writing, a kind of awkwardness in word-choice, contractions, interrupted syntax, unstable tone and other features which drew the interest of some modernist poets. I am more interested in a kind of slipping or release of control which opened moments of his poetry beyond the parameters which he had set for himself, to

Am I saying that Gurney was a better poet than Eliot or Pound? How could I possibly say that? It's not about better and best poets. It's about what we want from poetry as a whole.

form true realizations, both verbally and conceptually, such as the three lines I quote, which are not typical. And even within these lines the word *tiny* I find quite disturbing.

Poetic Practices

Ed Roberson

I had published three books, but had no indication anyone had ever read them. I felt that nothing I had ever done was of any consequence, was of any importance, or meaning to anyone. I wasn't writing.

I wasn't into that fatal tantrum phase of swearing never to write again. I kept my notes and did exercises with my thoughts. I just was not seriously writing when the call came.

As a background to this, I had lost my job, I had gone through a divorce, and was headed into custody court. Plus, I was told I needed to see a psychiatrist.

I decided to fill this emptiness by waxing the hard wood floors in my apartment. I had what furniture was left piled in the middle of the floor, the rugs on top, the phone on top of that.

The way things were, I had got into the habit of not answering the phone. But without thinking, when it rang, I picked it up.

I tell people about the encounter of this phone call all the time.

"Is this Ed Roberson?"

I didn't care. I said, yes.

"Are you the one who wrote—," and the voice listed all my books, as well as some individually published work. No one had ever identified me by calling off the list of my achievements. This was the first honor of a praise song I ever received.

Curious this time, I said, yes —

"You're one of the old guys —"

What?

He explained that he regarded me as one of the people who had carried the black literary tradition across the gap from Wright , Ellison, and Baldwin to the present restatement and reflowering.

He named Robert Hayden, and Clarence Major, Ishmael Reed, Al Young—names I had always wanted to be included among, but somehow never showed up in. And here was this person, Nathaniel Mackey, speaking from a world in which I had always thought I was working , but had never had any evidence of it existing, the larger world of black literature.

He said it had a magazine about its people that he edited, Hambone, and he needed some new work. We talked—

We been on that damn phone for years.

Please, Lord, don't let me ever have to hang up—

I called Nate last week to tell him Wesleyan had selected the cover of my eleventh book, and that I'd also won the big bucks Jackson Prize for Poetry.

He tells me about the Andoumbouloo.

I break into the holy dance.

The Renewal of Wrongness

Elizabeth Robinson

> Mystery is not despair.
>
> —John Jeremiah Sullivan

Not one encounter, but many. Slowly, over the course of the six years I worked with chronically unhoused people, I reconsidered almost everything in my life.

I thought that people living on the street were uncultured and incurious. Until B told me that he read the entirety of Dickens while sitting in the library drinking gin. J showed me a YouTube video in which he played trombone in an ensemble. S, when she got out of jail after assaulting a police officer with her prosthetic leg, used to stop by and discuss Nabokov novels with me. A beautiful man at the feed grabbed a tray and sat down to read the Upanishads. And after M was evicted, I found Kierkegaard, Watts, and Kerouac on the sidewalk where the Sheriff had dumped his belongings. K and D used to get the bus to Denver on First Friday to go gallery hopping—this was partly due to the ubiquity of free wine in the galleries, but they also liked the art.

I may have thought that some people were too far gone to get better, any better at all. I certainly thought, at first, that once a person was housed the problem was over. I had no idea that being housed is a skill. So immersed am I in the habit of being housed that the responsibilities that come with housing are invisible to me.

I had no idea that social service agencies at all levels are rife with casual, everyday cruelty. I expected that when a person said they wanted to come inside, it would be possible to make a checklist of all the documents that we would need and to methodically proceed through the process toward completion. I was optimistic that the process would be time-limited and relatively direct.

I did not anticipate that I would frequently lie, that my most effective work entailed circumventing the system, that I would apply myself diligently toward violating rules and laws. "You are so calm," I was constantly told, "that must be why you are good with homeless people." In fact, I lived in quiet rage. I learned to relish countering the eternal "no" with a resourceful fuck you. I built trust with disenfranchised people by flagrant violations of privacy, bad boundaries, and disregard of my employers' explicit instructions.

I thought that all people wanted identifiable location: an address, to be addressed. I thought they wanted ease and a place to live. I thought they wanted unity of narrative. I thought they wanted family. I thought they wanted what I want. I was wrong. I was sometimes right.

To be wrong about so many things. To experience a thoroughgoing change of ethos while in my fifties—in a word, to be completely humbled—was a salutary experience. All I'd ever really done or wanted to do was write poems. Making poems was a way to configure meaning, to construct a universe. It enabled me to pattern experience aesthetically. Then the world itself asserted its randomness and forced me to reorient. I found myself waking up in the middle of the night worried about who was outside, at risk of dying from exposure. I couldn't understand, frankly, how it was that so many people *didn't* die of exposure. I didn't have time to write poems or anything, until I stopped to inspect my laptop and found pages and pages of writing. To be wrong about so much.

This is an essay about the art of trauma and wrongness and how it is its own poetry.

* * *

Carlo has the face of an angel. He looks young and unmarked. Curly black hair, slim build. I'd never heard of him, and I know most of the unhoused population of Boulder, but suddenly he was a frequent flyer at the jail. When we held "jail court"—arraignments for jailed individuals, most of them homeless—he was quiet and alert. We always had to get a translator because he let the court know that he speaks no English. He responded appropriately, never elaborated. Like most homeless people, he'd do a couple of days and then be back out on the street. I later learned that Carlo understood English just fine, but in court he spoke only Spanish. Maybe insisting on a translator, something that dramatically slowed court proceedings, was his subtle protest, a way of gumming up the works. Maybe he just prefers the sound of Spanish.

One day, I got the word from two police officers that there'd been a stabbing. "Is the victim anyone I know?" I asked. "Probably not," they said, "Some young guy who's just showed up on the scene, named Carlo."

But, they assured me, I knew the perpetrator: Bug-Out. I'd known Bug-Out for years, but only as Bug-Out. The first time I saw his real name on the jail roster, I had no idea who he was.

Turns out that Bug-Out, who *never* under any circumstances came to general arraignments for his trespass and camping tickets, wanted to come to court, and he wanted to clean up a bit for the occasion. First he went over to the 29th Street Mall and tried to steal some pants from Eddy Bauer. He was chased from the store. He then asked the people hanging around his camp if anyone could give him a relatively clean pair of pants to wear to court. Carlo offered up a pair in exchange for—what?—a little meth, some alcohol, a joint, a couple of bucks? The deal was done.

Unfortunately, Bug-Out discovered that Carlo's pants weren't so clean after all. In fact, they were literally full of shit. So Bug-Out did what any person of honor would do: he stabbed Carlo. When the police showed up on the scene, everyone was mum: no one knew anything about the incident. Bug-Out had taken off. Carlo initially refused to go to the hospital, but he was bleeding out pretty profusely. Eventually, Carlo did agree to go and he allowed as how he had deserved to be stabbed. Asked why, he declined to specify his transgression.

Bug-Out got picked up and was indignant that he would be arrested under such circumstances. It looked like he might go to prison. People in the "Fam," his family of the street, bewailed his absence. They love him so much, he's the greatest guy—though he is one of the more difficult psychotic people of my acquaintance. So much for his housing prospects, I thought, but he spent six months at the jail and then was back at the encampment.

It's hard for me to account, really, why I wanted to tell this story here. But here's what I love about it: Carlo's quiet deception in the court that gave him just a little more agency, the new-to-me orders of honor and affiliation, the fact that I knew Carlo before the police officers did, the fact that I'd known Bug-Out for years without considering what his legal name might be, the fact that so many people love a belligerent, violent, schizophrenic man: the whelm and collage of absurdity that is the through line of this series of events. *Zing.* It hit me as a great example of poetry.

* * *

One day, Rebekah asked me if I would go to court with her for her custody hearing. Her toddler, Leah, had been in foster care since birth, and Rebekah was desperate to get housed and get custody. To get housed *so* she could get custody.

I said yes, even though I had doubts that this was the ideal situation for any child. Because I knew that Rebekah loved that baby and that the foster care window was closing: not only would she lose custody, but she would lose visitation rights. The family caring for Leah wanted to adopt. Rebekah would lose her child forever.

I'd known Rebekah for about six years, first when I worked at a day shelter and then when I began working at the court with people who live on the street. Rebekah was with a man, Stephen, who was a health nut with a meth addiction. He also had a rage disorder, he explained to me one day with relief. The diagnosis rationalized his own volatility to him. He wasn't just crazy. Well, he *was* crazy, but at least a diagnostician validated it in a way that helped him to acknowledge and respect himself.

Rebekah and Stephen were often fighting, or he was badgering and yelling at her to improve her life, to take vitamins, to do yoga. The police were frequently summoned. Rebekah was rail-thin because she insisted that she was allergic to food. Food, full stop. Water has chemicals in it that upset her stomach. She'd go to the emergency room complaining of terrible pain and they'd roll their eyes and kick her out.

So it was a miracle when Rebekah got pregnant. I know what you are thinking: two crazy, drug-addicted, chronically homeless people having a baby? Terrible idea. But they were both radiant with it. Fucked up people can fuck each other up and still love each other truly and deeply. You sure don't have to be homeless to live that truth. Stephen got Rebekah clean and sober. They decided to move into a gnarly trailer in a gnarly trailer park with Rebekah's "street dad" (street dads, moms, and siblings being, basically, any homeless or formerly homeless person with which an individual decides to claim relation). Rebekah's street dad was just barely unhomeless, with a long record of manufacture and distribution. But Boulder winters are long and cold. Stephen apparently chose to man-up and become a breadwinner, the better to support his kid, so he got on board with Street Dad's business. Whenever I saw Rebekah she was glowing with vitality and anticipation.

So, despite my doubts about her ability to parent, I showed up at what I thought was the custody hearing. I could, in good faith, say that Rebekah had worked hard, and quickly, to get a place to live. She had a job, sort of. She had been living in a car, but the good news was that she owned the car, it was insured and registered, and she had a license. None of this would have been possible a year earlier.

There was an extremely large audience in the court room and Rebekah's attorney hastened over to thank me. He thanked me with a sincerity and intensity that made me nervous. And then I noticed that there were news reporters and cameras in the court room. "All rise," the court clerk said, and the judge came in.

"We are here today to decide on sentencing for Rebekah Nero in the homicide of Stephen Gardner to which she was found guilty as an accessory. We will take statements from the defendant and her advocates and from the mother and aunt of the deceased."

OMFG. Rebekah didn't tell me that this appearance was a sentencing hearing on her *murder* trial.

All of a sudden, I was standing before a full court, in front of Stephen's ostentatiously grieving mother (whom I'd certainly never heard him mention in the five years I'd known him) stuttering that Rebekah was clean and sober and loved her baby and had worked really, really hard to get her housing documents together. Rebekah abetted this awkwardness by refusing the assistance of her attorney and getting up to ramble on in a made-up legalese about her innocence and her maternal abilities. In the end, the judge told her to stop talking or she'd be removed from the courtroom. Rebekah was sentenced to a year in jail and remanded to custody. So ended her life with Leah. Oh, and a person who is in jail for more than ninety days is no longer considered homeless: the federal government has declared they are *housed* in the jail. So Rebekah would have to be homeless for a year following her release before she'd qualify for a housing voucher again.

See, while Rebekah and Stephen were living in Street Dad's trailer, Stephen's temper got the better of him. Perhaps this is because anger disorders and meth don't mix well. It's also been said that Street Dad was a controlling asshole who had amorous designs on Rebekah. In the heat of an argument, Stephen grabbed Street Dad's product, a stash of heroin, and ran out onto the street. Street Dad raced out and shot Stephen several times point blank, then ran back into the trailer. While horrified neighbors looked on, Rebekah ran out to Stephen's prone body and yanked out many packets of "powdery substance" which she jammed into her coat. I imagine that she thought she was protecting Stephen from charges of possession when the police arrived. By the time she was done, Stephen was dead.

Again, I'm hard pressed to say why this story in particular rose to consciousness as I embarked on this essay. More absurdity, yes, but also terrible loss and injustice on every dimension. Everything about it is broken and irremediable. And simultaneously, Rebekah and Stephen loved each other. They wanted that baby. Rebekah's life was transformed by a child who was born while she was in jail awaiting trial. You could say she was delusional. You could say that at crucial moments her attention was totally misdirected. But her desire was true and enormous.

This, too, is a kind of poetry, if poetry is a vehicle that circumnavigates the abysses that can't be overleapt. My favorite poems don't try to pretend that grief can be consoled; they don't try to clean up all the debris of wreckage. The distress coexists with the desire. Poetry's attention, like Rebekah's, may seem to be focused on the wrong things, but our misdirected gaze can show, in peripheral vision, how out of kilter the "right" focus has always been. The small accuracies of what we really care about, what Hugh Kenner referred to as "an aesthetic of glimpses," is not only an aesthetic, it's an ethics.

* * *

When I was first learning to read, I remember seeing a poem that had misspelled a word in order to amplify rhyme or pun—I can't remember what it was. With the rule-obsessed zeal of an early reader, I reported this to my father. "That's poetic license," he said, "It's not a mistake." It dawned on me that poetry offered the freedom to be wrong, willfully wrong. My encounters and friendships with unhoused people has renewed wrongness for me.

For years, I had been fighting an internal battle against the idea of linear narrative as an overdetermining feature of art. I hated the narrative pressure to drive toward climax and resolution—as though anything is ever resolved. I wanted my poems to partake of non-narrative patterns and to create a new sense of constellation and balance that wasn't dependent on resolution. In unhoused people, I found my ideal conversation partners, for irresolution was their pattern and language. Yet they taught me that narrative has a place, because when your narrative has been stolen from you, you must survive great indignity and pain.

A traumatized person understands different orders, patterns, rightnesses. Need reaches through logic and takes what it can get. So many times, working with a chronically homeless (read that: chronically traumatized) person, I had the sensation one has while watching a horror movie and wanting to call out to the protagonist, "Don't go into the dark house where you hear screaming!" Ah, don't do that thing which will give you an hour's relief but a month in jail.

I think both poetry and trauma reveal, if we are susceptible to the revelation, that the range of possibility is much greater than we had anticipated. I love the woman who wouldn't stay at the shelter on even bitter winter nights because they had deemed her jewelry-making tools "deadly weapons" and told her she couldn't bring them in. I spent my own money to buy a lock so that she could secure her stolen shopping cart of belongings while she slept in the park.

I love the man who hesitated to get housing because he feared it would interrupt his work as an eco-performance artist. He had lashed a spatula to a discarded broomstick and used it to scoop up trash on a twenty-block corridor of the town. He moved inside when we found him a place within a block of his corridor.

I loved Robin for his profound and beautiful obstinacy, earning seventy-six camping and trespass tickets in a six-month period because he refused to stay anywhere but at the park a block away from the grocery store where his ex-wife (and best friend) worked. This too seemed like a creative performance—and a protest—because artmaking *is* obstinate, obsessive—a political (or at least politicized) protest against all the limited understandings and assumptions that ruin us. The cliché of the rebel can be a cliché that disrupts other clichés. As far as Robin was concerned, he needed proximity to a person he loved more than he needed to be alive. He was explicit about this.

Robin's record-breaking record of civil violations was an art of iteration that I observed among many people living outside, where to do a thing over and over was a way to make meaning in a world otherwise bereft of it. Agnes Martin's beautiful grids of repeating lines. A ballad with a reliable refrain.

I loved these people with whom I felt, finally, safe (except when I was terrified) and understood (or very earnestly liberated to be misunderstood), who welcomed me in indirect and direct ways to use my own trauma as a resource, to accept the deformations of my own trauma as a means of using the damage in my life to my own right/wrong ends. If this doesn't make sense, all I can say is: exactly.

Poetry's cultural irrelevance, its marginality, is something that I've always felt was an asset to the practice of making poems. In poetry, you show up where you need to show up and talk the way you need to talk and use whatever resource is available even if it isn't particularly well matched to your ends. In that way it is not unlike my life with people on the street. A man who never goes to court steals some pants in order to go to court. Another man agrees that he should be stabbed on account of having traded the aforementioned person a pair of trousers caked with shit. A woman fails to mention that the court appearance for which she needs an advocate is her murder trial.

If there is anyone for whom I feel contempt and anger it is those social service providers, shelter workers, counselors—those smug anti-poets of the world—who place bets on how quickly a person will get evicted, who say that another human is too messed up to benefit from help, that this person or that person is only going to die anyway.

We're all going to die. Not all of us will heal. But my friends of the streets, unpredictably, uphold the art and mystery of recovery. Jen, Kevin, Nathan, Josh, Diablo, Jeremiah, Shorty, Lori, Jesse. No one can tell who will recover or why or when. I revere this mystery. It comes from the same place that a good poem or painting or piece of music comes from: things come together into new meaning regardless of their dissonance. Good art and healing don't mend all breaches but incorporate the rifts. Loss and trauma don't just disappear. The partial, provisional wholeness of a person or a piece of art has no obligation to be beautiful or coherent. These retain the right to be whatever they are.

One day I met P. at her camp. We had worked for almost a year to get her documents together so she could get a housing voucher. As we turned to leave, she looked back at the mud and ice-slicked lot. She hesitated. "Is there something about being homeless that you're going to miss?" I asked. "Ah," she sighed, "I'll miss the freedom."

North Hill

Martha Ronk

When I first met Wayne Winterrowd we were newly hired faculty members just out of grad school who found each other alone in early morning hallways at Tufts University. Together we found ways of manifesting our deep connection around texts, humor, classroom performances, exhaustion, my failing marriage and the left-over ravages of his late nights out. How to explain King Lear's erratic proclamation to first year students. Now, I think of the bitter friction that came between us at the end, his drinking and my stupid, well-meant admonishments, but then I had found a mirror that allowed me escape into whoever I thought I might be. It was his voice with the slight remnant of Shreveport, and his ability to talk, tell stories, memorize passages I could hold onto, analyze texts—they caught me up and I concocted responses.

For much of my adult life his belief in my ability to write poems sustained me, kept me at it, gave me an unstinting audience and critic. I had lost both parents and divorced, so he and his husband helped me erect a cabin on their Vermont property and I went each summer (no phone, no car, no TV, no printer). Wayne had moved from the academic world to become the renowned designer of the garden at North Hill and of many other gardens, and an author of many books and articles on gardens, roses, and food. During my time in the cabin, we spent hours exchanging work, going over manuscripts, arguing about how to interpret particular texts. For two summers I borrowed their ancient Volvo to drive to the Bennington Writer's workshops and for three summers I went to the MacDowell Colony and visited before or after with my son. For years my most intense, perhaps most intimate, complex, and fraught conversations occurred at North Hill. They devoted their lives to things they deemed beautiful. We went to the Clark Museum, Jacob's Pillow, and to music at Marlboro. We went to junk stores and collected old kitchen bowls (now I make more at a ceramics studio in Pasadena, objects that hold air, and try to write about emptiness/silence/the air itself). Somehow, although the town was small and working class and in early years quite homophobic, the two men dug in, taught high school in early years, and made many local friendships. When I was elsewhere, we wrote long letters to one another and I have a paper stack of the handwritten, the typed, the emailed, full of details—the material world—Wayne's probing questions, commiserations, attention.

The antique trestle table was the center of their tiny kitchen, the meal, the guests, the food, the napkins ironed at the last minute, the flowers, the fireplace, brickfloor underfoot, talk. The wax on the table threw light in a sheen; dishes had to be handed to another never pushed across so as not to scratch the table. A fire in the fireplace, the dog lying next to the Jacobean chest. It sounds highly artificial now and seemed so even then, but it was a self-conscious fiction designed in the era of AIDS. Wayne, a great cook, made dinner and after much wine talked. His talk included long quotations of poems and plays, arguments over politics and preferences, explanations about how to plant and where the plants had come from (the blue Himalayan Meconopsis, for example), pointed questions about why I'd written what I'd written, pleasure in it as well, my own mind already into what would stay with me, what of his words would beget my words, his return to his favorite novel, *The Golden Bowl*. I had studied *The Golden Bowl* for a semester in graduate school and continued to read James although I never taught his novels. Still they are wrapped up with Wayne and with my own work, James's sentences and obsessiveness, his transitions, his knowing the eerie power of objects—as did Wayne who could walk into a dusty junk store and see the one unusual and "beautiful" thing. *For the subject in existence is logically constituted only by the object for which and to which and by which he lives* (James).[1] Wayne instructed me to pay the attention to objects as he did, waxing furniture, admiring plants, finding the exact gifts—for my birthday, a chartreuse glass vase:

> Someone has come in the room and moved the chartreuse glass bowl so chartreuse as to seem a giant smudge, and suddenly the room begins to swim. The bowl floats in a wobbly arc into the foreground, the rest of the room dims and you feel suddenly intimate with the glassy and sickly surface, glazed over by displacement. (*Transfer of Qualities*)

1. Henry James, Sr. as quoted in Bill Brown, *A Sense of Things*. University of Chicago Press, 2003, p. xiii.

The dead stay with us, but how I miss him, miss myself as I was then. This immersion in artifice at North Hill changed how I approached the page, conceived of projects and books, pushed me somewhat out of my own inwardness. My prose poems in *Transfer of Qualities* were imagined in the context of *The Spoils of Poynton*, in which objects had tropic powers and severely pressed on the people around them—objects, not psychology, changed behavior, emotions. Early on, in order to write about love I set the stage in *The Tale of Genji* which we had read obsessively together. I took up a process which I have used again and again: utilizing another's writing to frame, impel, and merge with my own. My book, *Vertigo*, adopted the long, parenthetical sentences from *Vertigo* by W.G. Sebald whose work I read and reread. His essay about being unable to recognize the streets and people when he returned home years later, influenced not only that book, but also the chapbook I wrote for Magra books, *Familiar/Unfamiliar* about LA. Most recently, when I was stuck and blank, I gave myself an assignment to write responses to Wallace Stevens's lines, "I do not know which to prefer,/The beauty of inflections/Or the beauty of innuendoes,/ The blackbird whistling/ Or just after."[2] Once I had worked on this task, I was unable to stop encountering silence; although I hadn't wanted to, I was somehow caught in a realm that became my newest book, *Silences.* Many of the poems in *Silences* are ekphrastic poems on, for example, Van Gogh, Poussin, Agnes Martin, Ann Hamilton. Each work allowed and compelled me to write and to write in what I think of as my artificial voice, the one in which I'm in a realm outside my ordinary life, a crossover into someone or someplace else. I seem to work in response, in dialogue with an absent presence.

On a high shelf that ran around the living room at North Hill was a series of pre-Columbian pots of various sizes and designs, the hallucinated zigzag pattern black and white, faded rust colors, a tail-like curl, the "kill hole" in the center. One statue stood in pride of place, a fertility statue I was shocked to see again in a museum in Cusco. Some of the pots were quite small, others somewhat larger, about thirty of them it seems to me who ought to remember exactly, having sat for many evenings listening to a CD playing *The Four Last*

2. Wallace Stevens, "Thirteen Ways of Looking at a Blackbird." *Selected Poems*, edited by John N. Serio. Alfred Knopf, 2009, pp. 58–60.

Songs by Strauss, but I don't, although I knew then that the hours were stolen expanses, and would one day be gone, I couldn't, wouldn't fully realize it, the pots floating up there on their shelf, white slip on the insides the face of a mime, a heart-line deer with branching antlers. Perhaps because I knew as soon as I arrived in Vermont in the summer that I'd have to leave in the fall, and perhaps because the experience of transience defined their garden and ways of thinking, my own obsession with what the Japanese call *mono no aware* was heightened; I know it is in much of what I write (but, of course, it is also in Shakespeare's sonnets, which I taught year after year at Occidental College.)

Der Garten trauert,
kühl sinkt in die Blumen der Regen.
Der Sommer schauert
still seinem Ende entgegen[3]

I sat on the floor in the crooked rectangle of sunlight coming through the front door of the cabin, a massive medieval door, heavy with iron studs, and moved to get whatever sun penetrated through the deep shade of the forest. Cold all morning despite a fire in the Franklin stove and now midday sitting in the rectangle in which time slipped by so infinitesimally slowly that I forgot to work, think, walk, plan, wash up my one plate. My chores were to feed and to close up the chickens and geese at night, to carry hay from the high barn to the Scottish cows in pasture (once to chase them back in before electric fences were installed), to deadhead day lilies, to do errands, to wash dinner dishes, *to stay alone* until dinner. A daze of sun on wide planks of pine so soft in the first years after the cabin was built no one who came in was allowed shoes. The ferns shifted in the movements of air. Rhododendrons opened their pale blossoms. Time stopped, my thoughts at bay, I didn't move even when my position made all my limbs ache and I couldn't straighten my right knee and I thought I'd never be able to move again. I returned to my desk.

The sense I had at North Hill: timelessness and loneliness: both fruitful and a bit maddening.

Despite visitors and other family, usually there were just three of us—a couple and me. The hours in the day often seemed endless. Yet out of

3. Herman Hesse, "September" from Richard Strauss's "The Last Four Songs."

that time and silence, I was able to write poems, as if I could see or hear something to respond to because of it. I dreamed every night as I never did at home. When I walked the hill, images, lines, conversations—so I told myself—fell out of my head like children's blocks, becoming available for use. The rhythm of walking turned into the rhythm of lines. In this liminal place boundaries dropped away. I had hallucinations (once, because of the tension with my teenage son, of Chronos eating his children), imagined hearing behemoths in the woods at night especially on my way to the outhouse, heard myself crossing into the lilt of a woman who helped in the garden, felt forces pressing on the windowpanes that rationally I knew were not there. Inside and outside interpenetrated. (The cabin was an A-frame with small window panes on the high sides, quite exposed to the dark.) As a child I most hated being interrupted and even now, if I am intensely focused, I startle. Even at my most uncomfortable and cold in storms, I knew I need to be where I was if I wanted to write.

I wrote many books in the woods, dedicated *eyetrouble* to Wayne, Joe, and their garden. Although both men wrote in what was a somewhat nineteenth-century style, I had taken up more experimental work. But Wayne always believed in what I was trying to do; uninterested in my academic essays on Shakespeare's plays, he was always interested in poems and insisted I also write short stories—so I did, the narrators often obsessive and conflicted, and of course several of the stories revised aspects of our joint life. My book, *Partially Kept* on Sir Thomas Browne's *The Garden of Cyrus* (1658) always referred me to the gardens at North Hill, to the rage for order and to the transitory nature of every plant as well as every garden. I selected certain phrases from Browne and wrote around them so that a reader would be aware of the loss of a way of seeing and writing, as in "Or" in *Partially Kept*, but also a way of describing the layering of memory:

Or on a morning
the wistful eyes which whilom glanced down upon the fields
Or on a morning
I wot not, what in mee is come to pass, In me this wilom
who most gladly was
Or on a morning that came after, after the fields
lanceleaf blue or only the fields
where I was distanced from the past and from the time I saw it,
eyes having changed in the meanwhile, who was walking the morning.

The gardens, they were the center of everything at North Hill, each garden room differently planted with different colors, each needing a different sort of care, and behind it all, physical labor. In the upper meadow, there was a vegetable garden—fresh peas in June. In late August before I returned to classes in Los Angeles, shadows fell deeply across the grass. I missed it even before I left and wrote often about that liminal state. I hadn't wanted to move to California and still longed for seasons, rain, grass. They had more flowers than I could learn the Latin names of, some ordinary and some such as the Australian, Xanthorrhoea quadrangulata, rare. My personal favorites because they grew large by my cabin were Rhododendron. Their first book, *A Year at North Hill*, like all their books addresses the fragility of a garden and time; I now know that the garden is gone, but in 1995 they were young, their shovels turning up shards of slate gray pottery that caused them to think about the past, and only imagining a future: "Now we, too, have added our subtle accretions to this land, first by making a garden on it, and then by writing a book about it. It will not easily shake off either imposition, though certainly the words we have written about it will go first."[4] We often talked about time standing in the vegetable garden, peas over and beans coming in, and although I never knew time in gardens, I did understand fragility. I didn't feel that my having chosen to be here summer after summer for twenty-two years was a choice; it felt given me and I lived in a time when we believed in creating chosen families.

All this raises questions of home and my own odd attachment to a place and rhythms that weren't altogether my own and were, I now think, too often, illusory. Or perhaps I think that because everything ended so painfully. Both men continued to drink more and more heavily and both ultimately died from it. Despite years of wealth and grand trips to opera, expensive restaurants, Europe, and other famous gardens, at the end they were penniless and dependent. They refused to manage money—and couldn't imagine dying until they chose to. I've never encountered such ferocious adherence to creed. For me, Wayne comes back in language and new poems and in gratitude that he chose to believe in my work long before my first book.

---

4. Joe Eck and Wayne Winterrowd, *A Year at North Hill*. Little Brown, 1995, p. 6

Discovery and Rediscovery: A Personal Reflection on Writing the Prose Poem

Ian Seed

My first encounter with small square blocks of prose presented as poetry was in the winter of 1974–1975.[1,2] I was in my final year of high school. My mother owned a few unusual books. One of these was *Love and War Poems* by the pacifist American poet Kenneth Patchen (1911–1972), published in 1968 in a stapled, but high-quality edition as "whisper & shout no. one." It sold for 2s 6d or 1 dollar.

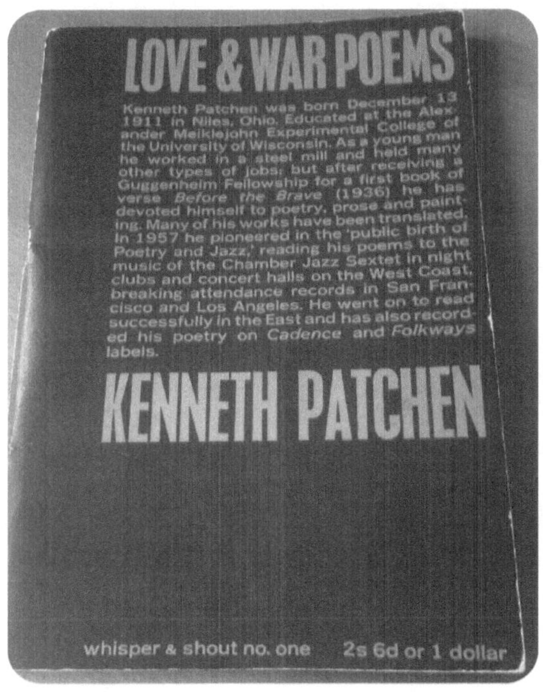

1. An earlier version of this essay first appeared online in the *Fortnightly Review*, October 2018.

2. For a discussion of what a prose poem might be, see, for example, Anthony Howell's article, 'The Prose Poem: What the Hell is It?', *The Fortnightly Review*, April 2016, or Jane Monson's illuminating 'Introduction' to the anthology she edited, *British Prose Poetry: The Poems without Lines* (Palgrave-Macmillan, 2018).

What I found so affecting was not only Patchen's passionate language, or his rich, sensory imagery, or his playfulness (often forgotten), or his utterly uncompromising style—which, granted, can at times result in terrible writing—but also the different *shapes* of the poems on the page: short lines, long lines (which like Whitman's do not stop before the right margin), poems written in a mixture of prose and verse, titles written vertically down the left side of the poem, and *those* poems written as small square blocks of prose, such as the following:

> Red grapes shielded from the sun by thick, velvety leaves. Vines strong with the strength of the loved earth, grapes like huge shiny drops of blood on the undersides of those green fingers. The air is rich with the smell of growing, womb-warm under the sun of the noon-day . . .
>
> Down the rows walk three men in single file...heads bent . . . hands tied behind them. . . . A few yards back a fourth man in the cab of a truck sprawled high with bodies listens to instructions over a twoway radio and yawns nodding at something said by a fifth man who is squinting wearily down the sights of a heavy rifle mounted in the cowling. . . . After a time the voice of the two millionth man gives the awaited order and the finger of a two-millionth and first man tightens on the trigger. And under the sun of the noonday the air is rich with the sweetish smell of the harvest. ("Vines with Their," p. 24)[3]

One thing that struck me here—although I would not have framed it in such terms at the time—was the way in which the poetic is contrasted with a more objective, documentary style to heighten the obscenity of the atrocities being committed—off camera, as it were. The poem ends where it began, with the sensory description of the air "rich with the sweetish smell of harvest." The lyricism of the language only reinforces a sense of horror, disgust and shame.

I was impressed by what could be achieved in so few words. And finally, there was the fact that this was called a "poem," but in terms

3. "Vines with Their" by Kenneth Patchen, from *Collected Poems of Kenneth Patchen*, copyright © 1952 by Kenneth Patchen. Reprinted by permission of New Directions Publishing Corp.

of shape it did not resemble any of the poetry that I was studying at school, although I had read and enjoyed Blake's *Marriage of Heaven and Hell*, which I had picked out on my own from the school library. Blake was in fact an important figure for Patchen. (In a short essay in the *Love & War Poems*, he memorably declares: "Thank God for William Blake! And thank William Blake for a very great deal of God!") Patchen's political prose poems presage Carolyn Forché's widely-anthologized "The Colonel" and the prose poems of writers such as Claudia Rankine.

The fact that I discovered prose poems through editions like this meant that for me they quickly became associated with a literature that was underground and subversive. Prose poems were outsiders. In spite of their square shape, they would not be boxed in by academic labels or commercial interests. Throughout the years, and through many a move from country to country, I have shed most of the books I have owned and read. However, I have hung onto my small press publications for dear life, always making sure they were safe somewhere.

However, while Patchen's work widened my sense of the possibilities of language, it never occurred to me that I too could write poems—if that's what they were—in square blocks of text, even if I was, of course, like many teenagers, trying my hand at lyrical free verse. The first prose poems that made me want to write my own were those of Pierre Reverdy, which I first read in 1979 as a third-year undergraduate student at Nottingham University. As with the poems of Patchen, I discovered them in a small press publication. It was simply titled "Pierre Reverdy," had a plain white card cover, and contained sixteen unnumbered pages of poetry on flimsy paper. Unlike the Patchen, there was no introduction, no afterword, no table of contents. Beyond the poems themselves there was only the information that the translator was Vivienne Finch, and that the pamphlet was published in an edition of five hundred by "The X Press."

I was immediately enchanted by the writing of Pierre Reverdy, and indeed remain so to this day.[4] The prose poems in these translations by Vivienne Finch subtly evoke the atmosphere of Montmartre in the years just prior to the First World War. They also conjure up another, alternate world somewhere between dreaming and waking. Reverdy uses a language which is elliptical yet simple and vivid, and always hauntingly beautiful. Take, for example, "Mascot":

> Little doll, good luck charm, is struggling at my window, at the mercy of the wind. The rain has soaked her dress; her face and hands are fading. She has even lost a leg. But her ring remains, and with it, her power. Winter knocks her against the glass, her little foot blue-shoed, and she dances, dances with joy, and with cold, to warm up her heart again, her wooden heart, the good luck charm. At night, she lifts up her arms beseechingly towards the stars.[5]

4. See, for example, *The Thief of Talant* (Wakefield Press, 2016), my translation of Reverdy's 1917 self-published "novel in verse," *Le voleur de Talan*.

5. "Mascot" in *Pierre Reverdy*, trans. Vivenne Finch (London: X Press, 1980), n.p.

I tried several times to write something like this, but the results were almost always selfconsciously poetic. It was in 1980 when I had left university and was working in series of menial jobs, that I discovered the prose poems of the British poet and editor, Cory Harding, who remains one of underground poetry's best secrets. It was Harding who had brought out Vivienne Finch's Reverdy translations. He also used his X Press to publish his own work, for example the A4chap-book, *Blue Yellow & Green*, which was, in the poet's own words:

> Typed on an Olympia portable typewriter (pudding face type) and dooplicated [Harding often played with spellings] on Armageddon (cheap & nasty) paper using exarmy stencils run off on a RoneoVickers 865 machine one rainy Sunday afternoon at the Cats Meat Warehouse, Tooting in a special limited edition of 75 copies only with a silk-screen cover by the author.

The title is perhaps unusual for a poetry collection, but it is an apt one. The prose poems make frequent references to colors and tell surreal stories that can be visualized as a painting, or as a series of paintings. Like many prose poems, Cory Harding's convey strong feelings of estrangement and a loss of identity, employing an inseparable mix of pathos and absurdity, and have an oddly biblical quality:

> I would like to ascend into that little blue hole in the sky until I no longer remember how I was once human and how my body once consisted of spare parts that have now become obsolete. I would like to float up into that hole at the back of the sky until small clouds enter my body and I forget how my voice once consisted of thousands of wires that burned and sparkled in the dark, and how my body was once controlled by electricity, and how my feelings were ruled by magnets, and my thoughts by poisonous chemicals. You had promised me I would see the beautiful birds beneath the water and the fish swimming thru the blue sky and the clouds floating beneath the ground. But after you gave me this new face it dissolved into a pool of water on a road bordered by high trees where I lay breathing into a rubber tube that sighed like the passing of clouds across my chest.[6]

For better or worse, Cory Harding's work compelled me to try my hand at writing something similar. One early evening in January 1981 when I was walking home in the snow, the draft of a prose poem formed itself in my head.

6. Cory Harding, "The Mystery of the Blue Sky (part 2)" in *Blue Yellow & Green* (Croydon: X Press, 1980), n.p.

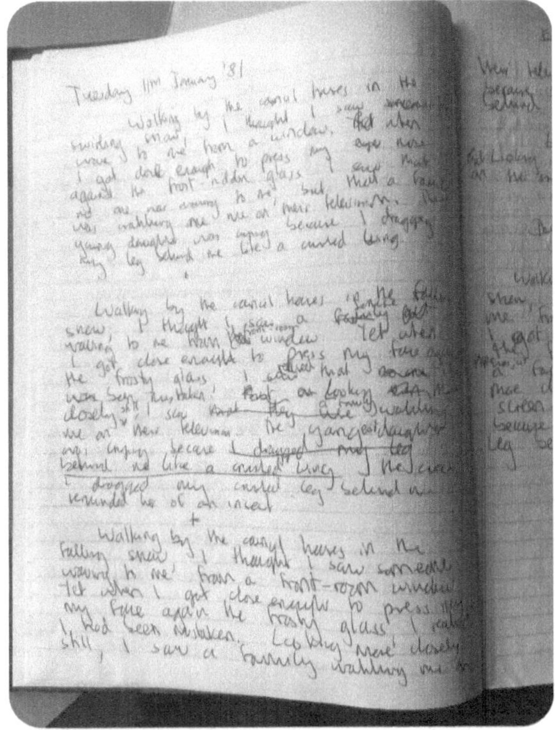

Tuesday 11th January '81

Walking by the council houses in the falling snow, I thought I saw someone waving to me from a front-room window. Yet when I got close enough to press my face against the frosty glass I realised I had been mistaken. Looking more closely still, I saw a family watching me

The final version came out like this, with the title "Insect":

> Walking by the council houses in the falling snow, I thought I saw someone waving to me from a downstairs window. Yet when I got close enough to press my face against the frosty glass, I realised I had been mistaken; there was only a family watching television. Looking more closely still however, I saw myself walking on the screen. The youngest daughter was crying because the way I dragged my crushed leg behind me reminded her of an insect.

The language here is very different from that of Reverdy or Harding, far less "poetical." It is stripped down to a minimum. The po-faced narrator does not express any emotion. Nevertheless, loss (perhaps grief), estrangement, and disorientation are conveyed through the storyline, the imagery, and the way the prose poem changes perspective, continually replacing one reality with another.

I sent "Insect," alongside some much weaker work, to Pete Mortimer, editor of the prestigious *Iron*. He had always rejected my writings in the past, but his rejections were kind and encouraging enough for me to keep trying him. He accepted "Insect,"[7] jokingly asking me if he should publish it under the name Franz Kafka. Astonishingly, I had not thought about Kafka when writing "Insect," even though in my nineteenth year, I had soaked myself in his work, and I now realize that his influence has lasted to this day. Kafka's very short stories, written around the same time that Reverdy was writing his early poetry, have been published both as fiction and as prose poems.[8]

However, a figure I feel even closer to is Max Jacob (1876–1944), friend and mentor to Pierre Reverdy, although I don't believe I had read his work back in 1981. While Kafka builds an alternative universe through the accumulation of seemingly realistic detail, Jacob is a writer who with just a few brushstrokes plunges us into a world we create for ourselves.[9] His language is plain, pared-down, almost conversational, like that of someone telling a jokey anecdote in a bar. Yet the pictures he paints are astonishingly beautiful, filled with a sense of mystery and loss, which is in no way diminished by their comic absurdity. Here is "The Beggar Woman of Naples," taken from Jacob's groundbreaking collection of prose poems, *Le Cornet à dés* (*The Dice-Cup*), like Reverdy's *Le voleur de Talan* published in 1917 and at the author's own expense:

> When I lived in Naples, there was a beggar woman at the entrance to my palace, to whom I'd toss a coin or two before getting into my carriage. One day, surprised she'd never thanked me, I looked at her more closely. It was then I saw that what I'd taken for a beggar woman was a wooden crate painted green, containing some red soil and a few half-rotten bananas.[10]

---

7. Over the decades, "Insect" has taken on a life of its own, appearing in various journals and anthologies, for example, in 1987 it was featured on BT's Dial-a-poem series. Most recently, it was discussed in *Literary Non-Fiction: A Writers' and Artists' Companion*, edited by Sally Cline and Midge Gillies (Bloomsbury, 2015). It appears in my collection *Shifting Registers* (Shearsman, 2011).

8. See, for example, *Models of the Universe: An Anthology of the Prose Poem*, edited by Stuart Friebert and David Young (Oberlin College Press, 1996).

9. Max Jacob was of course also a painter and art critic, but it was Picasso who persuaded him that his true vocation was that of poet.

10. From Max Jacob's *The Dice Cup*, in my own translation, due for publication

What makes us do a double-take here is the way Jacob makes us believe in the impossible, or at least the highly improbable. Even when afterwards we realize that at one level we have been tricked, at another level we have absorbed and internalized the prose poem's fictive logic. However unreal, it has become part of the reality of life. I attempted something similar in my own prose poem "Town Centre":

> A thin youth with tousled hair and a wispy beard was walking from car to car stuck in the traffic. He tapped on each window and held out his hand for money. One driver, perhaps to show off in front of the woman next to him, jumped out of his car. Shouting and shaking his fist, he ran after the beggar all the way up the crowded high street. I thought he would catch him, but the beggar, turning a corner, ducked unseen into an Italian restaurant. I found him sitting at a table there, looking at a menu. The tablecloth was piled high with coins he'd taken from his pockets. He invited me to join him.[11]

Like my earlier poem "Insect," "Town Centre" plays with perspective, and yet establishes a reality effect through its twists and turns. With the first two sentences, it appears as if the story is being told by an omniscient narrator. In the third sentence, the narrative voice becomes more hesitant with that word *perhaps*, which indicates that in fact the scene is being played out in front of someone who is watching. It is only in the fifth sentence that we realize that in fact this is a first-person narrative: "I thought he would catch him." Like a short film, the narrative jumps from one shot to another until the narrator is suddenly and unexpectedly face to face with the beggar in an Italian restaurant, although we are not told how the narrator got there. We then see that the beggar is a kind of trickster, almost a magician, as he piles high the coins he has taken from his pockets. The invitation that the beggar / trickster / magician makes to the narrator is most unlikely and yet seems somehow entirely logical within the context of the prose poem, where almost anything can happen, and which possesses its own truths.

---

by Wakefield Press (USA) in 2023.

11. From *Makers of Empty Dreams* (Shearsman, 2014).

Coins are, of course, a symbol of luck. In dreams, they are said to represent positive feelings about things that have been or can be achieved. They may indicate the birth of a relationship with the person who shows or gives them to you. There is the sense in this poem of some kind of reconciliation taking place, perhaps even a metaphysical one. A colleague of mine says that this prose poem reads like a secular version of a poem by George Herbert, and I can see what he means by that. When I read this poem back to myself, I am startled into a kind of warm feeling, whereas I am chilled by the earlier prose poem, "Insect."

Prose poems can be a great vehicle for exploring chance encounters. As outsiders, prose poems offer a space where what is strange, what is "other," can be welcomed in. Prose poems continue, as the poet Jeremy Over puts it, to throw "authority figures off the scent—pretending to fish for the moon so that they can be left alone to pull up the nets and see if they have snared any real fish."[12]

After "Insect" in 1981, I only wrote intermittently for a couple of decades: the odd poem, the very occasional short story, and around a dozen or so prose poems. The Italian writer Natalia Ginzburg has somewhere said that up until the age of around twenty-five, writers can rely on a kind of innate lyricism. After that, if we are to write at all, we have to make writing an integral part of our everyday lives. Absurdly, it took me until my early forties to realize that. Even when I returned to writing, most of it was in the form of a more realist poetry and longer short stories.[13]

I occasionally wonder why I abandoned the prose poem for so long. Perhaps some part of me believed it was somehow not a valid form of writing. What brought me back to the prose poem in late 2004 was an increasing interest in abstract, rather than narrative poetry, for example the work of Gertrude Stein, John Ashbery, Rosmarie Waldrop, Sheila E. Murphy, Rupert M. Loydell, and Jeremy Over. I began with a series of prose poems that depended mainly for their

---

12. See Jeremy Over, "Fishing for the Moon: Some Recent Prose Poetry in the UK," *Hard Times: Contemporary British Poetry Issue*, no. 80 (2006), pp. 39-44.

13. See, for example, my long short story "Amore Mio," written in 2004, published in 2010 under Lancaster Litfest's Flax imprint, available on Amazon as an ebook.

effect on rhythm and sound, and on the accumulation of disparate imagistic fragments.[14] After about a year, however, I felt I'd written them out of my system. Instead, I turned to cut-up and collage, producing both lineated and prose poems in this way, with varying degrees of success.[15]

And then, in 2010–2011, almost without any intention on my part, I began writing narrative prose poems on a daily basis. Or rather, it was as if they were writing themselves.[16] What surprised me was how similar they were in spirit to the few prose poems I had been writing thirty years before, as if they had just been waiting for me to open the door to let them out. It feels like cheating. I have not had to struggle with my narrative prose poems in the way that I do with other kinds of writing, and yet I believe that the best of them are the only writings of mine that are somehow genuinely themselves. They have needed just a little nurturing from me in order to make their own way in the world. Perhaps, like the friend in my prose poem "November," they were simply waiting for me to recognize them:

> I was sitting on a park bench, thinking of an old friend, of how I had never embraced him. I hadn't seen him for years, and yet as I was wondering about him, I saw him pass by in the light rain that had started to fall. He turned and stared as if he could not believe it was really me. He seemed to have hardly changed, while I had aged almost beyond recognition. I got up and ran to take him in my arms, to hold him so close I could stop his eyes from wandering over my face.[17]

---

14. See my collection *Anonymous Intruder* (Shearsman, 2009).

15. On occasion, I still turn to cut-up and collage now, but I believe that there are other poets who use this technique to much greater effect than I could ever hope to.

16. I should add that my prose poems were considerably enriched by my reading of contemporary authors of the prose poem, such as Linda Black and Lucy Hamilton. See, for example, Black's *Root* (Shearsman, 2011), and Hamilton's *Stalker* (Shearsman, 2012).

17. From *Identity Papers* (Shearsman, 2016). Oddly, I think another influence here is the poetry of Edward Thomas, which is permeated with a sense of regret at roads not taken, and which made me want to start writing in the first place when I was in my late teens.

My Catullus

Simon Smith

The first Friday in June 2000. I'd been working as Assistant Librarian at the Poetry Library on the fifth floor of the Royal Festival Hall in London since 1991, and a major part of my job was to answer questions on all aspects of poetry from the public, who turned up at my desk, wrote in by letter, or phoned, and increasingly, as time went on, via email. Mid-afternoon and the phone went. I picked up the receiver, and on the other end of the line a man asked, from what sounded like the other end of the world, if we had a poem by Catullus. Poem 8 was what he was looking for. The Poetry Library collection is really a library of poetry written or translated into English since 1912, but there were exceptions, and Catullus being a poet translated frequently in the twentieth and twenty-first centuries, often by poets, was one of those, and we had a pretty wide selection of versions to choose from. I asked my enquirer to hold, whilst I went into the reference stack to fish out a suitable translation. The Peter Whigham was my first call, it being the Penguin edition, but it seemed too idiosyncratic, the Zukofskys's versions too off-the-wall, James Michie's, in rhymed couplets (really?). In the end, I opted for the OUP edition, not translated by a poet at all, but by the scholar Guy Lee. Here I thought was a reliable translation, counted on by students, most likely, and so the "prose" meaning would be *fairly* true to the Latin. I read the poem down the phone to the anonymous caller, line-by-line as he jotted from my dictation. He read it back to me, checking for line breaks. I filled out the inquiry form for library stats as we chatted. He sounded happy and grateful, and put the phone down. He didn't offer his name.

It was a quiet afternoon, the sun out, warm, and a few hours before the main concert in the Royal Festival Hall, adjacent to the Library. The office workers, who congregated in the arts center from all over London and beyond at that time, would be enjoying happy hour, so few would venture to the fifth floor, even if they were interested in poetry, away from the bars at ground level with its live, free jazz. So, a quiet afternoon. I was up to date with inquiries, I might want to consider cataloguing some new books, an absorbing task, and one where I could keep my finger on the pulse of what might be going on in contemporary poetry at that time.

The Catullus volume sat on the inquiry desk, a hardback copy, still open at Poem 8, the Latin on the left-hand page, the translation to the right. Lee's version looked pretty faithful, and quite closely made, line-by-line, but also somehow flat, if serviceable, good for teaching purposes, if you were teaching Latin perhaps, but not really a good poem in its own right:

> Wretched Catullus, you should stop fooling
> And what you know you've lost admit losing.
> The sun shone brilliantly for you, time was,
> When you kept following where a girl led you [. . .][1]

I started to doodle with a pencil on some scrap paper, looking at the Latin, glancing over at Lee's version, and slowly started to form my own interpretation of some the phrases and lines I'd found most questionable. By the end of my shift I had my own draft, more a version than a translation, but what I thought was quite an exciting poem, with all the attributes, which I thought (and still look for in a poem/translation), of freshness, readability, challenge to other translations—a new "take" on the original, a form of reinvention, finding things in the text, which others hadn't spotted, or I might have followed a path, others had not trodden. Actually, I felt quietly excited about what I had found. I'd never "translated" a poem before, and I wasn't sure if what I was doing *was* translation or if I was doing it "right." (In fact, I had translated poetry before, in the form of "literal parsing," back when I was twelve years old—and it was Poem 8—for my Latin class. I couldn't remember the wording of the "translation," I simply remembered getting it down as a homework assignment, as some kind of chore).

So, with a sense of quiet excitement, and my scraps of paper in my bag, I caught the train home, to the suburbs for the weekend. And the weekends were long. I'd split with my long-term partner the previous Christmas (the Millennium), and had to scramble to find somewhere to live, and was trying to make the adjustments to

1. Catullus, *The Poems of Catullus*, translated by Guy Lee. Oxford University Press, 1990, pp. 8–9.

living alone after twenty-odd years of marriages and "significant" partnerships. So, having something to do, to find a "project" after several months of aimlessness was a godsend. I also had the double affliction of "writer's block," something I'd not endured before, and "translation" seemed like an interesting solution to think through the language problems of another poet, if I couldn't find my own poems for myself.

That evening I reflected on Catullus and me. Here was a writer who was the first I'd known as a "poet." A poet whose work I studied and parsed for exams, and qualifications. A poet, I then put to one side, as other school work took precedence—more qualifications—but over the previous twenty years Catullus had popped into consciousness at various key moments. Ezra Pound's enthusiasm had caused me to go back and reconsider the poems on more than one occasion. The Penguin translation had always been on my shelves, wherever I traveled, or settled. In fact, Catullus had always been a presence, albeit a background one. All of this life lived with Catullus there, but mainly out of my field of vision seems now, with hindsight, close to part of the process Walter Benjamin identifies as, a "translatable" work searching for its translator. In a very fundamental way Catullus's poems had chosen me to be their translator for this moment in 2000, and for many more moments over the following decade and more. As I continued to think on the past, the memory came back, that in 1998 I had toyed with translations of Catullus, as I was working on 14-line poem cut-ups, creating a homage to the great translators of Catullus in the twentieth century, in what now seemed a preparation for the new task of my own translation. So, I created a "new" Catullus poem:

CATULLUS #117

(takes #1–6)
(for Bernadette Mayer, C.H. Sisson, Louis Zukofsky, Peter Whigham & Frankie Howerd)

The schoolboy with his shining morning face on

—Tom Clark

Curious to learn how many kisses
at my own cost it is the pleasure to lick up

(three hundred) tomorrow when the shops open,
useless without loving: ¾ never steal kisses! Of all
light-hearted men and women none is
lighter than Catullus is today
(used in imaginable tomorrows)
sharpest of sharp hellebore, flower at the field's edge.

Love me so we'll laugh at all without return,
even if the formal field of kissing
sounds preposterous, sweet as sweet; all right, I'll
bugger you and suck your pricks (the guts melt).
I hate and I love ¾ you may well ask how:
as the fastest piece of timber or the passing plough.

10th March—12th September 1998

Here was a new poem, made from the translations of others, without a rhyme scheme, but using the acrostic "C-A-T-U-L-L-U-S" and "L-E-S-B-I-A" to anchor the poem to the left-hand margin.

I decided, on the Saturday to wander up the Charing Cross Road, where then (these have all gone now) every other shop sold second-hand books, and by the end of the afternoon I had accumulated a "Catullus library" of translations, commentaries, and literary and scholarly critical works. I decided I could use all of these books as an "apparatus" to assist with my translation project. On the Sunday, I returned to Poem 8, with my new-found translation experience and new sources of knowledge to complete my version of Poem 8, which appeared little changed in *The Books of Catullus* (2018):

Poor Catullus, quit kidding yourself just quit
now know you've lost by admitting the losing.

There was a time when the sun shone all day long on you;
when you followed where the girl led you loved by us all as well

as we who never loved no one before. No not never nor after.
Never.

There were plenty of the "good times" to go around
and you wanted them all and she wanted them

from sun up to sun down it was as good as it gets.
From here on in she's not up for it and nor should you be,

you jerk, don't scuttle after what runs away faster,
don't do it. It's make your mind up time and stand firm.

Ciao, my pretty. And so today Catullus stands firm
Won't say a word or come looking if you're not willing.

But you'll be sorry when nobody calls, mark my words.
God damn you love what kind of life are you looking for?

Who's calling you pretty now? What kind of guy touches you up?
Who will call you "my love" my love? Whose will you be called?

Who will you kiss? And whose lips do you get to bite at next?
But you, Catullus, you with your mind made up stand firm.

And so began a project that would run parallel to my other writing until 2014, from *Reverdy Road* to *11781 W. Sunset Boulevard*—with other translations of Reverdy, Apollinaire, Rilke, Martial, Propertius, Baudelaire—often acting as markers and anchors within sequences of my own poems, underpinning their history, their method, their aesthetic, acting as counterpoint to my own trajectories, allowing a new-found depth and dimension to the practice of each book, and within each book each poem.

But more than this aesthetic and historical underpinning, and dimensionality over time—giving the idea of writing the "book," or sequence a depth and heft, working with and through Catullus meant I could develop ideas and effects around "voice" (and there are many voices in Catullus—as there are many forms—and in such a small body of work. It's what makes him attractive to a string of what we might identify as Modernist writers from Horace Gregory to Peter Whigham and the Zukofskys). The encounter with Catullus helped me realize and release voices I hadn't encountered before or even knew where lurking there in the shadows and margins of his poems, but also my own poems as they came to occupy a parallel space. Indeed, the whole question of ownership became simultaneously problematic and fascinating: how far are my translations of Catullus's poems "his," how far are they my own? Ownership, in this context, also relates to "voice': is the purpose of the translation to "release" Catullus's voice into a contemporary English, or is the encounter with the Latin poet's work a way to shift or embody something new in my own work, and my own "voice'? The poem to be made to free up a space for Catullus's poem, or is it something to appropriate for myself? Related are questions of ethics and integrity, as well as acquisition: do my versions of Catullus smother out the original? Do they seem to be of their own purpose, rather than "true" to Catullus's own intentions and purposes? Is the translation a journey back to the "original" text and the culture it emerged from, or a place to take a riff and improvise from, to discover a contemporary reality through the bending and distortion of an old melody or trope—"One of My Favourite Things"?

Earlier in this essay I mentioned that my encounter and rediscovery of Catullus's "Poem 8" came at a time of emotional upheaval. That particular poem really struck a nerve, rather uncomfortably, like hitting the (not so) funny bone, and revealed an emotional state in myself, at the very moment where I was trying to reach the core of Catullus's emotional experience, at least as extreme, and demonstrable in the text of the poem. We seemed to be stepping together, in parallel, across two-thousand years.

Again, earlier in this essay, I have mentioned other poets, who I now had the confidence to encounter through the act of translation. One of these was Rilke. I don't actually like Rilke's work that much, but as I was translating Catullus and writing books such as *Reverdy Road* and *Mercury*, I started up conversations with some other poets along the way (translation is a form of conversation, as well as appropriation, and transformation). I also started to collect versions of the Eurydice/Orpheus myth. I had had trouble shaking off the memory and scarring of that relationship break up from 2000 when I re-discovered Catullus. By now, it was 2005. I don't hold to confessional writing: I think, like Jack Spicer, that poetry can be as harmful as it can be healing. But, I started to create a new version of Rilke's "Orpheus. Eurydice. Hermes." I struggled with the poem over three or four months, and something quite unexpected started to happen my dreams and nightmares about the previous relationship ceased, and, as I concluded my version of the poem, and through leaving the translation behind, as a kind of emotional slouching off of a skin, so the emotional damage was left behind too. Translation as catharsis.

I'll close with my version of the Rilke poem.

Orpheus. Eurydice. Hermes.

(after Rilke)
This bottomless pit of shadows.
Like silvery trails, they soundlessly
skated on into the endless void. Life-blood drowned
low-lying vegetation, following its route to the earth's surface,
where dusk fell, it solidified as feldspar.
Nothing redder in sight.

A precipice soared skyward,
and forests thick as fog. Swaying footbridges
reached into the blackness, and a huge, grey, sightless lake
mirrored the heights to the bottomless drop
of a sky over hills and valleys, filtered through gloomy daylight.
Across tranquil fields
a public bridleway unravelled like calico.

Down this road they came.

Leading, a thin man draped in blue –
silent, an angsty, shifty gaze, arrow-like, forward.
With long, fast strides he quick-marched,
eating up the distance; hands straight down
making tight fists, punching out the greatcoat's creases,
unaware of the priceless lyre
that grew from his left side, like a bunch
of lifeless roses taped around an olive branch.
His senses hewn in two parts;
his power of seeing far ahead like a sheep-dog
corrals and swerves,
upright, to attention, quivering at the furthest corner –
his listening like a smell motionless in the air it floats in.
Occasionally, he caught it, hung about
as far back as the footfall of the others
who ought to shadow him up the footpath to sunshine.
No, it was no more than his own echoing back,
no more than the breeze rustling his coat.
They're still with me, he told himself;
whispered out loud to die on the air.

They were there, he had to believe, grave doubts rushed
in to fill their lightness of foot. Desperate to cast his hungry gaze
behind, knowing the look would obliterate
the entire expedition, so nearly
realized, and if he did, if he did he could not help but see
the two, cautious, ghosting him distantly:

he, god of quickness, long-distance and Director of Communications,
the brim of his cap pulled tight over beady eyes,
his walking-stick thrust before him,
at his ankles tiny wings beating the silence;
at his side, upheld on his left hand, as pledged: she.

She, adored at such a pitch, one lone lyre sang
a full-throated sadness more sustained than
the entire profession of mourners since the earth was born,
the drone re-creating the earth, in its slopes
and copses and tracks and settlements
and meadows and rivers and beasts;
with its own sun orbiting this other world of sadness
parallel to this normal world, a second sun floated,
through this veil of tears pregnant with heavenly bodies.
She, adored at this pitch.

From here she stepped to the left of the god,
her little feet tightened by the winding-sheet,
unsure, timid, unafraid.
Deep in her own thoughts, as a woman expecting,
and recognized neither the other ahead,
nor the track rising to the places alive above.
Deep in her own thoughts. Her deathly state
shrouded her, her great prize beyond want.
Like fruit sugared in its own decay,
she was satiated with the enormity of death,
the shock of its newness beyond her comprehension.

She had entered her new maidenhood
where no one could touch her; her petals were shut
tight as a nightshade, her wedding finger
sore with the constrictions of wedlock
so the god's infinitely subtle attentions

scalded her, like cold lips unsought for.

No longer the bombshell
whose Being dictated poem after poem back to him;
she was his lost love-seat's perfume, and his rock:
a step away from him.

She was shaken free as long hair,
random and scattered as a rain shower,
sown far and wide as grain.

Rooted to the spot. She.

At that moment the god pulled up sharp.
Stopped her in her tracks and said,
voice quivering: he looks behind!
confused, eyes opened wide, she whispered: who?

Miles away, a shadow in the glowing exit,
somebody, A.N. Other in silhouette,
nose, eyes, mouth, unremarkable.
He was there, compelled to watch
the God of Communications turn back
on the path between the fields, weeping
soundless, tuck in behind the slight body
turned shuffling along the track,
feet tightened by the winding-sheet,
unsure, timid, unafraid.

The Babysitter

Donna Stonecipher

I started writing poems thanks to my fifth-grade teacher in Seattle, Mrs. Merlino, who taught us haiku. Fitting the contents of my fiery little heart into 5-7-5, pouring messy thoughts and desires into a miniature elegant form, changed me. (She also taught us calligraphy, remarkable for a mediocre public school.) For months afterward, I walked home from school composing haikus, which I then copied into an accounting book I'd bought for ninety-nine cents at the Fred Meyer up on 85th.

In high school, I took the only Creative Writing class offered, with a certain corpulent Mr. E, who was not shy about procuring for himself the benefits of student-performed back-rubs during class (we took it in stride, figuring it must be part of "poetic license"). For one assignment, he had us send fan letters to real, working poets from the Seattle area. From among Mr. E's books, I chose Colleen J. McElroy, then a professor at the University of Washington. I liked her poems' compression and their textures. I have no idea what I wrote to her in my letter, but I was overjoyed to receive a gracious reply in the mail not long after. (I still have her letter, with its kind encouragement.) My reading otherwise was random and slipshod, whatever fell into my hands from my sister or friends—*Flowers in the Attic* one week, *Clan of the Cave Bear* the next. My biggest poetic influence in high school was probably still Shel Silverstein until my first boyfriend, an older college student who lived in an apartment just behind "The Ave," the center of what there was of an alternative scene in 1980s Seattle, gave me a book of poems by Marge Piercy. Her short poems were accessible and enjoyable, about cats in Greece and feminist topics. Still, they felt remote, written by a middle-aged woman who could have been a teacher of mine perhaps, but not a peer.

There were no books in my house growing up, except for an ancient Webster's dictionary with a desiccated rose pressed between wax paper and stuck into the pages between the headers "jai alai" and "Japanese quince," kept in the same drawer of our Craftsman bungalow's built-in cupboards as the Christmas napkins and the used gift-wrap bows my mother was saving for the next occasion. My parents read the daily newspaper, but nothing else. They had not gone to college, and there was very little knowledge of, or interest in, highbrow culture in my family home. In fact, highbrow culture, which would have included poetry, was viewed with suspicion—not untypical for a lower-middle-class American family in the Far West. My mom collected rocking-horse Christmas ornaments, and my dad spent most evenings in his basement shop, working under the hood of a car or soldering something together that had broken around the house. We read poems in my AP English class, but none of them stuck in my head. I got much more out of the novels in that class, and spent many hours absorbed in Edith Wharton's *Summer* and William Golding's *The Lord of the Flies*. Riding my bike up to the public library each week, I would finger the rack of paperback classics, but although I was attracted by their air of august nobility, and sensed that we were predestined to spend time together someday, they intimidated me, and I chose young adult books about teenagers struggling with heroin addiction or broken families instead.

I graduated with a 4.0 grade average (at that time the best you could get), and an award for best student in the English department. And then I plunged headlong into the disaster of college.

I had cried and bullied my mother into agreeing to send me for one year to a small private liberal arts college near New York City, the mecca to which I hoped to escape from provincial Seattle, against my father's express wishes. *Your mother and I didn't go to college,* he said. *So you will go to a public university, and* your *kids can go to a private college.* This enraged me. *No,* I *will go to a private college, and I'm not having kids anyway!* I seethed to myself. When he heard that the two daughters of a famous movie star would be my fellow students, my dad hit the roof. I didn't understand it. Luckily or unluckily, my parents were about to descend into a bitter, years-long divorce, and my mother took the opportunity to play good cop, securing me one year of what I called "my dream school." What would happen afterward was unclear. The college was expensive, but my parents were exemplary savers, lifelong penny-pinchers and coupon-cutters. I had grown up in thrift store clothes and eating out of cans and boxes. And it was 1987; college costs had not yet ballooned into the obscene debt-generators they would become from the 1990s. With some scholarships and financial aid, the cost was just barely do-able for a two-income family.

Off to New York I went, woefully unprepared for exactly the devastating experience my father had feared for me. But my parents had never explained anything about class, and when I was eighteen, I didn't know it existed. Seattle was remarkably egalitarian in the 1970s and 1980s. Some of my friends lived in nice houses on Blue Ridge with backyard pools, and others lived with their families in apartments, and I didn't think twice about it. My family was somewhere in the middle, with our small Craftsman bungalow, bought by my parents for a now-laughable sum in 1969, the year I was born. Unless I misunderstood everything, which is entirely possible, I don't remember any particular friction over the socioeconomic differences in our homes.

My one precious year at my fancy New York college, I was placed in a year-long fiction class, though I had expressly written in my application that I aspired to be a poet. When I timidly mentioned this to my professor, he smiled, patted my arm, and assured me that I would like his course a lot. I had not yet learned how to advocate for myself with anyone outside my family, and so I wasted my year in his class, trying to write short stories with no innate interest in plot, characters, or narrative arcs. At our second meeting, the professor, who was a working fiction writer, said to me: "I see from your application that your mother is a blue-collar worker." (My mother worked as a checker in a supermarket.) "There are only a handful of kids at this school whose parents are working-class. How do you feel about it?" I blinked at him, confused. I genuinely had no idea what he was talking about. But I knew enough to know I should feel ashamed. As I taped up my posters of New Age fairies and lake scenes by Gilbert Williams, carefully wrapped and transported from Seattle, I stared at my new roommate's posters of someone named Paul Klee. The first time I said the name out loud, Paul "Clee," my roommate laughed. It's Paul "*Clay*," she informed me. I pronounced everything wrong. I didn't know any of the cultural references my new friends traded back and forth with ease. I had never sunbathed nude in the south of France. My clothes were too cheap. No one knew where Seattle was. "Is that in Or-e-gone?" they asked. I didn't correct them. I floundered in my classes. I didn't know what communism was. I had performed well in my public high school, but this college was oriented toward kids with a private school education, with educated parents. I secretly wrote poems instead of short stories and typed them up on my big electric typewriter shipped from Seattle. My one refuge was the volleyball team, since I had grown up playing sports. I felt comfortable smashing the volleyball into our opponents' side.

And meanwhile, my year was ticking away. I had to apply to transfer to another college. A big university in New York City could give me more financial aid, so the next fall I found myself there, taking writing classes taught by graduate students. One, a poet with long red hair and a bushy beard, assigned us *On the Road* and Gregory Corso's *Birthday Poems*. He told me I would like Audre Lorde, so I bought a book of hers in the university bookstore, and I did. I enjoyed reading everything he assigned. But it all felt like somebody else's literature. And basically, that's what literature had felt like, in toto, up to that point: somebody else's literature. I loved books. I responded passionately to them and I craved them. I laughed and cried over them, and ever since I can remember, I had always had "my nose stuck in a book," as my dad liked to say. But there was always a scrim between me and their authors.

My parents got divorced. I tried to transfer again, this time to an Ivy League school, but I didn't get in. My private liberal arts college offered to take me back with more financial aid, so I transferred back.

That summer, a challenge awaited me. One of my rich friends from the volleyball team had passed along the offer of a month-long gig as a nanny in Bermuda to a French family, acquaintances of hers. The family was obscenely wealthy, and had rented an entire house on a private beach. The next-door neighbor was a daughter of Ronald Reagan, I forget which. I fell in love with the six-year-old girl who was my charge, and with the daughter of the housekeeper, too; but, treated like a hired hand who nevertheless had to eat and socialize with the family, I have never felt more paralyzingly uncomfortable in my life. The first five nights, I cried myself to sleep, after marking off the day in the cast-off Pierre Deux agenda my rich friend had given me. Only twenty-eight days to go, twenty-seven days to go, twenty-six days to go, twenty-five days to go. In this rarefied world of extreme wealth, I felt gawky and gauche. The family wanted my charge to practice her English, so although I had been studying French, I was forbidden from using it, which made her think I was stupid. She was a beautiful little girl, but for some reason was consumed by the idea that she wasn't pretty. (Today, I know from fugitive internet searches, she is a model, with 42,000 Instagram followers.) When the husband and a houseguest friend bought matching Rolexes one day for fun, I fished the boxes out of the garbage for me and my sister. The husband expressed disgust at my feminist unshaven legs. I didn't know how to cook, but I learned to make a good vinaigrette salad dressing. I made bracelets out of the little shells I found on the beach and gave them to everyone but the stepmother, whom I hated. She—I'll call her T—was American, a gorgeous, cold, bronzed mean girl who seemed to take passive pleasure in my discomfiture. She had a walk-in closet off their bedroom filled with identical crisp white shirts that set off her tan, paired with tight black designer pants and stiletto heels.

I duly learned how to ride a moped so that I could ferry my charge back and forth to a half-day camp. I had one night a week off, Saturday night, and I made the most of it. I rode my moped through the fields to the bars in the town and danced and drank and flirted. Men bought my drinks all night, and I ended up half-naked on the couch of one of them.

My only recourse in the midst of my misery was writing. I wrote by the notebook-full—letters to anyone I could think of, long entries in the margins of the Provençal agenda, whose days I continued to X off, with little encouraging notes to myself—"Only twenty more days! You're gonna make it! Seize the day!" Night after night, once my charge had been put to bed, I poured out my dread like a tipped-over ink bottle.

From my second college roommate, who was from New Jersey, I had picked up the insult "pig-dog." One morning, I was composing a letter to a high school friend in which I had written, "T is a pig-dog." I was called from my desk to attend to something, and when I returned to my room, there was T, standing over my desk, reading the letter. I froze, then broke into a sweat. T retreated to her bedroom, closed the door, and did not reemerge for four hours. I rode off to fetch my charge on the moped, panicked. When T finally emerged, it was time for our daily trip to the beach, and to my astonishment, she came up to me and asked if she could apply sunscreen to my back. We walked into my bathroom, and as she rubbed lotion into my skin, I was trembling. "I read your letter," she said. I burst into tears, not knowing what was coming next. She apologized for reading it, and acknowledged it had hurt her. Between sobs, I gulped out that it wasn't really about *her*, it was just that I felt so uncomfortable with my job, and that writing was my way of coping. We had a long talk. I said I felt that being a poet made me different from everyone else, and she said that I ought to try to share more of my passion. "Maybe one day I will look back on this trip and say to myself, "thanks to Donna, I learned to like poetry.'" We ended with a hug.

That night, I copied out a poem from the book I was reading, wrote a note thanking T for the talk, and enclosed one of my shell bracelets in an envelope that I placed on her pillow while they were out.

Things got a little easier after that, but T soon retreated back into her inscrutable coldness. One day, we were all invited onto a friend's yacht. When one of the men showed interest in me, and for once I started feeling comfortable talking to him, T noticed and interrupted us to tell me to take my charge ashore for a swim in the shallows. I suppose I invited her aversion, in a way. I was still crossing the days off in my agenda.

Before we flew back to New York, T informed me that she was sorry, but that the guest room it had been arranged I would stay in their palatial Upper East Side apartment while I waited for my flight back to Seattle was no longer available.

After we landed in New York, they dropped me from their limousine at the subway. And I never saw any of them again.

When September came, back up the Hudson River I went. I had somehow been empowered by having managed to get through the trials of Bermuda. I had been pried violently out of my shell, and I found making friends much easier. And one day, in front of poet Jean Valentine's door, I fell into conversation with a young, petite blonde student who changed my life. Camille exuded a warmth I hadn't known I had been missing—Seattle warmth. She had grown up partly in a Seattle suburb, and her open, friendly, deeply sympathetic nature felt like a warm shower after two years of Eastern cold. Camille was the first aspiring poet I had ever met who was aspiring right. The walls of her dorm room were covered in collaged pictures of famous women writers. She hadn't wasted time in high school with Marge Piercy, but had gone straight to Toni Morrison and Virginia Woolf—she loved, and intensely identified with, Virginia Woolf. She had been a hero in her high school, standing up to bullying football players. She was writing poems of a sophistication I could only dream of. She had read all of Sylvia Plath, and couldn't believe I'd read none of Sylvia Plath. She handed me her copy of *The Collected Poems*, and said that I must read it. Immediately.

And so, that night, I sat on my dorm bed, opened *The Collected Poems* of Sylvia Plath, and started flipping through it. There was "Daddy"—turns out I *had* read that before, somewhere. But its raw fury didn't particularly move me. The poems were beautiful and engaging, but the scrim remained. Until I happened upon "The Babysitters." In "The Babysitters," Plath describes a nannying job with a rich family that sounded uncannily like mine in Bermuda. She writes about crying secretly in her room in a gorgeous mansion, about the difficulties of the job taking care of someone else's children, about not knowing how to cook, about the obscene wealth—there was even a yacht, too. But when I got to the lines

> Nights, I wrote in my diary spitefully, my fingers red
> With triangular scorch marks from ironing tiny ruchings and
> puffed sleeves.[1]

I stopped breathing. I couldn't believe it. I read "The Babysitters" over and over. That was *me* in the poem, crying myself to sleep and writing spitefully in my diary. At long last, after years and years of unconscious seeking, I had finally looked into the mirror of literature and seen myself reflected back. My experience, the experience of a young American woman, working in misery as a nanny for rich people, was worthy of being recorded in a poem, was worthy of being printed in a book. I gasped with relief.

I consumed everything of Plath's after that—her poems, letters, diaries, biographies. My poems changed. I grew more confident. I wrote my first really good poem—about being a nanny in Bermuda.

---

1. Sylvia Plath, *The Collected Poems*. HarperPerennial, 1992, p. 174.

Why do we read poems? I loved poetry before I saw myself reflected in it. I wrote and I read it with ardor. But it was only this encounter, first with Camille, and then with Sylvia Plath's "The Babysitters," that made me believe that I, too, could inhabit the mantle of "poet." I know that Plath's anger was formative for many women of my generation, who grew up in the residue of pre–Second Wave feminist conceptions of womanhood. Sylvia Plath performed American girlhood of a certain era to frightening perfection, and also revealed the devastating costs of that performance—but she had done the seemingly impossible: legitimized young female experience as appropriate material for poetry, told in that young woman's voice. Even though her life circumstances were notably different from mine, she was the closest I could get to evidence, cold hard proof, that the experience of my life was sufficient stuff to make for poetry. I could never be Keats, or TS Eliot, or even Emily Dickinson, but I could be a descendant of Sylvia Plath's.

I could belong.

Majesty

Cole Swensen

Encounter. It seems always sudden, even if just slightly, often a bit unexpected, and in some way revelatory. An encounter has all the power of a confrontation but none of the oppositionality. It opens rather than opposes.

Every painting offers an encounter—and a qualitatively different one from that offered by other visual media. In the case of representational painting, this has to do with a painting's inherent uncanniness and its temporal dynamics. An encounter with a representational painting has the signature quality common to all things uncanny in its fusion of the familiar and the strange—it confronts the viewer with something readily recognizable yet radically altered by painting's inevitable distortions, which adds a dose of shock to the encounter. And by shock, I don't mean that it's necessarily even startling; it's more likely a (perhaps unconscious) change in the body's electricity, caused by the simultaneous occurrence in the viewer's mind of the scene presented (by the painting) and the scene represented (out there in the world)—and the fact that they can't quite fit. It's a simultaneity that yet has a glitch, a shift, an offset—the real time of its subject out in the world (its representational time) gets set off against the presentational time, which is an imagined time, because a painting always takes place in an imagined time, which is always in the present; a painting has no past.

This is a very different temporal dynamic than that of, say, painting's close relative, the photograph. A photograph's two times—that of presentation and that of representation—fall on two points along the traditional temporal continuum, the one that we deal with every day. But with a painting, only one of its times—that of presentation—falls on that continuum while the other, being imaginary, does not, which cants ajar, and in that gap begins a reverberation that never stops.

Tacita Dean's series of painted-over photographs of trees offers a particularly uncanny encounter because it erases the distinction between painting and photography, thus fusing these two different temporal dynamics. Like the other pieces in the series, the work titled *Majesty* (owned by the Tate and easy to find through an Internet search), emphasizes, on the one hand, the tree's monumentality through tight framing and, on the other, its reality through close detail, but it also defamiliarizes the image through the white gouache with which she has surrounded the entire tree, using tiny brushstrokes that insist on the painted nature of the work as they pick out the thinnest twigs in the most minute detail, which, because white falls back, pushes the image forward—so much so that the tree seems to be straining against the front of the picture plane, pushing itself outward and into its encounter with the viewer. The combination of the force and the beauty of this encounter foregrounds the viewer's ethical relationship to the tree, requiring a response to its implicit address and engaging the series in an ecologically attentive conversation.

When I first saw *Majesty*, I felt the power of encounter in the sense of that barely perceptible shock of awakened electricity, but I also saw something that I've been trying to get to work in poetry for years, and that is the play of two different but simultaneous temporal regimes. We are used to the fact that a photograph occupies two points on the daily timeline, and we're also used to the fact that a painting manages, so strangely, to occupy both daily time and the timeless imaginary, but we're not used to negotiating both at the same time—it jars us out of our perceptual habits and, very subtlety, demands that we participate in two utterly different ways of constituting, and thus of experiencing, time, which creates a subtle vertigo, an irrepressible desire to leap—in this case, across the gap between the two.

I'd love to do this in and with language, but I don't know how, though I sense that it's precisely that leap that is central to the plot. The construction of time (always both highly personal and utterly communal) is a question I come back to again and again in my work; one way I've addressed it is by exploring historical frames and dimensions, in hopes of igniting that productive offset, but content alone can't do it, and even trying to "enstrange" content through linguistic slippage, syntactic play, and other ways of jostling meaning out of the stasis incurred by the habits of daily language and put it back into motion don't manage to incite that shock.

My strong response to Dean's tree project got me to thinking that spanning media, creating an offset of aesthetic perceptions that demands that the mind engage two different aesthetic regimes simultaneously might perhaps create both room and invitation for that vertiginous leap. This is, of course, simply a description of ekphrasis, so, clearly, I'm looking for something that goes much further than that, but it may well be the desire for this leap that has maintained ekphrasis as a persistent mode of exploration for millennia. It can allow both writer and reader to maintain the immanence offered by the experience of encounter while also facilitating a wandering in time that referential modes, either in writing or in another art, allow.

It's a balance—or rather, a teetering balancing-act—much more difficult to strike in language than in image, and while it's not a process that can be taken apart and studied, I'm hoping that repeated encounters with this series, as well as with certain other visual works—Gerhard Richter's *Overpainted Photographs*, for instance—will attune me to some opening that I'm currently unable to see, will direct my attention toward some other way of using language that can somehow allow it to incite that amazingly enabling temporal disconnect that makes you suddenly, though so briefly, aware of your place in time. That, too, is another encounter, an encounter with time itself, which is the constitution of the self, though it seldom occurs consciously. When it does, it gives that self a more rooted presence, which is to say, it adds another root, another avenue of nourishment and another anchor.

Encounter's relationship to attention is a theme that's been running along under the surface of the preceding comments. Encounter and attention—each causes the other, and Dean intensifies the encounter by accentuating the activity of her attention. Not even the closest observation can match a mode of attention that engages the active participation of the attender. We *attend to* something not just with our minds, but also with our hands, and her meticulous brushwork amounts to a kind of meditation on her subject, a way of attending to it without interfering with it. It also increases the surface detail immeasurably, giving the viewer that much more to attend to as well. This kind of active attention is something I would love to incite in poetry—how can we somehow read with our hands? Or at least make reading a kinetic experience? This is obviously what performance poetry has been grappling with—often successfully—for years, but I would love to engage it at the level of the page, within the silence and privacy, the intimacy, that a book—or a gallery or museum space—can create.

A kinetic poetry engaging an active attention would, of course, have to start with the writer, who must get the words to actively observe. I think back to Dean's use of detail, and though I can't say quite what, I sense that there might be an opening there, a way of using language, not to describe more precisely, but to evoke detail beyond that accessible through words. There is always energy in detail, as well as intimacy, in that it pulls us in, into the event-horizon of the work.

Something of that intimacy is conveyed by the fact that *Majesty* is also about an encounter with an absence that her white-out process makes very present, making presence an echo of absence. It's an extremely active absence that parallels the active attention mentioned above, and asserts absence as an intentional gesture, one that blends assertion and peace in equal measures. By painting out everything but the tree, she paints it into a different light, a different presence which allows presence and the absence around it to oscillate in a *mise en abyme* that constitutes another temporal distortion, or rather another, perhaps even unprecedented, way of occupying time. Poetry has made much of conscious constructive use of absence since Mallarmé's 1897 *Un Coup de dès*, but it has realized its function and power for centuries—every time a poet ends a line, they are beginning an absence. The relatively sparser forms used by poets from the Modernists on is a choice toward a positive absence, toward an absence that is not based on a lack of something or on a presumption that something *should* be there that isn't, but instead an absence that is an opening, like the emptiness of an open window, creating a light-space, in all the possible interpretations of that term. What might be thought of as the white-space revolution in poetry is based precisely on this redefinition of absence, according to which it becomes an invitation. And yet, it's an invitation that will never be, can never be, accepted, an invitation made in all sincerity, but that wants no response—an invitation to which there is no possible response—leaving this unacceptable invitation vividly alive, inviting, and constantly pulling us toward it on an asymptotic line. It's an invitation exuded not only by white space, but also by absences of all sorts once they're recognized as not-lacks.

In Dean's case, in addition to absence-as-invitation, there actually is something missing; her largely-opaque, chalky white field makes us acutely aware of what has been erased—it's more present now than if it had been left visible, increasing our encounter with a background that now only exists in our imagination—and therefore has been internalized; it now lives inside us. It acts as a metaphor for ecological erasure, which now lives inside us as well.

These issues of absence, invitation, and internalization are ethical ones involving recognition and participation, which, in turn, point to the ethical dimensions inherent in any encounter. As any encounter is always a matter of *being in relation to*, it challenges our individuality, disproving that illusion in a way that we must respond to. Unlike the above invitation, an encounter always requires a response.

This dense dovetailing of call and response and the fusion of the aesthetic and ethical orders are things I want to make occur in poetry as well. I often see in visual art, principles that I sense could take poetry elsewhere, principles that depend on non-linguistic moves; incorporating them into poetry would create a monstrous bridge that leaps kingdoms, just as Dean's *Majesty* does by bridging the animal and plant kingdoms, the viewer and the viewed, always reciprocal, creating a common tissue of them that recasts encounter as a networked participation with and in the other.

Sunken Sun

Anne Waldman

> The Middle East lives its destiny. No sound seems trivial or ordinary. The power of terror is totalitarian. Bullets crack and resonate in the amphitheater that is Beirut.
>
> —Etel Adnan, *Sitt Marie Rose*

> My body is a rag to be sewn to the earth.
> O you who sews worlds, sew me!
>
> —al-Ma c arri[1]

I spent the other day reading aloud—performing—the extraordinary *L'Apocalypse Arabe/ The Arab Apocalypse* by the poet, artist Etel Adnan, in a room of one.[2] I experience this text's magnitude of display and yearning and urgent alarm. Its measure of riot and desperation and power. The poem in its integrated sections shoots off the page, disrupts conditioned space, explodes in the ears and thrums the inner drums; it unleashes a linguistic slash/breach/upheaval. I made gestures, arms flagellating, and hands jabbed the air finding release in spastic display. I supplicated. I improvised finger-mudras and worked taut, awe-inspiring expressions upon my face. I let my mouth expand to hold the whole of ancient "Arabia," then I revised the map and considered all the turmoil continuing, now, ever, and the rest of the world's collaboration in that endless suffering of *problem-not-solving*: Israel and Palestine. I included Somalia, Libya, Tunisia, Syria, Yemen. I knocked my head with my fist, I looked up to pray again, then bowed and prostrated on the ground of the poem. My eye-mudras moved in all directions of space attempting to indicate . . . manifest . . . enact Etel Adnan's prophetic glyphs.

This ritual reading expanded a sense of my own ongoing kinetics and possibilities as a poet and performer. And I have traveled for

1. In Adunis, *al-A` mal al-Shi` riyya al-Kamila (Complete Works)*. Dar al-` Awda, 1988, p. 278.

2. Etel Adnan, *The Arab Apocalypse*. Post-Apollo Press, 1989, p. 12. All subsequent Adnan quotations in this essay are from *The Arab Apocalypse*.

years within themes around the interstices of war, exile, and editic memory. I have gathered repertoire from my own texts designed for or available to *agit prop/ street works*, musical accompaniment, including free jazz, choral, plus duets and word/sound constellations for other libretti, as well as recordings and performative film presentation. Examples would be selections from The IOVIS TRILOGY: *Colors In The Mechanism of Concealment, Songs of the Sons and Daughters of Buddha* (with translation from some of the oldest poems by women going back to the time of the Buddha),[3] *Jaguar Harmonics* (notes from an ayahuasca ceremony), and a libretto for David's T. Little's opera *Artaud in the Black Lodge* engaging the sound collages of Antonin Artaud. I have always been engaged with particular shamanic practices, with and without entheogens, I have always been drawn to cyclical artistic forms from India, Indonesia, indigenous Mexico. Etel Adnan's text was a new kind of contemporary initiation.

I put my whole body into the codes and lingual soundings of Adnan's animated and visual text, her *Codices.* May people of the future decipher these runes! I lay down for the arrow-like glyph between "Mexico!" and "bed undone" (II). I splayed myself on the floor before "great Inca." I stamped on the ground before "Ishi cried this morning" (IX). After "I painted the sun in the middle of the sky like a flag" (XII), I danced and swirled and repeatedly pointed to the sky and beyond. I held my belly, clutching it three times before singing out "the yellow sun of menopause" (XVIII). I stuttered and crawled after intoning "in the underground blackroom always black is experience" (XL). I groaned "There have been pounds and pounds of decomposed flesh tons of suffering" (L) and let blood symbolically gush from a wounded-long- gone body and moaned, and moaned. I took the text's ideograms as clues for performance and chanted "HOU HOU HOU HOU HOU" and "DOUM! DOUM! DOUM!"

An enactment of the battleground, measuring my own echolocation. An enactment of the psyche, measuring the relief the purge the terror this ritual mirrored. I spooked myself.

3. Anne Waldman, *The Iovis Trilogy* ("Problem-Not-Solving," "Coda: Beirut" (see letter by Etel Adnan), Coffee House Press, 2011

Who can say it, who says it, what are the words to call out and carry and implode this apocalypse? This is the closest to—Adnan's s text—I have come.

What she attempts to do in language is a crisis upon an altar, a *crise* of the heart.

I rested then took up the *agon* again, I retreated, then called to others.

They—apprehensive—left me in my retreat of poetry and prophecy and penance.[4]

I noted:

> "a blue sun receding a Kurd killing an Armenian an Armenian killing a Palestinian . . . "[5]

I noted:

> "What a purple and violent abyss broke loose on the Primordial land of Syria?"

I noted:

> "Treason floats down the smooth surface of the Euphrates like a woman"[6]

I noted:

> "When they eat the Palestinian's liver before he's even dead"[7]

I noted:

> "Imam Ali dances over nuclear blast"[8]

I noted:

---

4. Etel Adnan, Ibid.

5. In Hayan Charara, *Inclined to Speak: An Anthology of Contemporary Arab American Poetry*. University of Arkansas Press, 2008, p. 26.

6. Etel Adnan, Ibid.

7. Etel Adnan, Ibid., p. xxxix.

8. Etel Adnan, Ibid., p. xliv.

"we crucify Gilgamesh on a TANK Viking II reaches Mars"[9]

I noted:

> "And under the blue clouds of Babylon turtle doves announce a thunder"

I noted:

> "There have been meadows covered with human skin under the Arabian moon"[10]

I considered all the colors of Adnan's "suns," her *voyelles,* the red dots that are sunspots of the stuttering amplitudes of the poem, or a floral sun with petals of gold . . .

I noted her Mao and Rimbaud, the razor's edge.

I conjured my own physical/spiritual displacement. I recalled sleeping on the desert near Abu Simbel, sickle moon, in my young girl coven, 1962. I felt the sun's heat early in the morning.

I recalled the airport in Beirut, on my way to Egypt machine guns everywhere. The fear in people's eyes. Rain obscuring the sun.

The root of the Arab word *nashid* (song) is the voice, the raising of the voice and the recited poem itself. According to the poet Adonis, the Arabs of the pre-Islamic period felt the recitation of poetry a talent in and of itself, distinct from composition.

> ". . . listening was essential to the comprehension of words and to musical ecstasy (*tarab*)"[11]

> "The actual performance of poetry had its own rules in the pre-Islamic period which survived into later ages. Some poets, for example, recited standing up, while others proudly refused to recite unless they were seated. Some would gesture using their hands or their whole bodies, like the poetess al-Khansa

---

9. Etel Adnan, Ibid., p. xliv.

10. Etel Adnan, Ibid., p. 69..

11. Adonis, *An Introduction to Arab Poetics*. Translated by Catherine Cobham. Saqi Books, 1990, p. 15.

(sixth-seventh century) who, it is said, rocked and swayed, and looked down at herself in trance."[12]

I wanted that trance, wanted Cassandra invoked here in poem of wailing and ejaculation, and the explication of the harm out under a cruel desert sun. For the desert will consign all to dust and sand more quickly perhaps than we can imagine. *The lone and level sands . . . .*

Pre-Islamic: Rhythm evidently began with *saj* the root of which contains a reference to song, and is used to "denote both the musical call of the pigeon and the plaintive monotonous cry of the she-camel, alike in one respect of being continuous, unvarying sounds."

I rather punctuated with a vast array my imagination in a verisimilitude of Adnan's time and place. And thought of her, summoned her to inhabit her rage and the passions I would also enact on her behalf.

I had worked a decade ago with Berber (Amazigh) schoolchildren in Marrakech. They had been troubled and fearful after the bombing in Jemaa el Fna in April of 2011—sixteen dead, twenty persons wounded—drawing pictures of their responses to the tragedy. One had to keep the poetry transmissions, which were in English and French, simple. These brilliant youngsters had grown up in a culture vivid with some of the most sophisticated music and poetry and crafts imaginable and had so much more to teach me.[13]

We got through the first verse of "Tyger Tyger," acting out the poem with our bodies as we chanted it together, first in French, then English, then Arabic.

Tyger Tyger burning bright—we drew a sun with our hands in the sky, over the desert perhaps, not far from the door of the Dorm we worked in.

Suddenly we were *in the forests of the night,* hands and body trembling in the darkness, yet indicating the solace of trees, our bodies growing up from the ground.

12. Adonis, Ibid., p. 16.

13. Gratitude to the Tamaas Foundation and my colleagues working in Marrakech May 2011: Ha-Yang Kim, Alystyre Julian, Julie Klear, and Sarah Riggs. Educational projects continue there for aspiring young people.

What immortal hand or eye . . . lifting a right hand, palm outward, and then pointing with the other hand to our left eye.

Could frame . . . we drew a large rectangle in the air.

Thy fearful symmetry . . . we crouched then leapt up with fierce expressions, eyes wide and wild, embodiments of this magical challenged new generation's tyger-energy.

One thought in this exercise of apocalypse, of sanctuary, of life cycles, of disaster—plague, famine, endless war. Of reaching into other planet nexii and zones, cultures and languages to the trouble times of humanity in a spirit of empathy, of symbiosis and play.

I considered the symmetry or exact correspondence of form on opposite sides of a dividing line.

In the Cellular: Poetry in the Body

Felicia Zamora

A Galapagos tortoise's heart beats six times per minute; that's one beat every TEN seconds, or forty-two babies born in the world per beat, or the universe expanding ninety-two miles, or two blinks for the average person, or one thousand bolts of lightning striking the ground. At a cellular level, the tortoise's body know its capabilities considering longevity and time. Compare that to the human heart which beats about eighty beats per minute, or even the hummingbird's heart which beats up to 1,260 times a minute or as low as fifty beats during torpor. So much can be said about what the body knows, and how it prepares for its own existence.

In his essay, "Circles," Ralph Waldo Emerson speaks about the soul and its ability to leap over boundaries, "But the heart refuses to be imprisoned; in its first and narrowest pules, it already tends outward with a vast force, and to immense and innumerable expansions."[1] I'm pondering Emerson's "expansions" and my own heart; the ways in which poetry set-up camp behind my ribs and nestled in my aortic sack. Poetry began bodily for me. Poetry found me long before I knew how to articulate it, or that my life would be dedicated to it. More on this soon.

* * *

Let's first consider more fascinations, as fascinations are important. The medulla oblongata functions in delicate regulation of our breathing, our cardiac activity, our sensory neurons, our circulation. Inside the skull, this continuation of spinal cord makes up the lowest part of the brainstem and controls the heart and lungs. Nerve cells travel this superhighway between the forebrain and midbrain. The bulb in the ladder to the cerebellum and cerebrum. All this synapsing taking place under flesh. The interstates of us.

1. Ralph Waldo Emerson, "Circles." *Essays by Ralph Waldo Emerson*. Literary Classics Bookclub, 1945, p. 221.

This idea that we are, in many ways, stuck in the interior when it comes to our consciousness, constantly ebbs through my thinking. Emerson said, "The eye is the first circle; the horizon which it forms the second; and throughout nature this primary figure is repeated throughout without end."[2] This connectivity to the horizon and the body has always intrigued me; the role sight plays in our lives is a powerful consideration for how we understand the world and ourselves. I remember the first time I saw the movie, *Being John Malkovich*. The strangeness of how humans live through the portholes of ocular bone and cells sent a wave of acknowledgment through me. Our consciousness sits at the helm of a muscular ship as we steer through the physical world. I felt like I was seen for the first time. I turned to my partner and said, "See. See, this is how I feel all the time." The concept of boundaries that Emerson spoke of has always eluded to the interior versus exterior environments for me. I am this mind, but also this body, and with both I am present in this existence. The body as a container, home, vessel for the thinking that is done inside.

> Are you not the sparrow-s
> hadow you see above the
> meadow? How the pupil
> swallows light, for the mind
> to regurgitate pictorially. We
> refract: the lovely art of
> bending. Once you see the
> sparrow-shadow, is it not part
> of you . . . burnt upon the
> retina; captured inside tissues
> & tendrils of brain? There
> now, witness blueprint &
> design in form.[3]

In all this thinking, my mind drifts to the 1980s and 1990s when everyone was obsessed time capsules. Our tiny efforts to collect ourselves in a world that's so much larger than our singular bodies. These were our own contributions to archeology. The digging in, to

2. Ralph Waldo Emerson, Ibid., p. 218.

3. "& wings made of matchsticks," by Felicia Zamora from *Of Form & Gather*, University of Notre Dame Press, winner of the 2016 Andrés Montoya Poetry Prize

one day be dug up. In middle school, I remember obsessing about what to put in my seventh grade time capsule. Kids had school photos, Bart Simpson dolls, cut braids of hair tied with ribbon, Garbage Pail Kids cards, mood rings, you name it. Thirty years later, I can't remember *what* I put in the capsule, but only the feeling of obsession. What our bodies choose to remember creates paths of understanding for us to later access. What we know about our past is largely what we remember. Beyond cognition, our skin, cells, and muscles also hold their own memory. This memory is at the mercy of what imprints on the cerebellum, amygdala, hippocampus, and prefrontal cortex.

I've always been a personal excavator, a scavenger. As a child, I made forts out of teacup shards, electrical wire the city forgot, broken branches, dirt, and rusted pots left behind the woods just north of the Alden Motel where I grew up. I'd rummage through shoe boxes, cedar chests, drawers, under beds, jewelry boxes, and cabinets when my grandparents left the house. Perhaps my scavenging was the first echo of poetry inside me. No one spoke of history in the Alden Motel. No one spoke of why we stopped speaking Spanish in the house; or why we stood in line at the foodbank every week; or why we didn't believe in Santa because the church ladies called us every December to negotiate between our Xmas wishes and their donation budget; or why we gave my mother cards on Mother's Day and Father's Day; or why my sister was put in special ed for being Mexican; or the racial slurs both inside and outside the motel; or the whispers from parishioners; or why the carnations I bought boys on Valentine's Day were always sent back under another boy's shoe. No one spoke of history, our history: Melody, Joe, and me—three brown bodies who weren't allowed to have a history. So, I became an archaeologist of the Alden Motel.

* * *

Flashback to 1985. My grandparents had left the house for a trip to Penny's in Iowa Falls. I heard the wheels of the Dodge go from gravel to pavement and leapt from the couch. I slunk out of the diner-turned-living room, left at the motel office, past Cindy the biting Pomeranian (but I'd bite too if I was a dog on a leash inside), right at my grandparent's living quarters, toward the blue tarp tacked at the entryway. Grandpa hung the tarp up in winter to avoid heating the two bedrooms up the stairs. "Up the stairs" to this day is still a phrase of dreams for me; it's the place I was not allowed to go; the reliquary of my uncle's muscle car magazines, 1970s-collared-shirts, and my grandma's fake furs. Upstairs was off limits to me, so of course every chance I got, I pulled back the blue tarp.

For years, a door at the end of the hall haunted me. I stood before the door with wide eyes: my own Valley of the Kings. I began to dig and shift the blockade boxes, blankets, and magazines to create a sliver of an opening and wedged my gangly frame inside. The smell of mothballs stung my nose and I ran my fingers over hanging garments draped in plastic, handles of old vacuum cleaners, and felt hats, until I reached a pile of shoeboxes. In the Alden Motel, shoe boxes never contained shoes. They held the good stuff: photos, keepsakes, letters, pieces of lace from women I think were related to me. I grabbed the box on the top, stepped back into the light, and sat down in the hallway. Lifting the lid, revealed a conglomerate of photographs. In the hoard of images and faces, one sepia photo stopped me.

In the middle of the square, slightly askew, was a five-foot, two-inch man, tawny skin, thick black mustache, woolen flat cap, and my sister, just a baby, wrapped in his arms. The man held my sister in front of a barbed wire fence with a field beyond. Time stopped. The world lifted a veil and I could not look away. Entranced, I scoured his face. His eyes were my eyes. His nose bridged and flattened in all the same places as mine. My cheeks were his cheeks. I held my own chin in my hands in the drafty hallway of the Alden Motel and cried. Until that moment, I had not understood replication, genetics, aching, culture, or mourning. All of my cells went feral at one time, and my flesh an inadequate boundary. My heart rivaled the hummingbird's pounding, all my internal interstates synapsed and synapsed and synapsed. On one hand, *I came from somewhere,* pulsed between my ears, and on the other, *Where is he? Why did he leave? Was I not enough?* bullied their way out as well.

I pocketed the photo. This was the first and only photo I had ever seen of my father.

* * *

For many years, I was fascinated by the image of this person I had never known. I hid the photo in a sock drawer, then a jewelry box, then in book. Early on, I took the photo out and each gaze created a gaping hole behind my ribs. At the age of forty, I would finally write the words born inside me the day I found the photo in a series of poems titled "Dear Coyote."

> I stitch the stars in patterns of your
> chin, your kneecap, your rib, your gait: a constellation of
> absence. I map your body, a celestial
> cartography to understand my own echo, my
> own cave in the torso, cave of undoing.[4]

In my teenage years, I cursed the photo for my mustache, slanted eyes, my skin.

> witness & your head imitates,
> back/forth; how *brutal* & *bothersome*
> arrange us; how you, unable to look
> away, lick your lips in disgust of you.[5]

In my twenties, I couldn't look at the photo due to my rage of finding out about the cocaine in the couch cushions, the sex with women while married to my mom, the violence to my siblings and Mom, the radio dedication to "Melody" on her sixteenth birthday.

> When you beat my brother's face with a sack of
> potatoes, when he bruised & you drew the
> burlap back for blood, did you smell lilac,
> believe your fists made us into something
> beautiful? When you opened our mother with
> knuckles scented with other vaginas, did you
> believe in your gift, passed? I cup my breasts in
> the mirror & consider the tissues of violence; if I
> crack my neck, cleave at the thyroid & pull out
> the medulla oblongata, will I cross section the
> parts of you that continue to wound?[6]

---

4. The poem "Dear Coyote" by Felicia Zamora was first published in *Boston Review* online at http://bostonreview.net/arts-society/felicia-zamora-three-poems.
5. "Watching Breed," by Felicia Zamora from *Instrument of Gaps*, Slope Editions
6. Second excerpt from the poem "Dear Coyote" as above.

The photo is now lost. Lost physically and in the imagination where brain, desires and cellular history have created a time capsule. This was my first encounter with poetry—in my hands. Poetry seeped up from someplace in my cells, my cognition, my heart, my lungs. It has been waiting, waiting for me to be ready. The image of my seven-year-old bloodstream circulating words that would one day become the poetry I needed, comforts me. In that photo was a ghost of my face, but I was never his, and he was never mine. He has only ever been a specter lambent across my horizon.

I continue to feel Emerson's words, "I unsettle all things. No facts are sacred to me; none are profane; I simply experience, and endless seeker, with no Past at my back."[7] This is the work of the poet: to unsettle. We first are unsettled by the world that harbors us. We long for a world in which we see ourselves. We long for a world we can look at, full on in the face, without bursting at the seams.

> . . . origin
> lay only in a compass-less map and the bright bright
> burn against the dark {galaxies streaming inside
> out} forcing them to *look, look away, look again*.[8]

The past was, and in many ways still is, a mystery to me. We are products of both our genetics and our social constructions. Maybe I saw my snoopiness (as my grandma used to say) as solving a mystery? Aren't we here to discover? From moments of birth, we discover the world in a harsh and challenging way, but unable to fully comprehend what birth means until many years of evolving.

* * *

Letting go is also an allowance of influence from the artistic process. How can something come from you, but never truly be yours? The "not knowing" trance-like state when writing poetry. Letting your obsessions take over can be a frightening endeavor. Poetry, in its unique art form, asks the artist to relinquish some control, to give over to process, for the sake of the art, for *what must be said*. Emerson

7. Ralph Waldo Emerson, Ibid., p. 232.
8. "Broken Things," by Felicia Zamora from *& in Open, Marvel*, Parlor Press.

says, "The way of life is wonderful: it is by abandonment."[9] I believe these words. We must be willing to let go, to release that which contains us, either in the mind or in physicality, to embrace that which we cannot know. This is the risk of creation. In life as in the poetical, it is the moment of letting go that is essential to our true birth: a birth without boundaries, with all the senses open and permeable; a birth into finding comfort in the unknowing; a birth born out of wonder into wonder.

My eye was the first circle. The photo of my father another circle. Our slanting eyes mirrored through genetics, another. The urge to discover, another: a poetry of the body. See how we ripple as natural beings. It was through this slanted vision, the part of my body that once disgusted me because it was among the many features that made me *other*, that my poetical existence emerged. Internalized oppression exists in many marginalized people; a colonization of the DNA. I know it does for me. It's how we fight against oppression in the internal and external that matters. My eyes and their slant shape the way I see the world. They are what make me beautiful. A unique gift to have felt violence and still loved. To have been spit in the face and still loved. To have been told I was worthless, dirty, nothing, and still loved.

> brain, safe behind skull; think *walls,*
> think *what walls keep, what walls inhibit;*
> how you no prisoner & thus, *out out*
> *brave other,* into a world that throws
> stones, a world that beats & batters;
> how you, *other,* love bold, love bold.[10]

Poetry begins in the cellular, in one person's cognitions where the impossible becomes possible. I'm a product of impossibility. We all are. The odds of us becoming are not odds one would typically bet on. Every Galapagos tortoise, hummingbird, walking medulla oblongata, found a way here under astronomical conditions. Therefore, poetry cannot happen without our thinking (which Emerson thought was the hardest task in the world). Thinking comes from the

---

9. Ralph Waldo Emerson, Ibid., p. 234.

10. Love Bold," by Felicia Zamora from *Body of Render,* Red Hen Press, winner of the 2018 Benjamin Saltman Award in Poetry.

brain and the brain is made up of one-hundred billion neurons and glial cells. I don't know about you, but that fascinates me. Fascinations are important.

We might believe that everything exists without us, and maybe it does, but if a tree falls in the woods . . . well, the woods wouldn't exist without the trees. Poetry cannot exist without us, without our humanity, creativity, imagination, ingenuity, fascinations, cognitions, questioning, risk, and doubt. The doubt of my lineage, of who I was in that hallway in 1985 created a circle of thought that spiraled me into the poet I am today. We are a compilation of motor functions and non-living organs and tissues that make up a body that lives. We are the epitome of impossible doing the possible. Our bodies have prepared for us. Poetry begins in the cellular.

My Dog

Matthew Zapruder

When I was writing a lot of poems in summer 2018, I would go to my desk every morning and try to get at least a draft down. I was also taking notes all the time, in whatever notebook I happened to have, or on random scraps of paper. I had somehow blissfully stumbled into what Lorca calls the stage of leaping, flying, gathering treasure. All day, no matter what else I was doing, I was also gathering. Periodically I would land and return, classify and select, only to begin gathering again. It occurs to me now this is what animals must do all day.

That June, I went to Amherst, Massachusetts. I had been an undergraduate there, and after living in the USSR and then California, returned to UMass for graduate school. This year I was visiting just for the day to give a reading at the week-long Juniper Summer Festival. It was so strange and sad to feel like a visitor to a place that had been home. I had been one of the founding faculty of that summer program and went for the whole week for many summers in a row. One summer, I met Sarah, and we started dating. Now we live in California, and it is vertiginous to return to the place where I lived for so long before I met her, and where I met her, where my life irrevocably changed.

At the obligatory awkward dinner before the reading, I was sitting at a table with Eileen Myles, Joy Williams, and Dara Wier. It would be harder to be in the presence of three cooler people. Dara had been my teacher and mentor when I was a grad student. Sarah had been in Joy's workshop when we met. I love their writing, and Eileen is one of my favorite poets.

Eileen was missing a front tooth, and seemed to have no intention of fixing it. I bet almost everyone is afraid to ask her how she lost it, though if you did, she would surely just tell you. She looks even more like a badass without the tooth than with. I personally was feeling a little dead at that point, drinking as if it were my job, getting ready for my execution at the hands of a poetry audience. Eileen and Joy were talking, unsurprisingly, about dogs, and tattoos of dogs. Then we all walked together from the restaurant to the auditorium, the two of them a little bit away from us, still talking.

I started writing notes, as we walked through Dickinson's little town and then the familiar campus with its peculiar mixture of colonial brick holdovers and huge brutalist structures. When I sat down in the auditorium before the reading, I made a few more notes to distract myself. On the plane I had been reading about the progressive journalist I.F. Stone. I thought it amusing that his name looked like "if stone" so I made a little pact with myself to use that phrase in my next poem. I stuck that at the end of the first set of scribbles, figuring it might come in handy.

When I got back to California I took out the little notebook and wrote this poem. I had the sensory memory of that night still available in my mind, the calm evening and sounds of people talking as we walked past buildings I had seen without seeing many hundreds of times.

As I was writing the poem, I remembered Joy and Eileen at dinner were also talking about tattoos on someone who was dead, I don't remember who. The tattoo was of dogs, and they both laughed, and one of them said, of course.

In the final version of the poem Eileen's experience becomes singular, she's talking to herself and walking "away from joy" which obviously is a different kind of line than something like "Away from Joy Williams, who was also at dinner." I am always on the lookout for the symbolic, and a way to find in something from life a deeper resonance, but I don't want to overdo it, I am just as happy to have a real-world texture in the poem, to just let be the way it is in the world also in the poem, and resonate in a different way. Too much symbolism is dull, but I like it when it authentically appears.

As I was writing, I remembered our family dog, Dylan, who was hit by a car on Fourth of July sometime when I was in middle school. For some reason we used to let him just run around the neighborhood even though there were a bunch of busy streets. In hindsight this was obviously criminally negligent, we knew absolutely nothing about dogs at all, and should never have been entrusted with one. When we found out that he had been killed, my brother and sister and mom and dad and I all sat on their bed and cried for a long time. It was one of the only times we did anything remotely like that as a family. Expressions of emotion and general sharing of feelings was utterly curtailed in our family, leading to long periods of furious repressed silence punctuated by violently emotional outbursts. I was thinking about how, after that, we had never gotten another dog. What if that lack has just gone on inside me, an "unnoticed silence" that I have only finally become aware of?

Looking back, I found two drafts in my notebook of the poem. In the margins of the first draft I see that I have a note to myself to reverse the poem: write the lines up from the bottom, without changing anything, just to see what connections are made. This is something I learned from Agha Shahid Ali (my teacher at UMass Amherst, along with Dara and Jim Tate) who seemed to have a knack in workshop for taking an incredibly boring poem and reversing it and making it magical.

I did this myself for a long time, both as a poet and teacher of poetry (live, in class, it makes quite an impression). It can work for the same reason why taking lines from different poems or notebook writings over the course of days and weeks, and combining them, can reveal a continuity. Moments of great alteration, fundamental transition, in our lives are rare. Almost all the time we are working on the same problems. Sometimes our thinking about those problems comes to the surface, but most of the time it is below, in our pre-conscious minds.

Access to that material is possible in dreams, and also in a looser, more exploratory type of writing, gathering without purpose, with intuitive attention to what "feels," in a way that is beyond immediate explanation, meaningful. But then, when we land and begin selecting and classifying, a different impulse can take over, one that is sometimes helpful, and sometimes destructive.

As most writers eventually discover, the initial order that we get our moments (whether collected at the time, or recollected in tranquility) into the poem is not so important. And in our anxiety to make meaning, we can often clutter up the poem, and over-manage and over-organize it. Maybe some of us are imagining an ungenerous reader, poring over the poem with a magnifying glass, looking for flaws. This reminds me of watching the great singer and songwriter Mark Mulcahy, performing at a small house concert. He stopped after one song, looked up, and said, you know what my problem is? I'm imagining the person who least wants to be here, instead of the one who most wants to. That's my problem too.

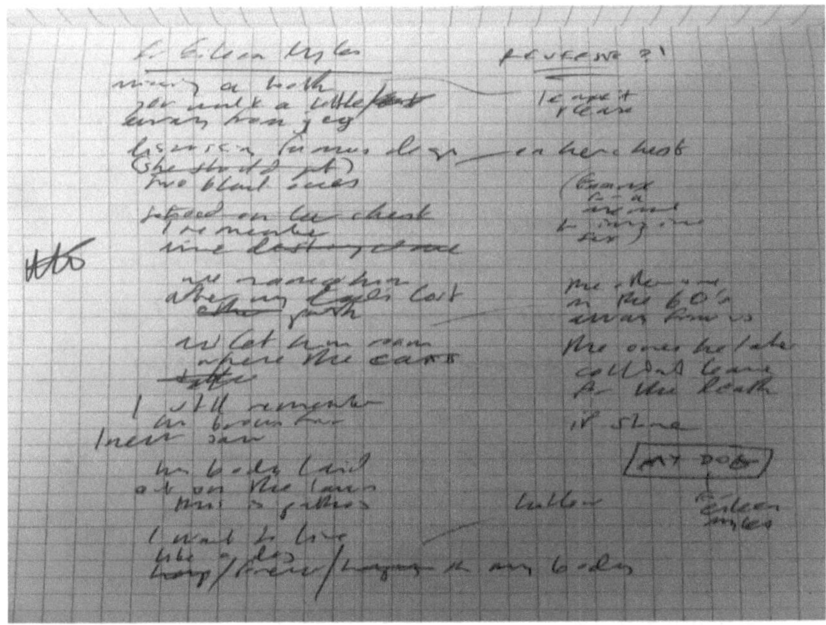

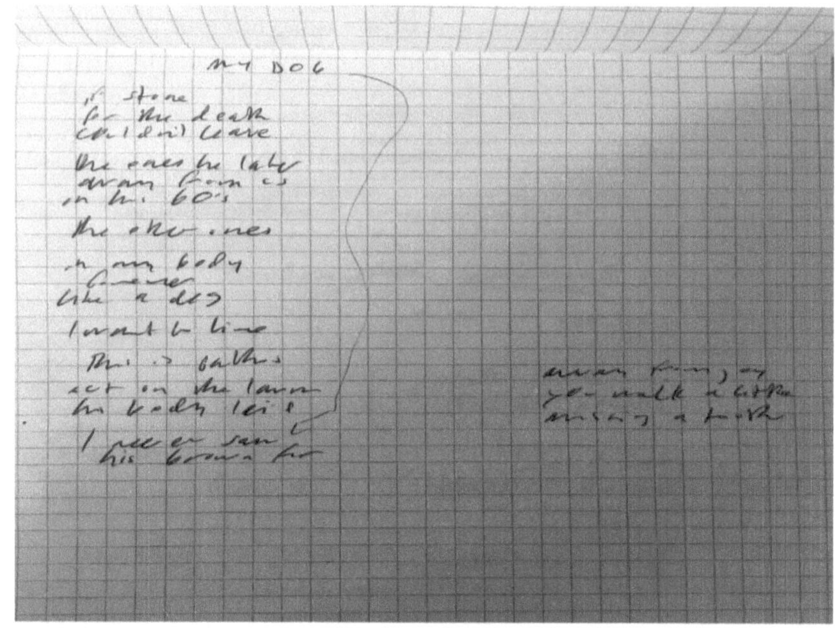

Figure 1. Composition notes for Matthew Zapruder's "My Dog."

MY DOG

away from joy
you walk a little
missing a tooth
discussing famous
black dogs
on the dead
chests of lovers
I just finally
heard
that unnoticed
silence
of never having
one again
it's been with me
all my life
I saw mine
named after
a god

his body laid
out on the lawn
brown fur
dried blood
yes it's wise pathos
this want to live
in my body
like a dog
not thinking
if stones
for human deaths
then what
for the other ones

(for Eileen Myles)

Contributors

Rae Armantrout's most recent books, *Versed, Money Shot, Just Saying, Itself, Partly: New and Selected Poems, Entanglements*, (a chapbook selection of poems in conversation with physics), and *Wobble* were published by Wesleyan University Press. *Wobble*, a finalist for the 2018 National Book Award, was selected by *Library Journal* as one of the best poetry books of 2018. In 2010 her book *Versed* won the Pulitzer Prize in Poetry and The National Book Critics Circle Award. In 2007 Armantrout received a fellowship from the Guggenheim Foundation. Her poems have appeared in many anthologies and journals including *Poetry, Conjunctions, Lana Turner, The Nation, The New Yorker, Bomb, Harper's, The Paris Review, Postmodern American Poetry: a Norton Anthology, The Open Door: 100 Poems, 100 Years of Poetry Magazine*, etc. She is recently retired from UC San Diego where she was professor of poetry and poetics. She lives in the Seattle area.

Jennifer Atkinson is the author of five collections of poetry—*The Dogwood Tree, The Drowned City, Drift Ice, Canticle of the Night Path* and *The Thinking Eye*. Individual poems have appeared in various journals including *Field, Image, Witness, New American Writing, Free Verse, The Cincinnati Review*, and *The Missouri Review*. She teaches in the English Department and the MFA and BFA programs at George Mason University.

Kelvin Corcoran lives in Brussels. He is the author of numerous books of poetry, including most recently The Republic of Song (2020). The sequence "Helen Mania" was a Poetry Book Society choice and the poem "At the Hospital Doors" was highly commended by the Forward Prize jury 2017. His work is the subject of a study edited by Professor Andy Brown, *The Poetry Occurs as Song*, 2013. He edited an account of the poetry of Lee Harwood in *Not the Full Story: Six Interviews with Lee Harwood*, 2008. In addition, his poetry has been commissioned to accompany traveling Arts Council exhibitions of British modernist art. He has collaborated with various musicians and composers both in performance and recording, producing the CD *A Thesis on the Ballad* with The Jack Hues Quartet. His work has been anthologized in the UK and the USA and translated into Greek and Spanish. He is the guest editor of the Shearsman poetry magazine.

Eduardo C. Corral is the author of *Guillotine* and *Slow Lightning*. He's the recipient of a Whiting Writers' Award, a National Endowment for the Arts Fellowship, the Hodder Fellowship and the National Holmes Poetry Prize, both from Princeton University. He teaches in the MFA program in Creative Writing at North Carolina State University.

Martin Corless-Smith is a poet, painter and essayist from Worcestershire, England. His recent books include *The Fool & The Bee* (Shearsman Books, UK 2019), *Odious Horizons: Some Version of Horace* (Miami University Press, 2019), and the book of essays, *The Poet's Tomb* (Parlor Press, 2020) and a collection of prose pieces, *The Ongoing Mystery of the Disappearing Self* (SplitLevel Texts). He lives and teaches in Boise, Idaho.

Laura Da' is a poet and teacher. A lifetime resident of the Pacific Northwest, Da' studied creative writing at the University of Washington and The Institute of American Indian Arts. Da' is Eastern Shawnee. She is the author of *Tributaries*, winner of the American Book Award, and *Instruments of the True Measure*, winner of the Washington State Book Award. Da' lives near Seattle with her husband and son and is a writer in residence at Richard Hugo House.

Carolyn Forché's first book of poetry, *Gathering the Tribes*, won the Yale Series of Younger Poets Prize, and was followed by *The Country Between Us*, *The Angel of History*, and *Blue Hour*. In March, 2020, Penguin Press published her fifth collection of poems, *In the Lateness of the World*. She is also the author of the memoir *What You Have Heard Is True* (Penguin Press, 2019), a finalist for the National Book Award and winner of the Juan E. Mendez Book Award for Human Rights in Latin America. Her international anthology, *Against Forgetting*, has been praised by Nelson Mandela as "itself a blow against tyranny, against prejudice, against injustice." In 1998 in Stockholm, she received the Edita and Ira Morris Hiroshima Foundation for Peace and Culture Award for her human rights advocacy and the preservation of memory and culture. She is one of the first poets to receive the Wyndham Campbell Prize from the Beinecke Rare Book and Manuscript Library at Yale University, and is a University Professor at Georgetown University in Washington, D.C.

David Herd's collections of poetry and chapbooks include *All Just* (Carcanet, 2012), *Outwith* (BookThug, 2012), *Through* (Carcanet, 2016), and *Songs from the Language of a Declaration* (Periplum, 2019), and *Walk Song* (forthcoming from Shearsman). He is Professor of Modern Literature at the University of Kent and co-organizer of the project *Refugee Tales.*

Paul Hoover has published sixteen poetry books including *Poems in Spanish, Edge and Fold, Sonnet 56, Desolation: Souvenir,* and *The Book of Unnamed Things.* His forthcoming book is *O, and Green: New and Selected Poems* (2021). He is editor of *Postmodern American Poetry: A Norton Anthology* and the literary annual *New American Writing.* His other works include *The New World Written: Selected Poems of Maria Baranda* (Yale University Press, 2021), which he edited and partly translated, and *The Complete Poetry of San Juan de la Cruz,* edited and translated with Maria Baranda (Milkweed Editions, 2021).

Ger Killeen is a poet, former professor of English and New Media at Marylhurst University, and digital humanist. He is the author of several books of poetry including *Lia A Léimfidh Thar Tonnta: A Stone That Will Leap Over The Waves* (Trask House, 1999), *A Wren* (Bluestem Press, winner of the Bluestem Award for Poetry), *Signs Following* (Parlor Press, 2005), *Blood Orbits* (Parlor Press 2009), and *JuarOz* (Headlandia Press, 2015). His work also appears in several anthologies including *From Here We Speak* (Oregon State University Press), *American Poetry: The Next Generation* (Carnegie-Mellon University Press), and *The Gertrude Stein Awards* (Green Integer). He recently edited *More Truly, More Strange: An Anthology of Poetry in Augmented Reality* (www.arspoetica.io) Ger works as an independent XR and web developer for the arts, literature, and digital humanities. He is a Snapchat Official Augmented Reality Lens Creator.

L. S. Klatt's poetry has appeared in various magazines and anthologies, including *Harvard Review, Denver Quarterly, Crazyhorse, Poetry Daily, The Believer, Best American Poetry, Image,* and *The Common.* His first collection, *Interloper,* won the Juniper Prize, awarded by the University of Massachusetts Press. His second, *Cloud of Ink,* received the Iowa Poetry Prize from the University of Iowa Press. He is the author of two other volumes, *Sunshine Wound* and *The Wilderness After Which.* He has also published essays on poets, most notably "The Electric Whitman" in *The*

Southern Review and "Blue Buzz, Blue Guitar: Wallace Stevens and the Poetics of Noisemaking" in *The Georgia Review*.

Éireann Lorsung makes texts, objects, spaces, and ideas in the company of many others. Her most recent collection is *The Century* (Milkweed, 2020); she is a 2016 NEA Fellow in Prose. More: ohbara.com.

Farid Matuk is the author of the poetry collections *This Isa Nice Neighborhood* and *The Real Horse*. He teaches on the MFA faculty at the University of Arizona and serves on the editorial teams for FENCE magazine and the book series Research in Creative Writing. Matuk's work has been supported most recently by residencies and grants from The Headlands Center for the Arts, the Lannan Foundation, and UC Berkeley's Holloway Visiting Professorship in Poetry & Poetics. *Redolent*, a book-arts project made in collaboration with Colombian visual artist Nancy Friedemann-Sánchez, is forthcoming from Singing Saw Press.

Rusty Morrison is co-founder, co-publisher of Omnidawn (www.omnidawn.com) since 2001. Her five books include *After Urgency* (won Tupelo's Dorset Prize) & *the true keeps calm biding its story* (won Ahsahta's Sawtooth Prize, James Laughlin Award, Northern California Book Award, and DiCastagnola Award from PSA). Her recent book: *Beyond the Chainlink* (Ahsahta; finalist for the NCIB Award & NCB Award). She is currently a fellow, awarded by UC Berkeley Art Research Center's Poetry and the Senses Program. Poems of hers have appeared in the Poetry Foundation website, and in their podcast series *Poetry Now*, in *Colorado Review, Fence, Iowa Review*, and elsewhere. Her creative nonfiction and poetry at *Entropy*, her nonfiction at *Harriet*. Her critical essays appeared at *Kenyon Review* and *Pleiades*. She is a recipient of fellowships from Civitella Ranieri, Djerassi, and other artist residencies. She has taught in MFA programs, been a visiting poet at colleges, and teaches workshops through Omnidawn and elsewhere. She offers private consultations. For more info, see her website: www.rustymorrison.com.

Sawako Nakayasu is an artist working with language, performance, and translation—separately and in various combinations. She has lived mostly in the US and Japan, briefly in France and China, and translates from Japanese. Her books include *Some Girls Walk Into The*

Country They Are From(forthcoming, Wave Books), *Pink Waves* (forthcoming, Omnidawn), and *The Ants* (Les Figues Press), *Texture Notes* (Letter Machine Editions), and the translation of *The Collected Poems of Chika Sagawa* (Canarium Books), as well as *Mouth: Eats Color—Sagawa Chika Translations, Anti-translations, & Originals* (reprint forthcoming, Wave Books), a multilingual work of both original and translated poetry. She is co-editor, with Eric Selland, of an anthology of *Twentieth-Century Japanese Poetry* (forthcoming, New Directions). She teaches at Brown University. Website: sawakonakayasu.net.

Eric Pankey is the author of many collections of poetry and recently *Vestiges: Notes, Responses & Essays 1988–2018*. At George Mason University he is Professor of English and The Heritage Chair in Writing, where he teaches in the MFA and BFA programs in creative writing.

Carl Phillips is the author of 15 books of poems, most recently *Pale Colors in a Tall Field* (Farrar, Straus, and Giroux, 2020). His prose books are *The Art of Daring: Risk, Restlessness, Imagination* (Graywolf, 2014) and *Coin of the Realm: Essays on the Life and Art of Poetry* (Graywolf, 2004). He is Professor of English at Washington University in St. Louis.

Donald Revell is the author of fifteen collections of poetry, most recently of *The English Boat* (2018) and *Drought-Adapted Vine* (2015), both from Alice James Books. Revell has also published six volumes of translations from the French, including Apollinaire's *Alcools*, Rimbaud's *A Season in Hell*, Laforgue's *Last Verses*, and Verlaine's *Songs without Words*. His critical writings have been collected as: *Sudden Eden: Essays*; *Essay: A Critical Memoir*; *The Art of Attention*; and *Invisible Green: Selected Prose*. Winner of the PEN USA Translation Award and two-time winner of the PEN USA Award for Poetry, he has also won the Academy of American Poets' Lenore Marshall Prize and is a former Fellow of the Ingram Merrill and Guggenheim Foundations. Additionally, he has twice been awarded Fellowships from the National Endowment for the Arts. Having previously taught at the Universities of Alabama, Denver, Iowa, Missouri, Tennessee, and Utah, Donald Revell is currently a Professor of English at the University of Nevada, Las Vegas.

Peter Riley was born in the Manchester area in 1940 and recently retired to West Yorkshire after living for twenty-eight years in Cambridge. In 1966 he was an editor of *The English Intelligencer*, the worksheet which first proposed a Modernist position in British poetry. Since then he has authored an heap of books and pamphlets, which have now been gathered into a two-volume *Collected Poems* published by Shearsman (2018). There are also books on music, and travel in Transylvania. In 2019 Longbarrow Press published a book of new poems, *Truth, Justice, and the Companionship of Owls.*

Ed Roberson's books have won the Iowa Poetry Prize and the National Poetry Series. In addition, he has won the Ruth Lilly Prize, the Lilla Wallace Writer's Award, the Shelley Award, the Pen/Voelcker Award for Poetry and the Jackson Poetry Prize.

Elizabeth Robinson is the author, most recently, of *Rumor* from Free Verse Editions. She is also the co-author, with Susanne Dyckman of the chapbook *Vivian Maier: 11 photographs in 20 poems*, from Dancing Girl Press. With Jennifer Phelps, Robinson co-edited *Quo Anima: innovation and spirituality in contemporary women's poetry*, published by University of Akron Press. She has been a winner of the National Poetry Series for *Pure Descent* and the Fence Modern Poets' Prize for *Apprehend* and has received grants from the Fund for Poetry, the Foundation for Contemporary Arts, and the Maison Dora Maar.

Martha Ronk is the author of eleven books of poetry, most recently *Silences* and *Ocular Proof* (on photographs). *Vertigo* was a National Poetry Series selection, *Transfer of Qualities* was long-listed for the National Book Award, and *In a landscape of having to repeat* was a PEN USA best poetry book. She has had residencies at McDowell and Djerassi, and received a NEA award. Her poetry has also been published in several anthologies and is included in the most recent Wesleyan collection of women poets; she also published a collection of short stories, *Glass Grapes*, and an ironic memoir, *Displeasures of the Table*. Her career teaching Renaissance literature and coordinating the creative writing program was at Occidental College in Los Angeles.

Ian Seed started writing seriously in his mid-forties. He is Senior Lecturer and Programme Leader for the BA in Creative Writing at the University of Chester, UK. As well as publishing fiction, poetry and essays, he has published four interlinked collections of prose poetry, all with Shearsman Books: *The Underground Cabaret* (2020), *New York Hotel* (2018), *Identity Papers* (2016), and *Makers of Empty Dreams* (2014). *New York Hotel* was a *Times Literary Supplement* Book of the Year. *The Thief of Talant* (2016), the first translation into English of Pierre Reverdy's hybrid novel of poetry and prose, *Le voleur de Talan*, was published by Wakefield Press.

Simon Smith's *The Books of Catullus* appeared from Carcanet in 2018. He took part in the BBC Radio 4 programme, "In Our Time," on Catullus, available online: https://www.bbc.co.uk/programmes/m000d1rg. His numerous books of poetry include most recently *DAY IN, DAY OUT*, published by Parlor Press (2018) and *some Municipal Love Poems* (Muscaliet Press, 2018). He lives in London and teaches creative writing, poetry and translation at the University of Kent.

Donna Stonecipher is the author of five books of poetry, most recently *Transaction Histories* (2018), which was cited by *The New York Times* as one of the 10 best poetry books of 2018. She has also published one book of criticism, *Prose Poetry and the City* (2018). Her poems have been published in many journals, including *The Paris Review*, and have been translated into seven languages. In 2018 she won a year-long writing grant from the Berlin Senate. She translates from German, and her translation of Austrian poet Friederike Mayröcker's *études*, for which she received a National Endowment for the Arts fellowship, appeared in 2020. She lives in Berlin.

Cole Swensen is the author of 17 collections of poetry and a collection of critical essays. She has also translated over 20 books from French and has been awarded the PEN USA Award in Translation, as well as the SF State Poetry Center Book Award, the Iowa Poetry Prize, and the National Poetry Series, and has been a finalist for the National Book Award. Co-editor of the Norton anthology *American Hybrid*, she divides her time between Paris and Providence, RI, where she teaches at Brown University.

Anne Waldman is a poet, performer, professor, editor and cultural activist and was a founder and co-director with Allen Ginsberg of the Jack Kerouac School of Disembodied Poetics at Naropa University and is currently director of its Summer Writing Program. She also directed The Poetry Project in NYC which she helped found in 1966. She is the author of over fifty books of poetry, including the book-length hybrid narrative poem *Manatee/Humanity* (Penguin Poets 2009), and the feminist epic *The Iovis Trilogy: Colors in the Mechanism of Concealment* (Coffee House 2011), which is the winner of the 2012 PEN Center USA Award for Poetry. Other books include *Gossamurmur*, (Penguin 2013), and *Cross Worlds: Transcultural Poetics* (Coffee House 2014), an anthology co-edited with Laura Wright. Her most recent books are *Voice's Daughter of a Heart Yet To Be Born*, (Coffee House 2016) *Trickster Feminism* (Penguin 2018) and *Sanctuary* (Spuyten Duyvil 2020). Forthcoming: *BARD, KINETIC* (Coffee House, 2021), and *New Weathers*, an anthology of essays co-edited with Emma Gomis, (Nightboat 2022). Waldman is the recipient of the Shelley Memorial Award, a Guggenheim Fellowship, and is a former Chancellor of The Academy of American Poets. She is a frequent collaborator with poets, dancers, musicians and visual artists and performs in festivals around the world, and has performed in recent years in Tangier, Marrakech, Madrid, London, Paris, Denmark, and Brussels. She is the founder which Ambrose Bye and Devin Brahja Waldman of Fast Speaking Music band and label, which has issued more than 30 poetry and jazz albums. Her album SCIAMACHY was released in 2020 to much acclaim. She has received the American Book Award from the Before Columbus Foundation for long-life achievement. She curated the Voz Alta poetry performance festival at Casa del Lago in Mexico City April of 2017 which included participants Raul Zurita of Chile, Guillermo Gomez Pena of Mexico/USA, and Thurston Moore of the US and UK. Over the years she has performed with Don Cherry, Steve Lacy, James Brandon Lewis, Melanie Dyer, Janice Lowe, Laurie Anderson, and Meredith Monk. The opera *Artaud in the Black Lodge* with libretto by Waldman and music by David T. Little will premiere at Opera Philadelpha in 2021.

Felicia Zamora is the author of five books of poetry including: *Quotient* forthcoming from Tinderbox Editions, *Body of Render,* winner of the *2018* Benjamin Saltman Award from Red Hen Press (2020), and *Of Form & Gather*, winner of the 2016 Andrés Montoya Poetry Prize. She's received fellowships and residencies from CantoMundo, Ragdale Foundation, PLAYA, *Moth Magazine*, and Martha's Vineyard, authored two chapbooks, won the 2019 Wabash Prize for Poetry and the 2015 Tomaž Šalamun Prize, and was the 2017 Poet Laureate of Fort Collins, Colorado. Her poems are found or forthcoming in *Alaska Quarterly Review*, Academy of American Poets *Poem-A-Day*, *American Poetry Review*, *Boston Review* online, *Crazyhorse*, *Georgia Review*, *Indiana Review*, *Lana Turner*, *North American Review*, *Poetry Daily*, *Prairie Schooner*, *Missouri Review* Poem-of-the-Week, *The Nation*, *West Branch*, and others. She is an assistant professor of English in poetry at the University of Cincinnati and associate poetry editor for the *Colorado Review*.

Matthew Zapruder is the author of five collections of poetry, most recently *Father's Day*, from Copper Canyon in Fall 2019, as well as *Why Poetry*, a book of prose. He is editor-at-large at Wave Books, where he edits contemporary poetry, prose, and translations. From 2016 to 2017 he held the annually rotating position of Editor of the Poetry Column for the *New York Times Magazine*. He teaches in the MFA in creative writing at Saint Mary's College of California.

About the Editor

Jon Thompson is a poet, essayist, and editor. He has published four full-length collections of poems, the most recent of which is *Notebook of Last Things* (Shearsman Books, 2019) and has published individual poems widely in journals such as *Colorado Review, Conjunctions Online, Carolina Quarterly, Interim, Iowa Review, Jacket 2, New American Writing, Third Coast, The White Review* and elsewhere. He is editor of Free Verse Editions, a poetry series and Illuminations: A Series on American Poetics, both published by Parlor Press. More on him can be found at www.jon-thompson.com

Photograph of Jon Thompson by Sofie Chester-Thompson. Used by permission.

www.ingramcontent.com/pod-product-compliance
Lightning Source LLC
Chambersburg PA
CBHW030905060726
47591CB00005B/1430

* 9 7 8 1 6 4 3 1 7 2 9 8 9 *